Always With You

Also by Gloria Hunniford

Next to You

GLORIA HUNNIFORD

Always With You

HODDER &
STOUGHTON

First published in Great Britain in 2008 by Hodder & Stoughton
An Hachette Livre UK company

5

A CIP catalogue record for this title is available from the British Library

Hardback ISBN 978 0 340 95396 9
Trade Paperback ISBN 978 0 340 96018 9

Typeset in Plantin Light by Hewer Text UK Ltd, Edinburgh
Printed and bound by Clays Ltd, St Ives plc

Hodder & Stoughton policy is to use papers that are natural, renewable and recyclable products and made from wood grown in sustainable forests. The logging and manufacturing processes are expected to conform to the environmental regulations of the country of origin.

Hodder & Stoughton Ltd
338 Euston Road
London NW1 3BH

www.hodder.co.uk

To my precious daughter Caron for her inspiration and my family for their boundless love and support.

My sons Michael and Paul, my husband Stephen, and Gabriel, Charlie, Jake and Beau.

And to Russ who is undoubtedly one of the best dads in the world – Charlie and Gabriel's hero.

AUTHOR'S NOTE

An extract from Caron's diary:

23 January 2004
Writing keeps coming up strongly over and over again.
Passing on and sharing whatever it is that I have learned
and passing on information through my journey. The
writing does not have to be A BIG PLAN – do it and see
what emerges. Let me pass across my learning and new
understanding of trying to attain peace and health through
believing.

Caron refers so much to 'writing' in her diaries, she was passionate about sharing what she had learned about coping with cancer and her seven-year journey to try to beat it. Now in a similar way, I feel as passionate in wanting to pass on what I have learned about 'loss'. In my case, the loss of a much treasured and deeply loved daughter who was vibrant, kind and good-humoured to the end of her life. People have written to me about losing a child or a loved one in their thousands, each one offering a different view point on how to deal with the all-consuming aspect of death.

Loss is something we *all* have to deal with in our lives. Open the newspapers any day of the week and the distraught, terrified faces of families in the first surreal moments of loss leap off the pages. A son or daughter killed in Afghanistan, another mindless stabbing of an innocent youth, a horrific road accident, suicides, or terminal illnesses. Desperate situations and horrific realities for the survivors. Dying is hard enough to fathom, but living with loss sometimes seems impossible. But what would life be like without the risk of loss? It would be a life without love – without colour, without joy. It would be no life.

Although my experiences are based on losing a child, many of the lessons I've learned are true for any form of loss.

On behalf of my daughter, Caron, and myself, I sincerely hope you find some comfort in the pages of this book.

Contents

PROLOGUE

My heart is broken. My soul is shattered. I ache, hurt, keel over with pain. I am bereft, cut loose, adrift, lost. I am no longer myself. I am empty, closed down. I am scared and angry. I feel out of control. I weep, sob, shout. I rage against an unjust world. There are so many words to describe the emotions imposed on us when a child dies: fury, terror, agony, shock, misery, loneliness, disbelief. We feel crushed, obliterated, overwhelmed; we are tossed into the chaos of hell, tortured, afraid and furious. I could go on and on about the effects of absolute grief; we are distracted, vulnerable, strangled, damned, useless, inert, irritable, trapped. Put together, these feelings might sound overdramatic, indulgent even, but as those of us who have lost a child sadly know, not one of these words, separately or together, comes anywhere close to describing the deep-rooted, agonising and searing pain we have experienced and continue to experience.

I cannot make those of you who do not know that pain understand, nor would I want to undermine other people's loss of *any* kind, but since death and loss are something we all have to deal with in life, there will come a time when many of us will need, for the sake of others if nothing else, to at least be able to empathise with it. How many times have we heard the phrases 'Time will heal' and 'You'll get over it'? Trust me when I say this – I will never get over my child's death, and I wouldn't want to. Caron's death is as much a part of her life as her life was. I cannot acknowledge one without the other, so when you ask a grieving parent to 'get over it' or 'move on', you may as well be asking them to forget their child. Go and stand over your own sleeping child or loved one and ask yourself whether you could simply get over it. As someone wiser than me said when they were told that they 'really should have moved on by now', 'Where is it that you want me to go?'

In the immediate aftermath of this intense loss, it is easy to believe that the pain might kill you. It is a completely holistic agony. You hurt on a physical, emotional and spiritual level. It is only later, after a sea of tears has fallen, that you realise, with a whole new surge of pain, that grief doesn't kill you. Sometimes that would seem too easy, because of course life does 'go on' around you; it has to. We have to learn to walk again among the fit, able and un-bereaved, but it is a mirage – we are quadriplegics on the inside.

So here we are, the nameless parents who have buried a child, or children. There is no word to describe us – we are not a widow, widower or an orphan, but somewhere in between, lost in no-man's-land, condemned to live out the rest of our days in purgatory. In the beginning we will be comforted and cared for to the best of anyone's limited abilities, but then we discover that long after the support has waned, we are still gravely injured. The wound is invisible to the naked eye, but it never, ever goes away. The plaster we place upon it to survive each day may conceal it, but the wound never heals. It is always there, always with us – a dull ache, a throb below the surface, a sudden twinge, a hollow wish – and may at any time be ripped open and exposed. Suddenly, months, days or even decades after the initial loss, we find ourselves back at the beginning – once again bereft, cut loose, adrift, lost, angry, afraid, alone and terribly, terribly sad.

> *Sometimes, when the sun goes down,*
> *It seems it will never rise again . . .*
> *But it will!*
>
> *Sometimes, when you feel alone,*
> *It seems your heart will break in two . . .*
> *But it won't.*
>
> *And sometimes it seems*
> *It's hardly worth carrying on . . .*
> *But it is.*
>
> *For sometimes, when the sun goes down,*
> *It seems it will never rise again,*
> *But it does.*

'Sometimes', Frank Brown,
sent by Fiona Castle

I must have read and reread the above poem thousands of times and have taken great comfort from it, but I now know that Caron's death is not something from which I will ever recover. It is more like a disability that I have learnt to live with, to live in and around. The pain is always with me, the memories are always with me, and her spirit, whether real or imagined (I no longer think it matters), is always with me. It is a complex, difficult, daunting and exhausting path to walk, and I personally could not have done it without the daily support of my loving family and friends, and also the extraordinary and unquantifiable help I received in the form of the eight thousand letters that started arriving the day after Caron died. At a time when I thought I was the only person on earth who'd experienced such immeasurable loss, I discovered there were literally thousands of us out there, all struggling as I was.

The backgrounds, experiences, 'stories', illnesses and accidents, murders and manslaughters, ages and sexes were different in every single heart-rending letter. Like snowflakes, no two people's experiences were the same, yet reading through that blizzard of loss, I began to recognise that, in one respect at least, we are all the same: we each gave birth to a child for whom we would have gladly died, but we were unable to.

I took extreme comfort in knowing that people had gone before me in this storm and survived, though I read over and over how easy it was not to. I knew that the snowflakes were continuing to fall. After writing *Next to You*, the story of Caron's life and secret seven-year battle with cancer, I realised that somehow by reading the book I had eased their pain for a moment or two, just as those letters and the process of writing the book had eased mine. I'm not naïve – I know that most people don't get eight thousand letters – and so I am going to try, in this book, to share what strangers were willing to share with me: their compassion, their understanding, their strength, their fears, their wisdom. I know now that I am not alone, I am not the only one, I am not mad, and this helps. No book can cure loss, however many you read, but being aware that snow has always fallen, and will fall again, may help you through the coldest, darkest days.

I packed up those letters tightly, built them up around me and used them to protect me from the short, bewildering days and long, terrible nights, from the icy cold that was always threatening to overwhelm me. Sheltered by them, I learnt how to survive in this frozen landscape. Every single personal account helped me on my journey back to the living, to join the warm-blooded species of which I had once been a member. I hope I can do the same for others.

Bereaved people are often criticised for not healing quickly enough, for seeming to mend too quickly or for dealing with their loss in inappropriate ways, but I say that until you walk in the shoes of loss, it is wrong to find fault. Whatever method of survival it is that gets you through the day is good enough for me. There are no rules when it comes to coping with a loss this profound.

When my worries threaten to consume me, when I doubt what it is I've been doing since Caron died, I return to her for advice, as I always did, and often still do.

I'm in the summer house writing at my new table – it's an overall gorgeous space. I feel very blessed to have it – quiet solitude. I could really write here. I don't have to write anything, other than what is in me.

Do not let other people's eyes become your cage. It does not matter what they think, say, feel. This is your life. Do not allow them to mould it. It is vital to be who you are – right now.

What an amazing teacher it [cancer] has been. Such a learning process about love, reality, being real, perception, sight and seeing my needs – voicing what needs to be said.

The big learning for me has been to live in the *now* – just in this present moment. When I stop the masochism of my mind to love myself, to 'stop' and be fully present, I have found that whatever is apparently happening within life, there is a stillness and a peace that are always there.

And I have a choice as to whether I spend hour upon hour invaded by fear and terror about what the future might bring, or whether I choose to be present in this very second – a second that I will never have again – and fully live my life in the *now*.

Caron's words, taken from her journal, not mine. I don't think she'd begrudge me using her memory or her hard-earned wisdom as a reason to get up in the morning. I hope she'd be proud. I have come a long, long way. It is my turn to pass on and share whatever it is that *I* have learnt, and I know one thing for sure: I wouldn't have learnt anything without her. I therefore dedicate this book to my beautiful girl, who is always with me. I thank her for being the wonderful daughter that she was and for leaving behind two spirited and phenomenal children, Charlie and Gabriel, whom I can love as I love her. It is written in her memory, and it is written so that I can keep her spirit alive.

I also dedicate this book to the eight thousand people who wrote to me and continue to write, who shared their grief and, on my lonely days, reminded me that I was not alone. And to those of you who are at this moment facing the monumental task of surviving loss, the death of a loved one is always with you, but so are the living . . . Thanks to you and Caron, this is how I found my way back to them.

My daughter, Caron, died shortly after 6 p.m. on Tuesday, 13 April 2004. She was forty-one years old, and she was my one and only baby girl.

I

The B✶✶✶✶✶d Cancer

'I'll lend you for a little while
A child of mine,' he said,
'For you to love while she lives,
And mourn when she is dead.

'It may be six or seven years,
Or twenty-two or -three,
But will you, till I call her back,
Take care of her for me?

'She'll bring her charms to gladden you,
And shall her stay be brief,
You'll have her lovely memories
As solace for your grief.

'I cannot promise she will stay,
Since all from earth return,
But there are lessons taught down there
I want this child to learn.

'I've looked the wild world over
In my search for teachers true,
And from the things that crowd life's lands
I have selected you.

'Now will you give her all your love,
Not think the labour vain,
Nor hate me when I call
To take her back again?'

I fancy that I heard them say,
'Dear Lord, Thy will be done,
For all the joy Thy child shall bring,
The risk of grief we'll run.

'We'll shelter her with tenderness,
We'll love her while we may,
And for the happiness we have known,
We'll ever grateful stay.

'But shall the angels call for her
Much sooner than we planned,
We'll brave the bitter grief that comes,
And try to understand.'

'A Child of Mine', Edgar Guest

In September 1997 my treasured daughter, Caron Keating, was diagnosed with breast cancer. She was thirty-five years old. I will never, ever forget receiving that fateful call from her husband, Russ, telling me the horrifying news. Caron lay upstairs in our house in Sevenoaks recovering from the biopsy, and I remember standing in the garden, staring at the big blue sky and thinking, This is it – whatever the outcome, life will never be the same again. And it wasn't.

A tight knot of fear lodged itself in the pit of my stomach that day, but when I walked into Caron's room, I forced my lips into a smile, willed hope into my voice and tried to shield her from the terror in my eyes. It became my mask and it is one that I still wear today. The knot of fear has become a knot of grief, but that too is still there. Thinking back on it now, I realise that the mask appeared immediately, as did the knot, and neither has ever left. Sometimes I think my former self is still standing in the garden, looking up at the vast expanse of sky, waiting for that call. When it came, it marked the end of one life and the beginning of another. I can see her, the old Gloria. Occasionally I can step back into her shoes, but I can't step into her skin.

I was such a lucky woman. I had a job I really enjoyed and was fortunate enough to have had a wonderful upbringing by marvellous parents. I had three amazing children; I was very happy with Stephen, whom I was living with and would marry the following summer; my children were having children; we were financially secure. I was having the most lovely time, really enjoying and relishing everything. It was a wonderful phase of my life, and then – whack – the steamroller came in: Caron had cancer and it kept on coming. In one instant you go from being in that joyous space, where everything is in place, to an alien world. Caron too: she was married to a fine man she loved; she had two beautiful sons; she adored living in Barnes and had an exciting job. She had started trying to come to terms with her father's death the previous January and was enjoying spending time with Gabriel, who was just nine months old, and Charlie, who was three. Everything was in its place.

When that question mark is placed over your life, you're left with it hanging there always. It takes away your carefree attitude for ever. All of a sudden everything's not quite in place, the axis has started to tilt a little, and even though you can have a wonderful approach to life and lead ten lives in one, it leaves you with a nagging worry. Consequently, no matter how well Caron was dealing with it and how ably she coped – and she was stoic and courageous and inspiring – there was always that 'What if . . . ?'

My incredible, beautiful, exceptional, brave child fought cancer with everything she had, and then went on to find more to fight it with. She did absolutely everything she could to stay alive. For her sons. For herself. For us. But it wasn't to be. In December 1999 an oncologist sat opposite my younger son, Michael, and me, and gave Caron eighteen months to live. She herself never wanted to know the prognosis, just what she had to do to get better. Then, after a lumpectomy, radiotherapy, a mastectomy and six sessions of double-strength chemo-therapy, Caron began to delve seriously, feverishly and determinedly into the world of self-healing. She could beat this thing if only she could work out what it was that was making her ill in the first place.

Sometimes I was nervous of the path she was taking. Sometimes I clung on to the healers' promises as dearly as she did. Often their message contradicted the advice of the doctors, and poor Caron was tossed about between an ever-growing number of disciplines, frantically searching for a cure. She had been told by a world-renowned holistic cancer expert that cancer patients who made changes to their lives often did better, so the family moved out of London to Fowey in Cornwall, where they had spent many idyllic holidays, with a view to slowing down and healing in peace. Russ likened it to driving with a chip in your windscreen: the slower you drive, the better your chances. It worked: for two years Caron, Russ and the boys had a wonderful life next to the sea despite fighting cancer, because at that stage the doctors were still going for cure. However, when the cancer came back, this time more aggressively, and Caron was faced with having to undergo a second mastectomy, she fled to Australia. She had previously visited Byron Bay, the sweetshop of complementary treatments and therapies for any condition, and had relished the positivity she had discovered there, as she confided in her journal:

> Finally arrived in Byron – in the rain. It feels very good to be back here – there is something in the fabric of this place which I recognise and connect with right away. Of course I miss my mum and the family, but this is where I want and *have* to be – at least for now.

In Byron Bay she tried everything, and I mean everything, that was available to rid herself of the b*****d cancer. We all flew backwards and forwards to Australia to help and support her and her family whenever and however we could. It was a terrible time, as anyone who has had to deal with cancer will know, but it was a wonderful time too and ironically some of my most treasured memories of my child are from that period.

Despite the million and one times I must have said, 'You'll beat this,' I knew in my heart of hearts that the normal trajectory of Caron's life had been altered. Even so, despite going over every possible permutation of events countless times, I could never actually imagine the cancer taking her life. Russ was incredible: he more than anyone knew deep down that his wife might possibly die. He had to see it, share it and live it every minute of every day for seven years; he probably faced up to what was happening long, long before I could, and he did whatever he was able and more besides, to make Caron's journey easier. Every day I am thankful for the compassion he showed his wife.

Deep in my soul I knew that the very word 'cancer' bred fear, but when we were all in the middle of it, we were so desperate to hang on to every glimmer of hope and the positivity that Caron had in abundance, that no one dared speak of the worst happening. Strange as it may seem, throughout the entire seven years of her battle Caron and I never talked about death, only about life. However, if you're really being honest, it isn't real. You say things like 'They caught it early', 'The drugs are so much better these days', 'You're resilient' and 'Your immune system is strong', but underneath it all there is always this huge knot of fear. Caron had it too. She fought cancer with fear for a long, long time. She never wanted Charlie and Gabriel to grow up without their mother. I don't know whether that knot of fear is somewhere deep in your gut or part of your whole being, but it feels like it permeates your mind and heart and takes hold. It was the elephant in the room that we could never acknowledge, but it was always there. I can't write about this without crying, even now, because it is still so raw.

I might have occasionally admitted to Stephen how afraid I was, but rarely to my sons, Michael and Paul, and certainly never to Caron herself. They may say I was in denial about what was happening to Caron, but it wasn't denial, it was survival. And anyway, even while you are airing your fears to someone, at the very same time you are doing the job of convincing yourself otherwise. After all, it is true that many people do successfully beat cancer – more and more every year. I simply couldn't go down the road of thinking that Caron's illness would lead to her death.

In all the letters I have received from parents who have been affected by cancer, there is the same talk of their child's bravery, stoicism, courage and determination. Caron was just the same. What else could we as parents do but match their positivity? So somehow you do. That instinct to protect the person you love takes over and you will do anything other than show that you're really, really worried, because there's an elephant in the room. The mask was always on for her, but the knot was there too, gnawing away inside me with an all-consuming, sickening fear.

Giving birth is the best thing you ever do in your life; to have that child taken away from you is, in my opinion, the very worst. It is actually unimaginable. Your brain cannot go to that place, so instead it answers your own fearful questions with the possibility of a miracle, the whisper of hope. That keeps you alive, and thank God. The two roads – fear and hope – ran parallel within my system. The fear never left me; as soon as I opened my eyes, it was there. My brain would say, 'What are we dealing with today? Is it really true that Caron's got cancer? Yes, it's real. It's the nightmare; it's not a dream.' I led my life in a conscious state of denial.

In the beginning I hated Australia for taking Caron, Russ and the boys away from our family unit, but it gave my daughter something spiritual, space, a place to forgive herself for what-ever wrong she thought she might have done to herself to get cancer in the first place. A question lingered constantly in Caron's mind: 'Is it something I have done or haven't done?' In Byron Bay she could battle on away from the cameras and out of the limelight. Life was good there – sunshine, sea and sand – but more importantly she was filled with new hope thanks to all the 'feel-good' therapies she could fall back on. She was offered fresh hope of a continuing life. Despite the terrible setbacks and pain and fear she continued to face, she was living in a positive environment and her family flourished. In Byron Bay it's enough just 'to be' and it's always a brand-new day.

13

I think her sons' memories of their time there will be happy ones, with lots of sing-songs and adventures, but my little girl was getting progressively more ill. The cancer moved from her breast to her bones and for the first time since diagnosis an oncologist gave *her* a prognosis, and that prognosis did not include a cure. Now we were talking about management.

In the middle of the night, when I couldn't sleep and I was on my own, and there was no one to don the mask for, a lot of churning and turmoil went on that I couldn't admit to anyone. What would I do? I used to think. How would I deal with it? I couldn't imagine how I would cope, and I still don't know how we got through it. Even though most of our family knew Caron had breast cancer, they didn't know its full extent. As for Caron and Russ's friends and colleagues, they thought Caron was suffering from a bit of post-natal depression. I would try to imagine the shock when it was announced; it was a dark, weird and horrid place. I would rerun the scenario of her possible death in my mind, the permutations, what would happen with the boys.

At night, it is harder to resist being drawn into the enormity of it all, of death and its impact. There came a point when I had really to say to myself, This is the cut-off point: I cannot go on worrying about what *might* happen however many years down the line, because tomorrow I could go under a bus, so I will channel all my energy into Caron coping with it and hopefully recovering. I wanted more than anything to be strong for her. I got into that by clawing along bit by bit, but every piece of bad news was another wallop. Now there's that question mark hovering above your body, the sword of Damocles over your head: a simple headache appears sinister; a sore knee seems ominous; you fret over the slightest pimple. Even now, night-time continues to be the worst: at least back then I could call Australia and hear that voice that I miss so much.

Her life, her husband's life, my life, my husband's life, my sons' lives were all ruled by cancer. She was in pain and I couldn't ease it. She was sick and I couldn't cure it. She was scared and at times I couldn't soothe her. She was my child and I couldn't make her better. I have said this before, but if I could have, I would have willingly taken her place. The steamroller kept on coming. In 2001 the cancer moved up her spine. Caron's sternum fractured, her back was agony, and she lost the ability to walk freely. At times she needed a stick for support. I can still hear the stick reverberating on the wooden floorboards, the pause as she was faced with taking the next step, the gathering of will and strength, then thump, a great sigh, and she was on her way again. Surely I knew deep inside that this might be our last Christmas with her, and yet there again came the same voice of hope, the same heartfelt wish: she had surprised us so many times before, so why not again?

I *will* walk properly again – I feel content and thankful my back is clearing and healing. All seems steady again.

I need to go slow – get a good healing programme. Now is the time to do that – no point delaying. Get on with it! No more distractions, excuses – do what you need to do now. Whatever that takes – give it to yourself now. Do *all* you can – you will heal.

A timetable, I think, will be the thing – so it's good that everyone goes and we have the space to get it all sorted. I need the empty space as well. Remember, 'anxiety' is just that – a sensation in the body which I find hard to accept. I do *not* feel I am dying. I feel like things are turning again and I am getting better. My strength is improving, breathing is good, energy better, flexibility – I still get a bit tired, though, so too does everyone else.

Maybe I push myself too much and I am bothered about what people think, though less so increasingly. Switzerland Clinic in March will happen and I have a real vision of getting clear of all of this once and for all and it never coming back. How fab would that be? Will I be free of all PAIN – that is also what I'd like. Who knows?

On 17 March 2004 Caron arrived in Switzerland. She'd found a clinic offering progressive, record-beating cancer treatment and had visited at the end of the previous year. Although it had not entirely worked out that time, she had been re-energised by the process and, as ever, was hopeful. I met her off the plane with our wonderful family friend Judith, who escorted her over so that Russ could stay at home in Australia because Caron didn't want the boys to miss school. After a twenty-four-hour flight my beautiful girl walked off the plane. We went shopping virtually immediately. We were in busy, busy shops in St Gallen; she bought some red shoes; we went to restaurants; we dressed up for dinner at night. I'll never forget the head waiter in a restaurant we'd visited before, back in October. Caron was dressed in her new red shoes and fishnet tights, and he just looked at her and said, 'You look *bellissima!*'

Caron had such energy about her. We went up into the mountains to enjoy the view and a delicious apple strudel. Her zest for life was contagious and I was overjoyed at the improvement she once again was showing. I allowed myself to believe that my indefatigable daughter was by some miracle going to survive.

The following week she went into the clinic to undergo a new course of treatments. We were due to stay a month. I don't know what happened, whether the treatments were too hard, whether it was a coincidence, but one day I picked her up after she had had an electronic treatment up and down her spine and she was in floods of tears with pain. She never really recovered. In the bedroom she said, 'There is no strength in my hips. I'm standing at the basin but I have to hang on.' Suddenly, or so it seemed to me, her health started to slide, faster and faster, into decline. All the strength in her lower legs left her. The weakness had set in. It was at that point she was taken to the cancer hospital. She needed a wheelchair to get there.

I remember the doctor looking at me in disbelief and saying, 'Do you know how ill your daughter is?' He thought I was really stupid, that I didn't understand. I knew how ill she was – I had seen the printouts; I knew where the metastases were – but she'd seemed so well, and because she had been so defiant and strong in her approach, I *still* thought she'd be OK, that she'd manage it. The doctor agreed to do another course of radiotherapy to ease the pressure on her spinal cord. She was going for radiotherapy in the morning and other 'feel-good' infusing treatments in the afternoon; right up to twenty hours before she died she was having treatments. I knew something had changed. Thankfully we were all due to be in Switzerland together for the Easter weekend: Russ, Charlie, Gabriel, Stephen, Michael and me.

Only a week earlier it had been just Caron and me. It was Mother's Day and she had given me a beautiful painting of tulips that she'd done months before. She'd written on the back of it, wrapped it carefully in tissue and brought it over in her suitcase to give to me. I was staggered by my child yet again and reminded of the enormity of her spirit. Despite being trapped in the midst of hell, she was still able to think of others. That day was probably one of the most special days of my life. It was a window of time. It was a blessing.

There was more to come. Easter Saturday fell on 10 April, which happens to be my birthday. Looking back, I can hardly believe it was such an action-packed weekend despite Caron's pain. It was the first time we had all been together for a very long time and she wanted things to be different over that Easter period. She insisted that we drive over the border into Constance in Germany for lunch and then spend a leisurely afternoon around the town. That evening I had organised dinner at an Italian restaurant down the hill from our hotel back in St Gallen. The pavements were packed with snow and ice and yet she was determined to walk down rather than be driven. Safely settled in the restaurant, she had a glass of champagne and relished a change of food. Unbeknown to me, the next day Caron had planned a surprise breakfast party for me. Stephen was detailed to get me out of the way first thing. When we returned to the hotel that morning, I walked into the room and there was Caron sitting among presents and Easter eggs, balloons and flowers, all of which she'd organised. There was an egg-painting competition to be held, breakfast to be eaten, gifts to be unwrapped. The room looked beautiful, and she'd even been out to buy a scarf that I'd admired a few days earlier. How did that girl – in the middle of radiotherapy and pain so excruciating that it left her breathless, plus everything that must have been going on in her mind – have the strength, the love, the determination, the warmth, the selflessness to en-sure that I, her mother, had a lovely birthday? Wouldn't the majority of people just have shrugged it off? I'm sure I would have – it was just another birthday. Instead, she'd organised a party. I will never ever forget it.

It is still an unacceptable fact to me that three days after walking on snow and the egg-painting competition, my daughter was dead. I cannot and I don't think I ever will be able to reconcile that the same girl who was painting Easter eggs on 11 April was gone on the 13th. It sums up how Caron had lived with cancer. She had always wanted everyone, including herself, to carry on as normal, and normal for us, no matter where we were, whether it was Australia, Ireland or Switzerland, was to mark celebrations in a big way. That indomitable spirit is sometimes the only thing that gets me through the day. I think of what she endured and how she found the courage to carry on, and I know that I have no choice but to do the same. It would be an insult to the memory of my child if I didn't. My God, though, it is so very hard.

In the middle of the egg-painting Caron suddenly felt unwell and had to go to bed. I don't know what happened, if something moved, shifted, expanded, but she never really improved from there. Although I didn't know it at the time, that was the beginning of the end. Her body had started to shut down. Caron made her first and only reference to losing her fight: 'Promise me,' she said to me, 'that if anything ever happens, you will look after my boys.' That was also when she said she never wanted to go to hospital or a hospice, that was just the way she felt; that was when Stephen tried to massage some warmth into her legs and couldn't find any sign of life in her limbs; that was when we all made the decision to return home to England.

2

13 April, 6.15 p.m., Caron Leaves Her Body

We give our loved ones
Back to God,
And just as He first gave them to us
And did not lose them
In the giving,
So we have not lost them
In returning them to Him . . .
For life is eternal,
Love is immortal,
Death is only a horizon . . .
And a horizon
Is nothing but the limit
Of our earthly sight.

Helen Steiner Rice

Stephen and I arrived home in Sevenoaks from Switzerland on the evening of Easter Sunday. Michael was to fly back the next morning with Charlie and Gabriel. He recalls the deeply emotional moment of going into Caron's bedroom before leaving – there she was sitting up in bed, having mustered every ounce of strength in her body with that huge smile of hers, with an even bigger hug for her gorgeous boys. 'See you back at Nana's,' she said.

It was very late by the time we walked through the door on Sunday night, tired from all the travel, exhausted by worry. Caron and Russ planned to return to Cornwall for the summer holidays but would stay with us first, so the next day was all about planning, shopping, getting the beds ready. Caron had been out of the country for almost three years; finally she was coming home and I wanted everything to be perfect. I wanted the house to look lovely and welcoming. I wanted her to want for nothing. Back in Switzerland, Caron kept saying, 'Why does Mum keep asking me about what I want to eat?' I was fussing, obviously, calling all the time to ask her questions: 'What do you think you'll feel like? Is there anything special I can get you?' I was trying to think of her favourite things. She liked melon because it felt so refreshing, so we went out and bought all the food she felt able to eat, including melon. It would turn out to be the last thing she ever ate. When we were in Australia, the first thing we'd go and do in the morning was buy fresh juice and bring it back to her, and we were trying to recreate that in Kent. Stephen is still a dab hand at juicing.

Amid the excitement and worry of getting Caron home, I had this stupid complication hovering over my head. I knew I had some major work commitments ahead of me: I was supposed to be presenting *This Morning* all that week. The decision to bring Caron home had been made swiftly and it was much earlier than expected. It took hours just to get Caron out of the hotel in Switzerland and into the car. Being in the condition she was, we'd decided it was best for Russ to drive her home; we didn't want to put Caron through the indignity of a flight or the threat of recognition in a busy airport, as Caron's illness was still a secret. (Although we didn't realise at the time, most press agencies did in fact know, as they had had photos of her entering the Royal Marsden Hospital since very early on in her treatment, but had agreed not to publish them.) We had no idea how long it was going to take for Russ to drive her to Sevenoaks.

I couldn't contact anyone at *This Morning* over the Easter bank holiday, and even if I had been able to, what could I have said, given that we hadn't told anyone how ill Caron really was? I trundled on, busying myself with getting the house ready, stupidly thinking, Well, I'll dash into the studio, present the show and be back before she's awake. It was only when Russ's car finally pulled up outside the house at one o'clock on the Tuesday morning that I realised there was no way I could go to work just a few hours later, no way I wanted to.

The previous day, Easter Monday, we'd been frantically getting things ready. There had been constant phone calls between my sons, Russ, doctors and a few select friends who knew what was going on in our family: 'Where are you now?' 'We've crossed the border,' 'How's she doing?' 'Sleeping,' 'Chatting,' 'Sleeping,' 'Better,' 'Sleeping,' 'Chatting.' I was filled with a taut, frenetic, expectant energy, mixed with the hideous paralysis that comes with an interminable wait. The journey took longer than expected, but then suddenly the wait was over and there she was. It was incredibly exciting to think she was in the car at the front door, the most euphoric feeling I've ever had. Though I'd seen her so recently, had spent weeks with her in Switzerland, it was nothing compared to her coming home. I'd dreamt about the moment she'd turn up at my front door for nearly three years. My heart was beating incredibly quickly. I almost couldn't believe it. This was what I had wanted for so long, I was so excited, and yet this was also the most terrifying feeling I'd ever experienced. Why? She looked beautiful sitting in the car, smiling up at me, but she was fragile, immobile, changed.

We had to work out how to get her into the house. In the end we found a chair with arms and lifted her on to it. It needed to be sturdy to lift such precious cargo, but it was very heavy and poor Russ and Stephen had to try to manoeuvre her in. In its own way, it was funny. At the time we were actually laughing about getting her in on the chair. Her sense of humour was still there, virtually in her dying hours. They put the chair down at the kitchen table and there she was, my daughter, home at last. The preceding years melted away; she was home and she was safe. I could look after her now.

Caron was hungry after her nine-hour drive, so Stephen served up the vegetable soup he'd made. She looked around the room, admiring the pictures, pointing out one we'd bought together, taking it all in and noticing the changes, down to the smallest detail, like the cushions she was sitting on, which we'd also bought together in Australia. We sat there for a long time. I was thinking, I can't believe she's here again in the kitchen, just the four of us. I can remember it so vividly that there is something of the time capsule about it; in hindsight, it was, like Mother's Day, a very, very special time.

We sat for about two hours in the kitchen. She ate a bit more, some wheat-free bread, drank a little rice milk. Mostly we just talked. She was obviously tired, so the men had to get her upstairs. First we got her into a lighter chair, which was scary to watch because it looked like she could topple out at any minute, but again Stephen and Russ did brilliantly and got her safely into the room at the top of the stairs. Then Stephen and I left, so Russ could put her to bed. Caron had always taken great pride in herself, and it was as much the case at the end, so when it came to dressing and undressing her, it was only Russ who was allowed in. I would never have asked to see her breast, for example; in fact I only saw it once, by default, because we were at the doctor's. She was quite demure by nature – wacky, but quite demure. I waited outside while Russ got her ready for bed. It seemed like a terribly long time. Finally Russ stuck his head into the corridor. 'You can go in now.' Donning the mask once more, I walked in. Caron was sitting up in bed and I remember remarking how fortuitous it was that we happened to have an electronic bed that you could go up and down in – at least I knew she would be comfortable. It was 4.20 a.m. when I finally kissed my child goodnight and went to my room.

I didn't sleep. I would close my eyes for five minutes and then open them with a start: Caron is back in the house again! Even with all the worries, it was such a great feeling. Like the previous seven years, I again experienced two utterly opposing, forceful emotions: hope and fear. I was confronted by a mixture of terror of the unknown, of what would come the next morning, when the doctors would arrive and more prognoses would be made, and the joy, the sheer exhilaration of the dream fulfilled that she was home.

I remember thinking, Of course there's no way I can go to work. I had only a few hours before I was due in. I waited until 5.10 a.m., then called the overall boss. What could I say? I told her I was terribly sorry to disturb her at such an hour, but that Caron had just come home and wasn't very well, so I wouldn't be able to come to work. She said, 'Don't worry about it,' and asked after Caron. I remember saying, 'She's not very good . . . I've got to stay here today.' She said, 'No problem.' I put down the phone and tried to get back to sleep. I dozed on and off for five minutes at a time. Eventually I abandoned all thought of sleep and got up. I operate better in 'doing' mode. I laid out breakfast, got things ready, cleared away evidence of Caron and Russ's heroic drive the night before, made phone calls.

Finally the marvellous moment came when Russ said I could go in and see Caron. The mere fact of being able to go into my daughter's bedroom and serve her breakfast gave me such unfathomable delight. As parents, we have a *need* to care for our children. It doesn't matter if they are one or forty-one, as mine was. When Caron was a child and ill in bed, I used to bring her a little magic teapot and bite-size squares of toast, so I'd arranged these and other things she loved on the tray now, just as if she was nine years old. Caron ate some of the melon; her throat was dry.

Bringing her on a tray all the things that she liked, seeing her grateful smile, knowing I was feeding her, was a salve to an ache that went deeper than I even realised at the time. I still have that aching need. Caring for someone who is no longer there is a huge part of the grieving process. I have now found my own ways to carry on caring for Caron. I had to; I am her mother and it was what I was put on this earth to do.

All too soon, though, the cocoon was broken and the mood changed as the house went into medical mode with the arrival of our GP, Richard Husband. He told me later that he had found it hard to hide his utter shock at Caron's deterioration. Ours had been a gradual adjustment to the havoc cancer had wreaked on her, how her body shape had changed, her weight, how everything had changed, really, but he hadn't been prepared for it; he just thought he was coming to visit someone with breast cancer. The degeneration of her body told him this had gone far, far beyond breast cancer.

I don't know what we did all day, but we were constantly busy. I suppose Russ and I talked about specialists whose help we might enlist. The ringing around started in earnest. Caron had more or less finished her radiotherapy, but we were keen to get cracking on the next thing: you always think the next doctor has the answer. The only reason I had called my GP was to register Caron. I never dreamt she was going to die. We were very worried about her of course, but all our conversations were still about when she got better, so we began making plans for the house in Cornwall, where they were to spend the summer. We even talked about converting the downstairs loo into a shower, for example, about turning our office into a bedroom so she didn't have to cope with the stairs. However, we were very worried about how we were going to manage to get her to the house in Fowey because it was perched on a cliff and there was a very steep descent down to the house. I knew there was no way she'd be 'housed' as such, and anyway, I had promised we would never allow it. It occurred to me that all the things she'd dreaded about coming back to England were suddenly very real. It was bad enough when she had been walking with a stick, but now that she was so ill, maybe she wouldn't even be able to do that. What would become of her life? Of course, as it happened, we never got the chance to worry about that any further.

Mostly I spent my time going upstairs and just looking at Caron in bed. I'd smile to myself, despite all the worries and phone calls, and hold that warm feeling close: My baby is back; my girl is here. Her dying was still not in my head, not anywhere on the horizon. I just thought she was particularly tired because of the journey. Once she'd recovered from the trip and from the latest onslaught of radiotherapy, she'd rally, as she always had. The doctors would reassess her. A new programme would be planned. I will say it over and over again: her dying was simply not in my head.

My GP sent an experienced nurse to give Caron a bed bath,

26

to make her comfortable and organise a drip to help with her breathing. I got the softest bath towels I could find and left her with the nurse. My GP had told me the nurse had a good feel for these sorts of things and she would be able to tell us what was going on. I waited nervously in the corridor again. When she came out, the nurse began explaining that Caron didn't have very long and that we should get the boys. She was telling us things that terrified my very soul. 'What do you mean, not long? A lifetime isn't long enough, so what is not long?' Earlier Caron had been sitting up in bed, eating, talking, so what did this woman mean when she told me my daughter hadn't got long? I couldn't, wouldn't accept it. Caron was simply sleepy because we hadn't gone to bed until very late. It wasn't a death sentence; there was nothing untoward about it; she was just resting.

Even though I still did not believe that Caron was dying, that morning I decided to ring Paul, who was on a skiing holiday in France, and tell him that Caron wasn't well. He promised to return home as quickly as he could. In keeping with Caron's wishes to carry on as normally as possible, Michael had gone into work that morning and was having lunch with a journalist when I called to say he really should get to the house. You might ask why he'd gone – his sister was making this epic journey from Switzerland and he's at the office? – but it demonstrates where we all were at the time, how we'd programmed ourselves to think. There had been so many instances in the past when she had been in the final stages that it had sort of become our norm. Caron would rally and that was that. He was eating pasta, took the call, went back to the table, and the woman he was dining with simply said, 'You have to go, don't you?' so he paid the bill, walked out of the restaurant, went to the train station and headed to Sevenoaks. As ever he didn't know what to expect, but at the same time knew it was serious because I wouldn't call and say, 'You've got to come,' if it wasn't.

Stephen opened the door for Michael, who ran upstairs. I was so pleased to see him. Russ and I were by the bed. Caron was alive, but her eyes were closed. Michael didn't get a chance to talk to her, but he was able to lie in the bed with her for a little while and tell her everything he needed to. Like all of us, he walked in and out of the room a couple of times, keeping a close eye on the rise and fall of her chest. On one occasion, he noticed a shift in her breathing. There was a gasp of breath and then silence. Michael, like all of us, was terrified. It was rather like when you lie next to someone who's snoring and you find yourself waiting for the next snore, but they go silent. Well, Caron was silent. Michael waited, his own breath held. Then there was a gasp and then silence again. He called for us to come back in. She took another breath and the moment seemed to pass. There was clearly a problem with her breathing, though. Whatever words of reassurance were spoken between us, we were all secretly thinking the worst. We knew she was very, very poorly, and it was becoming increasingly apparent that she wasn't getting any better, but still we didn't dare acknowledge that this was it.

That day Stephen was running around looking after me and making tea for us all. There was a girl ill in bed, loved like the daughter he never had. Busy on the periphery, he was desperate to help in any way he could. When the nurse told us Caron needed some special medication, Stephen went to the chemist to get the prescription. There was no way Russ or I could have gone. Stephen was invaluable to us, since because of him, neither of us had to leave her side. I had also asked him to buy the ingredients for a health drink, but when things took a turn for the worse at home, I called and asked him to come back. He was in the supermarket, queuing with his shopping, but he simply left the basket on the floor and ran.

Russ had a terrible time getting the children home. They were at a fairground for the day with his parents, who didn't have a mobile, so he got the owner to call them over the Tannoy. While none of us could accept Caron's death was imminent, somehow we knew it was vital to get them home. Russ, once again, managed the impossible and the boys were brought back to Sevenoaks. At the same time they arrived at the gate, the nurse called us into the room. Something was happening. I started screaming, but somehow found the strength in me to make the noise stop. I didn't want to scare the boys. Charlie and Gabriel were rushed up to see her. We were all hovering, panicking. I was still screaming inside, but for the boys, I kept the tearing of my soul inside. I couldn't believe what I was being told. It was suddenly happening so quickly. My child was dying. The boys kissed her, said their goodbyes and went downstairs.

I was shaking all over, unable to stand. Russ, Michael and I sat on the bed with her. She was wrapped up in our arms and we clung on to her body as the life force left her. After everything that had gone before, when the end came it happened so very suddenly. The shock was immeasurable. It is a feeling too incomprehensible to describe. As the very last breath left her body, this soft radiant smile spread across Caron's face and a curtain of peace seemed to fall gently over her. Her body eased. She was no longer in pain. I buried my head into her still warm, soft skin and wailed. I wanted to thrash and shout and scream, but the boys were downstairs, so I pulled on the mask that I had donned for Caron and for myself. This time I did it for the two little boys downstairs who had, unbeknown to them, just lost their mother. Stephen,

Michael, Russ and I clung to one another in despair, but how can you hold up another when you cannot hold up yourself? The hard work of grieving is something you do alone.

Not long afterwards, following a hideously delayed journey from France, Paul walked into the house. It was silent. The boys were watching telly. Paul remembers looking at Stephen, who stared back at him in silence. He wanted to shout, 'Why aren't you saying anything?' but something in his soul told him the worst had happened and of course Stephen couldn't say anything. There was nothing he could say. Paul came upstairs and there we were, Russ, Michael and me, still huddled on the landing, like lost children in a museum, not knowing what to do, where to go, whom to turn to. As Paul walked up to me, I finally managed to speak the nurse's unrepeatable words, which had been clawing at my throat. 'She's gone,' I said, though I didn't believe what I was saying. The pain seared through me. A sharp, jagged shard of pain that took my breath away. Where had she gone? Why couldn't she come back? How could she be sleeping one minute and dead the next? How were we going to tell her sons? How was Russ going to cope on his own? How was I going to cope? We all stood there staring wild-eyed at one another until finally we could not put it off any longer and Russ went to tell the little boys.

I have written before, and I believe it still, that watching Russ tell Charlie and Gabriel that their mummy was no longer with us, that she was an angel now, hurt as much as seeing my daughter die. I watched and felt the same pain sear through them that was still ripping me apart. The worst thing had already happened, and yet, just a few moments later, when I had thought it couldn't get any worse, it just had. I learnt at that moment what the term 'secondary losses' means; it wasn't so much a double blow, but an exponential increase of loss. My daughter had died and her family unit had died with her. Now they were three, and they were as lost and frightened as me.

My diary for that time is just empty page after empty page. I was utterly incapacitated by grief. I did, however, make one entry on 13 April. I wrote in capital letters, '6.15 p.m. Caron leaves her body.' At the time I wrote it because I physically wasn't able to write that she had died. How interesting it is to me now, knowing what I do, that I had left myself a vital clue to unlocking the mysteries of grief. Caron had left her body, yes, but she hadn't gone. In that moment when her last breath left her and she smiled, she gave me the greatest gift she could: the gift of hope. Hope that it wasn't over, hope that I would see her again, hope that love survived even death, hope that I wouldn't lose my faith, and in that hope I found the tiniest chink of light. I found something to hold on to when suddenly I was plunged into the blackest night. It was very small and very, very far away, but it was there. In the violent storm that engulfed me, her mother, there was a miniscule flickering candle on a distant shore. One solitary star in a vast black universe.

As the unbridled misery of the following years unfolded and I would fall, fast and furiously, time and time again, back to that moment of terrible realisation that my child was dead, seconds before I crashed to the ground and broke beyond repair there was that smile to catch me and remind me that, however dreadful I felt, all was not lost. It just felt like it.

Had a strange sensation last night about what would happen if death walked into the bedroom and I saw it – 'Come on' – and it felt OK. It will be just that – a moment. If this moment happens, it's the most 'now' you'll ever feel.

i carry your heart with me (i carry it in
my heart) i am never without it (anywhere
i go you go, my dear; and whatever is done
by only me is your doing, my darling)
i fear

no fate (for you are my fate, my sweet) i want
no world (for beautiful you are my world, my true)
and it's you are whatever a moon has always meant
and whatever a sun will always sing is you

here is the deepest secret nobody knows
(here is the root of the root and the bud of the bud
and the sky of the sky of a tree called life; which grows
higher than the soul can hope or mind can hide)
and this is the wonder that's keeping the stars apart

i carry your heart (i carry it in my heart)

'i carry your heart with me', e. e. cummings

3

Beyond Pain

One night I dreamed I was walking along the beach with the Lord.
Many scenes from my life flashed across the sky.
In each scene I noticed footprints in the sand.
Sometimes there were two sets of footprints;
Other times there was one set of footprints.

This bothered me because I noticed
That during the saddest scenes of my life,
When I was suffering from anguish, sorrow or defeat,
I could see only one set of footprints.

So I said to the Lord, 'You promised me, Lord,
That if I followed You,
You would walk with me always,
But I have noticed that during the most trying periods of my life,
There has been only one set of footprints in the sand.
Why, when I have needed You most,
Have You not been there for me?'

The Lord replied, 'My precious, precious child,
The times when you have seen only one set of footprints in
    the sand,
Is when I carried you.'

'Footprints in the Sand', Mary Stevenson

In the immediate aftermath of Caron's death there was this strange holding period when nobody else knew except very close family. The few friends who had been told about the cancer might have been aware of the trip to Switzerland, or at least that Caron was planning to spend the summer in Cornwall that year and we were looking forward to trips down to the house in Fowey, but to most, she was somewhere in Australia, living an enviable life in the sun. The unbelievable truth of course was that upstairs the warmth was already slowly, imperceptibly starting to leave Caron's body. And mine.

My heart froze over when Caron died. In those awful, piercing, panicked moments before she took her last breath, it froze. As the evening wore on, that punishing, numbing cold started to seep through me until I was as cold as ice. All I could do from that moment on was watch as unreality took over. My overwhelming feeling was one of utter disbelief. I could not take on board what was happening. I could not believe my daughter was dead. I could not accept the fact because it would surely kill me, so I froze. I went into deep shock. I was numb. I remember all of us being together as Russ told the boys downstairs in the sitting room. I don't remember much after that. I think Charlie and Gabriel went outside. Did they play football that evening or another evening? I am sure Paul brought his wife, Sandy, and their boys over, but I don't actually remember. I suppose the block of ice is a form of self-protection. If the pain you were feeling were to manifest itself fully, it would probably kill you. I think something much, much bigger took over: survival, an instinctive *need* to live though I had temporarily lost the *will* to live.

The cold spread through me, then encased me, until I was locked, or perhaps preserved, in my block of ice. I don't know scientifically what happens when you experience something like this, but the block of ice allows you to go through the motions in a daze for weeks without a clear, sharp sense of what's happened. Thank God. Is it strange or encouraging that something or somebody gives you the strength to deal with the practicalities of life in the midst of your deepest despair?

Did I sleep? No. Just as I used to lie awake in the night when Caron was sick, running everything over in my mind, hoping it was all a nightmare, now I did again. She was home, in that room, but she was gone . . . Where had she gone? Why had she gone? How could someone go from painting Easter eggs to dead? And so the questions began. Can't someone tell me why this has happened? Well, the simple truth, in this case, was no. It just had. Caron had got a terrible roll of the dice. But then again, was the car journey back from Switzerland too tiring? Or perhaps the flight to Switzerland was? What if she hadn't been turned for a bed bath? Was the electronic treatment on her spine too much? Should I have kept her resting in bed? The questions went on and on and on. No, I didn't sleep.

Charlie has always been an early riser, so that first morning, as dawn crept over the skyline, I got up and managed to dress. I didn't want that little boy to be on his own for one minute. I walked to the bedroom window and looked out on to a whole new landscape. This was the first day I had woken up to a world without Caron.

How do you make breakfast for a child who has just lost his mother? In exactly the same way you make breakfast for a child who hasn't. The kettle goes on, water boils . . . Incredible. Bread is dropped into the toaster and pings out again as toast . . . Remarkable. How can water boil and bread turn into toast when my daughter's body lies lifeless upstairs? I realise now that what was happening was that our survival mechanisms were already kicking in. In those first glaringly impossible hours, certain practicalities still had to be seen to. It started with breakfast. Little boys get hungry: shopping was going to have to be bought; food was going to have to be cooked. Undoubtedly our concern for the boys was so great that indirectly they helped us cope, or at least gave us a focus. In fact, only the evening before, when we had been desperate to know how to break the news to the boys, the GP had said, 'Watch, the children will lead you,' and they did, because small boys need to be fed and watered, and they had to be occupied too. At first we were waiting for the outcry, almost, but it never really came. I suppose they had been transported into a block of ice of their own. It certainly seemed to me that for a while they were knocked back inside their bodies.

The second, stranger, practicality was dealing with the press. Because Caron's illness had been kept quiet for seven years, her death from cancer was going to come as a shock. Few knew she had been ill, so not only did news of her death have to be made public, so did something of her tenacious struggle. A news release had to be written. Peter Powell, Russ's business partner, arrived at Sevenoaks and we sat round the kitchen table, Russ, Michael, Paul, Peter and me, and tried to put into a few words the shocking fact that Caron Keating had lost her battle with cancer. Peter then got on the phone and released it to the Press Association and instantly it went around the news agencies.

In the end every news channel covered it. It was a shocking, defining moment when the radio we were tuned into, read out the headlines for the lunchtime news. It was like a bolt of lightning struck the house. Reality hit. We were all up on the landing outside Caron's room when we heard it: 'The *Blue Peter* TV presenter Caron Keating died yesterday at her mother's house. She was forty-one years old . . .' We stood huddled together, hugging one another, listening appalled as the solemn newsreader expanded on what a few hours earlier we had put on paper. It was real. Caron was dead. Yet I could see her, lying there in the next room, out of the corner of my eye, as if only asleep. It was horribly confusing. It was almost an out-of-body experience. What you're hearing and seeing is all happening far away to someone else and isn't real. Tragically, though, that's just wishful thinking. There was a terrible sort of brutal finality about hearing it on the news; it confirmed she was gone.

When it came to the six o'clock news, it was almost more surreal. I remember Russ saying to the boys, 'Come on, we're going to watch Mummy.' It may sound utterly bizarre, and it was, but we all filed downstairs into the living room and watched the telly. Suddenly there she was, dancing and singing on *Blue Peter* on TV, and the boys were sitting on the floor watching. It was somehow comforting to see her move and smile. We were heartened by the lovely tributes that came pouring in from people about their favourite TV presenter, their friend, my daughter, Charlie and Gabriel's mum. Paul was upstairs holding Caron's hand while he watched her on the telly.

We were temporarily sucked into a parallel universe in which Caron was still alive. Then the news programme ended, the television was switched off, and bang, we were back to the present and our gorgeous girl lay lifeless upstairs. It was like having a bubble form temporarily around us and then burst. It felt as if we were being thrown forcefully against a wall. The bubble would reform, then burst. Bubble. Burst. Bubble. Burst. On and on until we were wrung out with emotion and exhaustion.

On the second evening after Caron's death my friend Jackie remembers opening a bottle of wine and us all sitting round the dining-room table. *Blue Peter* had just shown a compilation special and Gabriel had never known or seen his mother do any of those active, brave, adventurous things. After the programme there were a lot of dare-devil antics to share and with them came laughter. Caring for the boys took away the edge as the searing reality of Caron's death very slowly began to seep in.

This Morning also did a special. Watching the tributes became almost like an event. I gleaned a strange comfort in seeing life in her body. If I could, I would have climbed into the television set and stayed there. Instead I went back upstairs, lit another candle and stared and stared and stared at Caron, willing her to take just one more breath.

Everyone stayed. I've no idea where they all slept. Things had to be done. There were so many practicalities that had to be dealt with. Once again that 'something else' took over. Michael went out with Russ to make arrangements for the funeral. Of course, Michael and Paul had done it before, for their dad, seven years earlier. When Michael was only twenty-six years old, he flew to Ireland by himself when Don died, on 24 January 1997. The rest of the family were en route. Don and I had long been divorced. Michael went to the registry office before anyone else arrived. I remember him and Caron going to Marks & Spencer to buy Don a new shirt, and them having a slightly bizarre, comical conversation as they tried to work out whether Don would prefer the yellow or the cream one. I think they chose cream in the end. Here was Michael doing it again, this time for his sister, this time aged thirty-three.

Now Paul went with Michael to the registry office. The news was being repeated every half an hour: 'Caron Keating died yesterday at her mother's home . . .' The woman behind the desk noted the boys' surname, put two and two together and started commiserating with them. It wasn't normal. It wasn't private. The grieving process was sort of interrupted at that point, almost overtaken by the flood of emotional out-pouring that followed. It was extraordinary.

All of a sudden the world knew about what had happened to our family. The phone started to ring, the doorbell sounded over and over, and flowers began to arrive. Suddenly there was this huge onslaught of emotion from fans who had loved her on the telly, friends who had thought she'd gone to Australia suffering from a bit of depression, family who had believed she was getting better. Everyone was suffering from the same shock, asking the same questions. The phone never stopped. In the end we asked Jackie, a family friend, to be at home to answer the calls.

Caron's death was on all the news programmes and on the front page of every newspaper. People were saying such lovely things about her, paying tribute to her, recounting stories I had never heard. While I may have found a grim comfort from it, I know that my sons found it too much at times. The story of a young mother's secret seven-year battle struck a chord with many, but at the end of the day Caron was their sister and she was dead and that had nothing to do with anyone but them. I know now that grief is what we feel when someone dies, and mourning is what we do with those feelings, and the truth is that everybody grieves differently and everybody mourns differently. Part of me wanted Caron's story to stay in the headlines for ever, to keep her alive. In the depths of my despair, the only thing that gave me the slightest comfort was the kind and heartfelt words that were being said. Hearing 'The multi-talented Caron Keating . . . Beautiful, clever, witty . . .' and all the other lovely things people said about her were, in a stupid way, comforting. Does that make sense? No. Did anything make sense? Absolutely not.

None of us had the energy to talk on the phone at the time,

unless it was a really close friend, and even then it was short, but at the end of each day I would sit down with Jackie's meticulously made notes and read all the messages. It was nice, but if I am being absolutely truthful, in those very early hours I couldn't take any of it on board. It was all happening to somebody else. It was like watching a film. I was just waiting for the moment when the production manager would whisper in my earpiece that we were off air and I could go back to my real life, the one in which Caron didn't have cancer and hadn't died.

The very next day the mail began to arrive – first in a sack, then in crates. That too was very comforting. Like when I listened to famous people and newsreaders saying how much they had adored Caron, I was touched by how many people had loved my daughter enough to write. The letters came from far and wide. Emma Thompson sent a picture her little daughter had drawn of Caron, in vivid colours, just as she had dressed, with a bright sun in the background, and also wrote:

When the worst that can happen has happened, there is
little to say but to acknowledge that the landscape has
changed for ever and the world is a lesser place. I
remember Caron as the warmest, most beautiful girl, and I
believe that in the space she has left behind only the best,
most loving, most fruitful things can happen.
With so much love and sympathy,
Emma T.

The Secretary of State for Northern Ireland sent a note. Cherie Blair and a lot of leaders put pen to paper. But the letters also came from Caron's old school friends. There is one I still treasure from her classmate Andy White, now living in Victoria, Australia:

I first remember Caron at Methody. In the school band, where she played flute beside my sister. In the drama society, where she shone as a special person onstage. At school concerts and discos. Hanging out in the music department and later at the Arts Theatre. A lot of time spent talking and dreaming about the future. Looking back, it was such an exciting place to be, and Caron was at the heart of the people who made it like that.

I think, above all, when I first met Caron I could not believe that someone so talented and beautiful could be so unaffected and friendly. Years later I think the same thing. How friendly you are defines a person for me, and that would always knock me out about Caron every time I met her.

I wish you strength and faith, and know that you will see her again. I am sure her spirit is in a really good place, for she was such a great person.

Reading the letters was wonderful, overwhelming, humbling and life-saving. It was also hard, because every letter started with the bald fact that the sender was very sorry to hear that Caron had died. You would have thought that after reading those words a few hundred times it would begin to sink in, but it didn't. The letters from work friends, school friends, from the Girl Guides all lent me a new memory. Those shared memories confirmed what sort of girl she was and they really did bring comfort.

Unless you've been in that position, I don't think people truly appreciate how much comfort a letter can bring. You want to hear people saying how much they loved your child, husband, wife; you want to hear people pay tribute to the person who's died. That is why it is so important to go to the funeral, because that support means a great deal to the family. It means, 'We loved her too. We will remember her too. We will think about her too . . . and maybe, just maybe you can keep her alive a fraction longer.' My advice to anyone who knows someone in the ghastly position of just having lost someone is to ring, write, either, both, and if you're a very close friend, just turn up, deliver food. It doesn't matter. Just do something. Every act of kindness helps, and some more than others.

Over the next few days the volume of letters increased. I found I needed them daily. I simply couldn't wait to open them. I would almost get excited: 'Look, two crates today!' I'd delight in each accolade, somebody else extolling her virtues, saying how marvellous she was, what a great girl she was, how much they loved her. I opened every single one. It gave me such help just knowing how much my daughter was loved and admired. I appreciate rereading them still. In years to come the boys will be able to read them too, if they want. I'd hear over and over again on the phone, 'Can't believe it . . .' 'Wish I'd known . . .' and 'I had no idea . . .' but the letters were where the real feelings came out. That's why they are so important. Memories, snippets that you didn't know – those are the really fabulous letters that return to you a missing reel. Others were about why particular friends sought out Caron's company. Never underestimate what those letters give to people.

The letters weren't just from people who had personally known Caron or our family; from that first day after the announcement of Caron's death, letters from people I had never met started to pour in. At the time I thought that nothing could soothe me more than reading the generous words friends had written about Caron; I was wrong. I believed I was completely alone in my suffering. I was empty and desolate, broken but apparently still breathing. Surely no one had lost such a phenomenal child. Surely no one had felt pain like this and survived. How very, very wrong I was.

By far the greatest volume of letters came from women, like me, whose child, old or young, had died. An enormous part of my attempting to heal has come from those strangers whom I will never meet who wrote to me just after Caron died and continue to write to me still. I also received letters from women in their forties who had read about Caron and found themselves looking at their own children with new eyes, asking themselves, What would I do if that happened to me? Phillip Schofield went home from the funeral and hugged his children even tighter. Women wrote about how they had re-evaluated their lives. It is often said that we only appreciate something after we have lost it, and in this case it seemed that Caron had done the losing for them. I cannot stress enough what it was to be thrown such a lifeline. Every day I think of the wisdom people have shared, words they've written, things they've said that have helped me again and again. It is a huge part of why I am writing this book. I feel it's my duty to pass on that survival kit to the people who still write to me, who say, 'I don't know what to do. I don't know how to get by,' and more importantly I want to pass it on to those people who haven't written to me.

If ever I doubt myself, I remember with poignancy a letter I received some time later from a young woman who was facing illness herself: 'You saved a life today . . . If you can do it, I can do it.' That was exactly how I felt when I read those strangers' letters, because at the time I was convinced that I couldn't survive my loss. Then a letter would arrive that would make me weep with admiration, from someone who had faced an even deeper loss than mine and survived. Her son was only 33.

Dear Gloria,

I am so sorry to hear about the death of your beautiful daughter, Caron. She was always a ray of sunshine on the TV and will be sadly missed.

I lost my own son, Philip, aged thirty-three, to leukaemia in January and know a little of what you are going through. It is very hard to lose your child.

We have found that we have gained our strength from Philip's. I am sure you feel so proud of Caron's courage and the love she bestowed on those close to her, and we find we can draw on that. Philip told us he didn't want us to be unhappy as he had had a full and exciting life so we should be happy for him.

I am sure all these brave young people feel the same and I hope you will find this a help in the coming months, as we do.

Yours sincerely,

Brenda

There are chunks of that first week that I don't remember. I was freefalling in a spin, but I do know that I opened every single letter and read every single one. I absorbed each word like life blood itself. Though I couldn't recall the details now, they carried me through that first week and well beyond. 'Dear Gloria, I hope you don't mind but I felt compelled to write. You see, I know how you feel because I too have lost a child . . . I too . . . I too . . .' The message was clear: yes, I had lost an irreplaceable child, but I wasn't alone, I wasn't alone, I wasn't alone.

In the beginning I received some letters from people who had lost their parents. They'd write, 'I understand what you are going through.' I wanted to scream, 'NO YOU DON'T! I've buried my mother and father, and it doesn't feel anything like this!' Others would tell me about their partner dying:

'. . . thought it might help . . .', 'Life goes on', 'My husband was only sixty-two when he died suddenly. We had so many plans.' I wanted to shout, 'Sixty-two! YOU'RE LUCKY! Sixty-two! I'd give you everything, my beating heart, to have Caron live until she was sixty-two.' I know better now. I know that grief rarely takes the same shape or form, but the weight is still the same. Grief is grief.

Dawn from Kent wrote:

I watched my husband die of cancer. It took just sixteen months. He passed away on a beautiful summer day. The sun was shining through the window. He seemed to relax and give in. I told him he could go and he did. My priest told me I was wonderful to tell him to go. I gave him my blessing. He couldn't fight any more. The alien that grew in his insides had won. It came to destroy my family and it did. Night-times are the worst, morning never seems to come, but it does.

Take every day as it comes! If you feel like crying, then cry! If you feel like screaming, then scream! Do what your body tells you!

Grief is a process we go through to incorporate loss into our lives. It is completely relative. For one person, losing a parent is as painful as losing a child, or so it feels, until, God forbid, you lose a child. It is only then you realise how very different it is. As Boo from Cambridge wrote, 'There are no words to describe it; it is beyond pain.'

I know that people's intentions were only good, but I was in too raw a place to see it. I have reread countless letters, and now I can truly sympathise with the woman who lost her husband at sixty-two, who is entering her twilight years alone, who, like me, has had to redraw a future without a loved one.

The letters took over the dining room. I would sit at the table surrounded by stacks of envelopes. It became the hub because it was the only room big enough. In fact, still under the table there is a massive wicker basket full of cards sent by people who didn't include an address. I haven't had the heart to move it. It used to be a cardboard box, but I bought a basket because the box didn't do the cards justice. Keeping the basket there is a symbol of that time when the table was groaning under the weight of letters. I'd marvel at those crates, marvel, and at a time when I was destroyed by grief, that was truly a gift. And yet so many arrived with an apology, 'I hope you don't mind . . .' 'Please excuse me . . .' 'Sorry for intruding . . .' In those early days, when I was still firmly locked up in ice, I wasn't able to respond or file the letters adequately so that I could respond later, but I would like to say to everyone who wrote that it wasn't an intrusion. It was a godsend.

Walton-on-Thames

Dear Gloria,

I just felt I had to write to you. I lost my beautiful daughter Amanda to breast cancer. She was only just thirty-two years old. She died in my arms in her own bed in November 2001. She first had cancer aged twenty-six. She had part of the breast removed, then chemo and radiotherapy, and we held our breath for almost five years.

Amanda married Richard, her schoolboy sweetheart, and one year later she gave birth to Ella Louise. I was with Richard at Ella's birth, because like you, I was so close and proud of my youngest girl. She was so brave and never made a fuss when Ella's birth was over. Amanda and I cried together to think at last it was all behind us. Her dream of becoming a mother had come

46

true. This was the one baby she didn't have to hand back, as she had been a full-time nanny all her working life.

For two and a half years her life with us all was wonderful and then the Monster C was back. She had a further six months of chemo and then in the August her doctors told Richard and me she had just a few months to live. She was so brave – she said goodbye to all her dear friends and then she told me she wanted to die at home. I packed up my job and between us – my elder daughter, Ashley, Richard and myself – we nursed her together. I was told in late October that her time was running out, so I slept at their home for the last few nights of her short life. Like you, I didn't want her to leave me. My baby. Her pain was unbearable.

The final night her breathing changed. Richard said his goodbyes and little Ella kissed Mummy goodnight for the last time. I undressed and got into bed with my wonderful girl. I told her how much I loved her and how dear God I wished it was me and not her leaving us. I know they say the hearing is the last thing to go, so I held her close and took her back to the wonderful childhood we have given to both our girls, to places she loved in Devon, and talked and kissed her darling face and hands and fingers, frightened to let her go from me. The room was so peaceful. My baby had died in my arms in bed with her mummy, safe and secure in my love. Gloria, you also gave Caron that love and that safe and secure place, which is why she got home to be with you. You gave her life and you were there for her last breath.

I know the pain you are feeling. I still feel it two and a half years on, but I also know the love and friendship we shared as mother and daughter. I hope you find some peace and comfort soon. I have also now lost Ashley, my

other daughter, to sudden adult death. She was found dead in bed by my eldest granddaughter, Danielle, aged eleven years. So I have lost them both. I get some comfort that Ashley died in her sleep and both my darling girls are together. Caron is now with her daddy and at peace.
Your pain will ease in time and you will find you can talk about her without crying and laugh at the things she said. You have four grandsons to love, and I have three granddaughters to love, and that is a blessing – to look into their eyes and see their mummies'.
I hope you find peace soon, Gloria. Until they lose a child no one can begin to know how you feel. You should not have to stand by your child's coffin. It is so cruel, and for myself and my husband we have had to do it twice, but you do get the strength to go on, if only to care for grandchildren, because we know that would be our daughters' wishes.
I have no faith left in God, but I hope you do. God let me down by taking both my beautiful girls. My thoughts are with you, and I share your pain.
From a sad mum,
Sincerely,
Sandra

There is no question that over the coming days, weeks and months each letter that came passed on a bit of information that little by little helped me to thaw. The letters were from people who walked just ahead of me on this knife-edge, from 'one devastated mum to another'. Sometimes it wasn't even advice that gave me the impetus to get through another day without Caron: I got a letter from a woman in Battersea whose son had died. 'I feel as though a part of me has been taken away,' she wrote. Yes, that's it, that's how I feel. A part of me has been taken away. I wondered then if it was ever going to be returned. Perhaps it has been, but it isn't the same part. It has shrunk a little, got a little wiser, a little harder. It doesn't quite fit, but I am learning to live with it. It's like walking in shoes that are a fraction too tight: after a long day the blisters have cut to the bone, but you remain standing.

While downstairs became a sorting office, a reception, a canteen, a playroom, a planning office, upstairs Caron still lay quietly in her bed. In true Irish tradition, she stayed in the house for a week. She died on 13 April and was buried on the 20th. During that time she was taken away once, for one day, so the undertakers could do what they had to do. I remember saying, 'You have to have her back before dark,' as I didn't want her gone longer than a couple of hours. My friend Jackie remembers me getting very agitated while Caron was away and I made her call the undertaker to remind them that I wanted her home that evening. I didn't want her being any-where else but home. When she came back, it was in a coffin. It stayed in the room where she'd died, open, so that we could still go and look at her and talk to her. I didn't like the way the undertakers had done her make-up, so I retouched it. I know that may sound macabre, but strangely enough it wasn't.

Honestly, if I could have kept Caron at home for ever, I would have. We sat for hours and hours with her, talking to her. We never really left her alone, except at night-time. We didn't let the little boys go in: we thought that was too much, which they seemed to accept without question. They obviously knew she was in there, but they never tried to find the key and never asked to go in, except for one occasion when Jackie overheard Gabriel knocking on the bedroom door and saying, 'Mummy, you've been asleep too long – it's time to wake up.' Candles were lit all day long, particularly the one scented with tuberose, which was her favourite. I only blew the candles out when we went to bed. I may have gone to bed, but I still didn't sleep. Endless night followed endless night, as the hours since Caron's death became days, and the days became a week.

In amongst the letters, the tears, watching and caring for the boys and the visitors, there was a funeral to arrange. On one level the world had combusted, and on another we were looking at the practicalities of orders of service and choosing music. What reading would she like? Which typeface should we choose? On one level such decisions seemed utterly pointless – who cared which typeface when Caron lay dead? – but on another were absolutely necessary. It had to be done for Caron; we wanted everything to be as she would have wanted. Maybe even the formality, the process of a funeral, provides a reason to get up in those first few days. Without it you might come to a grinding halt, and it is harder to restart from a static point, so you keep moving, albeit like a zombie, taking in only a fraction of what is going on around you. So, yes, in one sense it's nonsense, but in another it is paramount. You want to give the person you love the most beautiful, respectful send-off you can, and you also need something to occupy your raging mind. It is so bizarre, so utterly surreal. What time would be best? One lengthy discussion. How would Caron have liked it? More discussion. Then there is the music to choose, tributes to write, flowers to order, times to plan, who to invite, where to hold the service . . . The dichotomies of death seem never-ending. One moment you don't care if food never touches your lips again; the next you're choosing what canapés to serve. The doing takes over, but always at the back of your mind there's one question that you cannot answer: why? Why? Why?

Nevertheless, your survival instinct and strength come from somewhere deep within. This envelops you and carries you forward in the middle of your darkest days, when you feel you literally haven't got the strength to stand. The other thing that keeps you moving are the friends and family that gather around you. People kept coming to the house; they never stopped. It was unseasonably good weather, so there were endless cups of tea on the terrace, in the conservatory, around the kitchen table. An old family friend, Michael Ball, asked if he could visit. He went upstairs, talked to Caron, said good-bye, then came downstairs for tea on the veranda. We sat outside roaring with laughter at his jokes, stories and memories of family times with Caron. It was amazing because just a few hours earlier I had stated with absolute sincerity, 'I don't think I will ever laugh again.' Caron was still lying upstairs and yet there I was able to share a joke. The human framework is incredible in how it deals with such shattering loss, how it learns to cope, despite itself. Even Caron would have approved. I had her own words to comfort me:

> The thing I love about the human spirit is that no matter how dire the circumstances – there always comes a point when you can have a laugh and forget about what is happening even for a minute – realise you're still alive and all things are possible.

The biggest saving grace, but also the embodiment of what we had all lost, were the boys, Charlie and Gabriel. They were amazing. The doctor who had told us that the children would lead us could not have been more right. Children live in the moment. One minute they would be talking about Caron, and in the next breath they were out on their bicycles, swimming or kicking a ball. It made me gulp when I heard Gabriel saying to the housekeeper, 'Did you know my mummy died yesterday?' but then he hopped on his bicycle and rode off into the garden. Children can be crying one minute and the next they're on the trampoline laughing. It amazed me how they could jump from one thing to another.

Fortune was, Charlie and Gabriel were in a house they'd known since birth and we were all around. Our study was their playroom. They had all their toys and drawing things there. A woman called Sarah from County Derry sent a card just before Caron's funeral. Her husband had died of cancer when their youngest son, Jack, was only ten weeks old. Like many others, I held on to her words tightly: 'Caron's two beautiful sons will make you smile in spite of yourself in the future. The magic of life. I hope that the "beauty" that was Caron inside and out will help sustain you in the future.' She was right: they did sustain me, despite myself, and they still do make me smile – a lot.

In many cases I think that children cope far better than you expect, provided they are being loved and well looked after. All our energy went into making sure they were. I had promised Caron I would, back in Switzerland. For seven years I had donned a mask for the sake of my sanity and my daughter's positivity and well-being, and the moment Caron died, it automatically transferred to the children. In the depths of your own despair you're thinking, How are the children going to cope with this? We lived second by second that first week. The children became our prime worry. We were all watching them. The doing mode moved into a caretaking mode . . . You slip yourself into gear and continue to grind up the mountain. You hide your pain behind your mask to protect the children, you dry your tears to protect the children, and somehow life continues. Like Caron, the children are still never far from my mind. For them, I kept buoyant; for them, I kept the mask in place; for them, I got out of bed and continued to breathe in and out; and for them, I give thanks.

In many ways life for the boys continued as though Caron was still in Australia. In hindsight those years in Australia had given the boys something that is very rare: a father at home all day, every day and some very very special times. He was, and continues to be, the best dad in the world as far as I am concerned, and I think that in the days that followed Caron's death he was something that was vital: a very present father.

The days leading up to the funeral were so intense, but then, in the middle of it, I have this daft snapshot of me asking Stephen to do practical things like painting the garage doors and front door because I wanted everything to look nice for our girl. It is a small insight into how deranged you become. I even asked my good friend Jackie, who had arrived at seven one morning to be with us, to try on some of Caron's clothes that had come in her suitcase from Australia. I needed to choose something for Caron to be buried in, but I'd become suddenly angry with the clothes, and the futile lifelessness of them. I wanted them to have a purpose, so I asked Jackie to try them on. She now says that if you are in the peculiarly privileged position of being near a grieving family, you go along with whatever they want: there is no right or wrong. When we had chosen the clothes, Jackie recalls that it was her job to iron them. She stood with the iron in her shaking hand, terrified of burning a hole. Michael walked in, noticed the tension and broke it with a touch of black humour: 'Caron always wanted to get you to do her ironing – funny way to go about it.'

And so the week went by in a total haze of feeling distraught, being brave for the children, being comforted, then practical, furious, everything, and underneath it all there was this total disbelief. Round and round we went in a cold vacuum, unable to take it in. I still can't take it on board. I look at Caron every day in photographs. If I didn't believe that I will see her again one day, I would have lost my mind by now. I have to believe that. I have to. I want to.

In the rawness of it all, you can't think or make decisions; you don't care what you have to eat and can't consider food shopping. The best thing that friends did for us was to bring us food. Surinder and Sunita Arora are a lovely couple who own hotels and they rang to ask if they could come over. Though I like them very much, at that point I wasn't quite ready to see people outside the immediate family. Heeding my words but wanting to help, they brought endless portions of delicious food. My friend Merrel Thomas made meals for three days and we all sat round the kitchen table every day and thanked God for the Aroras and Merrel. The idea of shopping for food and cooking was simply unthinkable at that time. Thanks to them, though, food was just there. Without them I don't think we would have eaten. If you're ever looking for something to do for someone who is under great stress, either death or sickness, just make food and bring it whether they eat it or not. Merrel would bring great casseroles that just needed to go in the oven and be heated up. Her desserts were ready to be eaten and required no preparation. One night we had a three-course meal, all Merrel and the Aroras' food. I was returning saucepans and dishes for months afterwards.

The letters kept arriving, each one giving strength when I thought I had none left, and people kept coming to hold me while I sobbed. We were visited by Johnny Comerford, Caron's oldest friend, and his wife, Cathy, who is godmother to Charlie. We all sat talking to Caron, drinking tea. The endless cups of tea.

Richard Madeley and Judy Finnigan also came. They had been in the Florida Keys when they got the news. Their first instinct had been to find a church where they could reach out to her and pray. They were due to be on air back in the UK on the day of the funeral, 20 April, so Richard suggested they fly by helicopter so they could go to work in the afternoon. Channel Four said they were crazy and would be in no state to work, so just gave them the day off. Richard called to tell us they were going to stay in a nearby hotel the day before the funeral, rather than risk the traffic. Richard vividly remembers being on the phone to Michael and him putting down the handset and saying to me, 'Hang on a second, Mum,' Michael said, 'R and J are coming down the night before the funeral . . . Yes, that's what I thought . . .' Then he came back on the line and said to Richard, 'Caron's still here. Would you like to see her?' They readily agreed. Like so many friends, they'd felt like they'd been robbed of seeing her again, as of course she and Russ had planned to spend the summer in Cornwall.

They drove down to Sevenoaks, went up to the room with Russ and sat and talked. Then Russ left and each sat alone with her. Richard recalls her looking peaceful, and has always said it was extremely emotional, moving and a very generous thing to be allowed to do. They hadn't seen Caron since they had worked together a number of years earlier, and though I've never asked Richard or Judy, seeing her again might have been a shock. The illness had changed her, the steroids and radiotherapy had taken their toll, her hair was shorter, gone were the long tresses, but she looked beautiful. Beautiful. In fact Russ said at the funeral that she had never looked more beautiful than towards the end of her life.

Richard's recollection is that the atmosphere in the house was reflective and sensitive, following Caron's lead. We ate together. Dinner was almost joyful, warm and moving, and we spent a lot of time sharing memories and laughing about her. It was while talking about Caron that Judy said, 'Think of her life as a complete life and not one that has been cut short.' That triggered something in Russ and gave him an idea about what he wanted to say at the funeral the following day, because Judy was right: Caron did live such a rich life in her forty-one years; it wasn't enough for me, but no amount of time would have been.

Russ then asked Richard to be a pall-bearer. Richard and Caron had worked side by side at *This Morning* for many months while Judy had been ill. They had tried out other presenters, but there was no question that it should be Caron. For one, she didn't take the job too seriously, and also she was a natural talent – there was something effortless about the way she presented. So Caron stood in for Judy for three months and within weeks Richard says she had become one of his best friends. He was honoured to be asked to be pall-bearer, and honoured to do the job.

If I make the time leading up to Caron's funeral sound jolly, it is not my intention – it wasn't – but there was something comforting about having Caron in the house with us and the visitors filled a void. Even so, there were times during those first few days when the fact that I was still breathing seemed staggering to me. Inside I felt that I had died with Caron, but no one else had noticed. I had been sentenced to death, but the guillotine had not yet fallen.

Little did I know that it was about to get worse. For the time being, Caron was still at home. Simply being able to look at her face and touch her cheek meant the world to me. We all spent hours and hours with her, and in a way I got used to her being there. Even though she wasn't moving and she was cold, she was still with us. I don't know how to describe it, really, but we drew a strange comfort from her physical presence. It was like she was alive, only sleeping. Maybe this all sounds silly, but it meant everything to me that she was at home. I was allowing myself to be lulled into a false sense of security, because she couldn't stay at home for ever, as much as I would have liked to have kept her there. I remember having exactly the same feeling about my mother when she died: I would have happily kept her home for ever. When the day of the funeral finally arrived, it all changed again and the grief reached a completely new level.

On the morning of the funeral I was consumed by a feeling of sheer, overwhelming panic. Even now I can remember it as though it was five minutes ago. The sun was shining, and the children were in the gazebo in the garden with their former nanny, Ruth. As I got ready, I could see through the window that they were drawing, painting and writing letters for Caron to put in the coffin with her, as we all did. Eventually we had to say our final, final goodbyes. Caron was dressed in her lovely silk clothes from Australia. She was buried with her wedding rings. We put our notes in the coffin and a video of Frida Kahlo that she had taken great strength from in those last days in Switzerland. It was particularly poignant looking at the children's drawings and little notes. Still to this day they make birthday cards for Caron. When I see the cards at the grave-side, the savage sense of loss that rips through me is equal to what I experienced as I watched the boys filling the coffin with things she would have liked. I felt a rising, suffocating panic, because I knew that soon I would never again see my daughter's face or hold the hand of the child I had known from birth. It was devastating and heart-wrenching. I kissed her for the millionth and final time, and then they closed the lid.

4

The Funeral

Do not stand at my grave and weep;
I am not there. I do not sleep.
I am a thousand winds that blow.
I am the diamond glints on snow.
I am the sunlight on ripened grain.
I am the gentle autumn rain.
When you awaken in the morning's hush,
I am the swift uplifting rush
Of quiet birds in circled flight.
I am the soft stars that shine at night.
Do not stand at my grave and cry;
I am not there. I did not die.

'Do Not Stand at My Grave
and Weep', Anon

Funerals are not events; they are a function of death; they force punctuation on an ever-growing sense of disbelief. And yet, amid the haze and pain, what is really odd is that you want to look your best. You want it to be a 'good' funeral. You want to pay tribute to the person who has gone. You want to let those who loved them take part, and as terrible as you feel, you want it to be a celebration of that person's life.

I have received wonderful, uplifting letters from brave women who have found a way to bury their courageous young children in a way that honours them and befits childhood. One mother wrote to tell me about her *Dr Who*-mad son, Joe, who sadly died aged eight. She had his casket made to look like a Tardis, with a second, smaller one for his ashes: 'A true time-traveller now.' They planned a huge 'tribute' day for Joe at which over three hundred people came dressed in his favourite colour, red, and let hundreds of messages for Joe tied to red balloons float up into the air. In her wonderfully descriptive letter she wrote about how the sea of red balloons disappeared into a stunning blue sky, and I feel that her son was well honoured. I suppose that is what the funeral is really about: honouring the dead. And that is why we find the strength to do it even when all we want to do is crawl into a dark place, curl into a ball and weep.

Many found that their loved ones had left comprehensive notes about what was to be said, sung and done on the day. Not in our case. Caron left us no clues. Coupling that sense of occasion with abject loss can be difficult; for us, it was almost like hosting a wedding but with no joy and dressed in black. All the time you're thinking to yourself, I want her to be proud of me and I want to look nice for her funeral, just as you would for a celebration. In the same way we bedecked the steps from the front door with hydrangeas and tulips because we wanted the house to look lovely, so I wanted to do her proud. We wanted it to be as beautiful as it could be because we were paving the way for everything to be lovely for her.

It was another stunning, clear-sky day. No April showers for Caron. Stephen's freshly painted doors glistened in the sunlight. The lawn was cut. There was colour everywhere. All her favourite flowers. The coffin was all draped in white lilies in the drawing room. It took hours to cover it, it was dripping with them, but it was still a box and she was still inside it and it was dark and she couldn't get out. It was the most terrifying, suffocating sensation because of course the part of me that died with her was in there too.

On 20 April 2004 we climbed a mountain of lasts. Everything that day was the last of everything that had gone before: the last time she was in that room; the last time down the stairs; the last time in the sitting room where the flowers had been so carefully laid; the last time she'd ever be at home in Sevenoaks; then we left the house for the last time and had that awful crawl up the long, wooded road that we'd walked with the dogs, then children, so many times. We covered the miles inch by inch, all the way from Sevenoaks to St Peter's Church at Hever Castle, where Caron and Russ were married in their fairytale wedding a meagre thirteen years before. The drive itself was purgatorial, but as terrible as it is to follow your child's coffin, arriving is worse.

As we had arranged, the cars stopped just inside the gates of Hever Castle. I could hear the bells tolling, over and over. They had been ringing steadily, mournfully since 1.45 p.m. Just then an explosion went off in my head. Enough was enough. I wanted it to stop now. We'd come far enough with this nonsense. I wanted my daughter back. When would this reel end? When could we go home for a nice cup of tea and a chat round the kitchen table? Instead we stepped out of the cars and the heavy wooden gates to the castle finally opened. The eight pall-bearers were Michael, Paul, Stephen, Richard Madeley, Johnny Co-merford and Roy Heayberd, an old friend, who spoke at Don's funeral, plus two of the undertakers.

As they carried Caron out, I remember looking up and seeing a bank of photographers and rows of people. Suddenly the flashbulbs started going off. I didn't know what was happening. I appeared to be walking behind the coffin, but it was just like being in a film. I was in somebody else's nightmare, not my own. I was sobbing uncontrollably by now because this was the last of the lasts: the last walk. I clung on to Charlie and Gabriel and somehow managed to put one foot in front of the other.

Seeing all Caron's friends who hadn't seen her for over two years was very hard, but also wonderful, I suppose, though I don't recall thinking that at the time. When you see people collectively like that, you see the person's life in microcosm. It's a living photo album, three hundred people to remind me she had lived a full and fabulous life. That's why it is so important to go to the funeral – more than anything you want to know your loved one's life meant something. If their death has had an effect on people, it is because their life did. On the day of the funeral that is all you have to hold on to. As overwhelming as it is to face a crowd on what is the worst day of your life, seeing an empty church would be worse. As well as the three-hundred-strong congregation, there were many people outside too. It meant a lot to me that they'd made the effort to come to Hever to pay their respects. The choir who'd sung at Caron's wedding was there. In many respects it was like a rerun of that memorable day, complete with the groom in his kilt, except the princess was missing.

Russ, Caron's Prince Charming, has shown strength and valour way beyond the call of duty. He absorbed years of Caron's pain, fear and tenacity. Bar climbing into her skin, he shared it all. He proved to us what he was made of when he stood in the same spot where he'd waited for his bride and said his wedding day was 'the best day of my life so far. The irony is that I stand here on the worst day of my life so far.'

There was still quite a lot of confusion surrounding the last few years of Caron's life. Many thought that Caron had suffered a mini-breakdown after Gabriel was born and that was the reason the family had got out of the fast lane and moved to Cornwall back in 1999. The truth about the cancer was of course now widespread, but I think very few people knew what Caron herself had been through. Russ told the congregation he was going to 'ramble on' for a while, and though it was going to be very hard, I think he really wanted everyone to know what we had all been through. First, though, he read out a letter that I had written to Caron:

My dearest and most beautiful Caron,
    What a joy and privilege for over forty-one years to have you as my most precious and loving daughter.
    I feel so proud to be your mum and I could not have wished for a more glorious daughter: spirited, caring, loving and full of fun. You showered endless love and joy on our lives and brought light and rainbows to us daily. Although our relationship has always been exceptionally deep, during the last seven years there have been constant new depths and discovery, but through all your pain and suffering you have brought such warmth, love, laughter and friendship.
    Watching you bravely battle with cancer has taught me so much about positivity, tenacity, dignity, spiritual growth and integrity. You are a total inspiration, not only to your family but to all those lives you have touched.
    You and Russ have given us the precious and ultimate gift in two beautiful boys, Charlie and Gabriel, and you will live on through them. They will be a daily reminder of your spirit and individuality and all the values that you have taught them. Alongside Russ, Paul, Sandy, Michael and Stephen, I will for ever love and look after your cherished boys, as you would wish.

Always With You

*I miss talking to you every day; you were the girl I
loved talking to most in the world. The heartache of losing
you will never be healed, but you have left us with
millions of exquisite thoughts and memories.*

*In Australia you used to say that you could not wait to
have a cup of tea out of your favourite cup at the kitchen
table in Sevenoaks, and with your incredible instinct and
typical Irish timing, you made it back. Perhaps out of the
endless memories, a few of the more recent ones will
always shine out. Four weeks in Switzerland when, in the
middle of concentrating on your healing and treatment,
you also managed to organise my birthday celebrations,
the Easter-egg-painting competition and a blissful Mother's
Day, just you and me. It was the first time in three years
that we had spent Mother's Day together and what a
glorious day we had in the Swiss Alps, scoffing apple
strudel and chatting non-stop.*

*How I treasure your gift, which you managed to paint
in Australia despite your pain and frustration – beautiful
tulips in a country frame, which you carefully inscribed
with love and kisses and lovingly placed in your suitcase
for our special day together. Yet another example of your
generosity of spirit, which you radiated in abundance. You
always did believe in angels and now you are one of
God's brightest and most beautiful, so fly freely, my
darling Caron, in your release from pain, and know that
every second I will carry you in my heart.*

With all my love for ever,
Mum

Russ went on to recount how he and Caron had met and fallen
in love. He talked of the work Caron had done, the impact

63

she'd had on the television, and he recalled that he, along with practically the entire male population of the country, had fallen in love with her when she was on *Blue Peter* and had, again like many, fantasised about winning the heart of the staggeringly beautiful girl with the Irish lilt. He said that the fact that he had been picked sometimes still seemed to him a wonderful mystery.

He told the congregation that when they had decided to get married, they had turned up at Hever doing the celebrity thing – 'Hi, can we get married in your church?' – but the vicar had said no. So they had brought Gloria down, but he had *still* said no. Cue for much-needed laughter. Instead the vicar told them they had to come to church for six months, which they did. 'With hangovers on a Sunday morning we worshipped in the church for six months and got to know the congregation and the choir, which made it so important on our wedding day.' Holding Caron's funeral at Hever brought so much back to Russ about what that church means to him and our family – Hever has been a venue for birthdays and weddings in our family for many years – and as Russ said, 'Caron will be well cared for here.'

He said, 'The one word that summed up Caron most was "rollercoaster", and boy, we all loved being on it with her.' He used the words that others had written in letters and cards over the course of the week – vivacious, out there, inspirational, a breath of fresh air, wild, funny, clever, caring, charming – but added that those who knew her well also considered her angelic, warm, special and loving. Towards the end she became brave and courageous. Russ added, 'I particularly remember all of these things about Caron, but of course on top of that, she was bewitchingly beautiful.' Then he went on to sum up their life together. He described them as a 'golden couple', recalled the birth of the two boys and said their life in Barnes was idyllic – constant open house, logs burning, food in the Aga, 'though not necessarily Caron's'. And then the horror of cancer. 'Shattered and fearful at first, she opened her heart, took a deep breath and got on with it. She would face and accept the challenge, whatever it was. She had such courage; it never faltered. This is a mark of the woman I love and will stay with me for ever. She made it so easy for the rest of us, and she kept fighting it, but it kept coming back.'

By February 2000 they knew it was lymphatic cancer. On their way back from a week in Cornwall, with the boys asleep in the back of the car, they decided to change their lives completely. 'Fowey was a haven,' he said. Caron had anonymity, could walk on the hills and, even though she was very ill, planned Russ's fortieth birthday and parked a Harley Davidson and a surfboard in the reception of the hotel in the town. Then Russ talked about Australia, explaining that she went there 'not to beat what she was going through, but to accept it. Byron became another haven. She wasn't running away; she never ran away,' he said. 'She just wanted to find peace and solitude. What affected her deeply at the time was that she left so many friends behind, almost without a reason. They didn't understand – sometimes I didn't understand – but we hoped that something good would come out of it. Though there were many difficult days while we were there, something good did come of it.'

Stephen and I went to Byron Bay whenever they needed us, and as I have said, though always close, my relationship with Caron deepened. Russ said Caron's quest to heal was 'beautiful to see, hard to see. Gloria was there for me too, and that made it easier.' The people they met were very spiritual, and 'between the mountains, the rainforest, the people,˙ we grew . . . They were saviours for us. We had great times and grew in spirituality.' He talked about the monks whose help Caron sought and told how Caron had insisted he go to hear them, even though she was in too much pain and could not go herself. 'Afterwards we brought them back to the house – six Tibetan monks sipping tea with Caron on the sofa.' They brought warmth and spirituality to Caron and came back six or seven times, sometimes staying for three days, sometimes a week. Once, they did a puja, chanting non-stop for four days for her strength and her soul. 'During the last forty-eight hours of her life, around the world Tibetan monks were chanting for her, to help her cross between the two worlds. It is a tribute to whatever in her shone. They saw it, I certainly saw it, we all saw it.'

Russ wanted to reiterate, because Caron would have wanted him to, that Caron's journey was her journey, the outcome for her was not necessarily the outcome for others, and just because she passed on doesn't mean others will pass on. 'It's worth fighting.' We all closed our eyes and prayed for those people who were fighting or close to someone fighting this disease.

He then went on to read a letter from her friends in Byron Bay.

We loved Caron like a sister, and it is hard to reconcile her being gone because her energy remains so strongly. We are grateful that we never knew her as a celebrity, but as the essence of a deeply aware, vibrant being who embraced every challenge with love and the commitment to live beyond what her cards had dealt her. Hers was truly a brave heart, and we were always humbled by her courage to sing and laugh and dance in celebration with the energy she had left in her body. We loved her songs

and we are honoured to have sung with her. We feel
blessed to have known you and Caron and the boys in
that place of surrender. And all that was left at times was
love; we have all been awash with it. The journey that
she took and the depths to which she travelled on her
inevitable path became the focus of many of our lives and
we will be for ever indebted to her for making our lives
more precious.

Finally Russ started talking about the end: the red shoes, Mother's Day, the birthday surprise, the Easter-egg competition and the sudden change that came across her, the drive home, the last day. He told everyone how Charlie and Gabriel came in to cuddle their mummy and say beautiful things, but now he was really talking to them. 'She knew anyway, guys, but the way you sat with her and held her hand and kissed her was a memory I'll take with me for ever. The bravery of you two has been outstanding.' He told everyone how she slowly slipped away, how peaceful she was, very, very peaceful. She knew that she had the love and warmth of her family and friends, and was in a familiar place. She'd done so much work on herself in terms of spirituality that she had no fear. She arrived at a stage of enlightenment from the darkness of cancer. She reached personal peace and calmness. A smile came across her face and stayed with her. 'She'll still be smiling – she'd say I was ranting, but she'd still be smiling. And that was it, but it's not it, because she will live through all of us and she will inspire many in the future.' Prophetic words.

At the end of his eulogy, he read the following poem. Faultlessly. He did Caron proud.

You can shed tears that she is gone
Or you can smile because she has lived.
You can close your eyes and pray that she'll come back
Or you can open your eyes and see all that she has left.
Your heart can be empty because you can't see her
Or you can be full of the love that you shared.
You can turn your back on tomorrow and live for
    yesterday
Or you can be happy for tomorrow because of yesterday.
You can remember her and ache that she has gone
Or you can cherish her memory and let it live on.
You can cry, close your mind, be empty and turn your
    back
Or you can do what she would want:
Smile, open your eyes, love and go on.

'She Is Gone', Anon

Then he ended, 'Caron was everything a man could ever wish for – beautiful, intelligent, witty, fun-loving, caring, honest, loyal and loving – and I was the luckiest man in the world because for sixteen and a half years I was the one walking the path with her. Caron.'

I have heard bereavement counsellors and other parents who've lost children talk about the terrible pain that a premature death inflicts. Over and over we obsess about all we and they are missing out on. A woman once asked me if, back on 5 October 1962, a stork, angel or delivery boy had arrived with a package containing Caron and said, 'I bring you this child to love and care for, but you can only have her for forty-one and a half years,' whether I'd send the package back. Would I turn the stork away? Never. Not for one split second.

68

I understand those women whose babies have died within hours of birth and who say, 'I would rather have known them for those precious minutes than not at all.'

When Russ stood on the same spot he married Caron and said those extraordinary things, he must have asked himself, If I'd known, would I have changed a thing? Well, like me, his answer would be a resounding No. Not only had he met the love of his life, she'd given him two exceptional boys. When she'd then been diagnosed with a terminal illness, their love was tested, no doubt, but it grew deeper, wider and stronger as a result. It was a privilege, he said, to love like that, and that is what came over in his eulogy more than the extended catching up, the filling in, the joining of dots; what came across was love. You can't see love and you can't hear it, touch it or smell it, catch it or hold it, but it is there. The room vibrated with it, and slowly the tears retreated and an extraordinary feeling of joy oscillated through the church.

After we all listened to Russ and Caron's song, the Van Morrison classic 'Have I Told You Lately . . . ?' it was Richard Madeley's turn to speak. He has since recollected to me the rapidly swinging extremes of emotion he experienced that day. It was unbearably sad and painful. Then there'd be a burst of laughter, then more pain as it finally hit him that this really was goodbye. There was no more putting it off. In a few short minutes she would be taken to the graveyard and be gone. Richard says he felt that they were witnessing the closing scenes of a wonderful life, but it didn't feel as if her life had ended, more that the final paragraph was being written in front of them and it was awful. First, everyone was feeling their own pain; then they saw our pain, which made them feel twice as bad, but Russ's eulogy helped. It was a *tour de force* and very generous. Russ knew that people were in great pain, and like

69

Caron had done during her battle, he tried to make it easier for everybody else.

Richard had written down what he was going to say, but every time he had rehearsed it he had broken down. His daughter Chloe had taken him in hand and told him in no uncertain terms that he was going to have to do a lot better than that! She said, 'You're doing this for the family. You have to be strong and get this right. You've been given a job to do.' So when he walked to the pulpit to give his speech, he had his daughter's no-nonsense advice ringing in his ears and, if that were not enough of an incentive, he had the image of Caron standing behind him ready to kick him in the arse if he didn't get it right! He did of course get it right, and said what was in our hearts.

After Richard there was more music. Then Judy spoke beautifully and sensitively about her closeness to Caron and their special friendship. Lastly Cliff Richard spoke, 'It's great going last on the bill, but you've all said everything I was going to say,' so he put down his prompt cards and spoke from the heart. He quoted from the Bible about the greatest gift of all – love, which gave great comfort and was a truly beautiful finish. Then, as Richard says, 'The bell went, the coffin was lifted out, and we all went back to Hever and raised a glass to a very special girl.'

It had been a magnificent service and a phenomenal tribute to Caron. Her friends and the entire family circle really appreciated being filled in on those 'missing years' while Caron valiantly fought her cancer in secret. The letters I was to receive from Caron's friends in the days and weeks following the funeral showed just how much people had been affected. One of these was an extraordinary letter from Shaun McIlwrath, an old boyfriend of Caron's from when they were teenagers growing up in Northern Ireland and someone she'd always kept in touch with.

Always With You

Dear Glo,

Sorry about the typewritten letter, it looks so formal, but it's only because my handwriting is so illegible. Anyway, it's me – Shaun.

This is just a short note to say how sorry I was to have to meet you again, after all this time, in such tragic circumstances.

I had not seen Caron for seven years and yet I would say I probably thought of her, on average, two or three times a month – every time I heard a passionate opinion, unrestrained laughter or an original and imaginative thought.

She ate up life. We all adored her. At an age when most of us were posing around trying to look bored and cool, Caron would find wonder and excitement in an empty room. She would challenge and charm, and could draw from the driest of minds rivers of dreams. That was her gift.

You see, the more I think about it, the more it becomes clear that whatever has happened, Caron is in a safe place now. Nothing can harm her or upset her ever again. Which is why I actually want to talk about you.

Everything Caron had came from you. I always thought of the two of you as being like suns. Big, radiant characters around whom the rest of us are pleased to simply orbit, enjoying the warmth and the life that your presence brings. To have one sun temporarily obscured from our view is terrible. To have the other's light diminished by that is sadder still.

It is now over twenty years since Caron and I were running around Hillsborough, or discovering Sevenoaks, and yet it seems like yesterday. And you know what . . . the next twenty years will pass in a heartbeat too. So soon enough we will all be meeting up again.

If Caron's experience has taught me anything, it is life is short and in the brief time we are here we should be the best, the boldest and the brightest we can be.

You were Caron's inspiration and she would not have wanted you to live any less of a life because she was not there – on the contrary, she would have wanted you to have lived more.

I know that it will be hard for those of us who knew her only briefly to learn to live in the absence of such a big life, so I can barely imagine how difficult it will be for you. And this is the real reason for my letter. I want you to know – as someone on the outer reaches of your galaxy – that the hundreds of lives you've warmed already, while not beside you every day, are with you now, and will be with you wherever you are and whatever you're doing.

You are always in my thoughts,
Lots and lots of love,
Shaun

Not that I knew it then, but his words were very prophetic. That letter would offer the first inkling that there was life beyond those terrible days. 'Life is short,' he wrote, 'and in the brief time we are here we should be the best, the boldest and the brightest we can be.' It was enough just to hold those words, unspoken but there, just inside, on the tip of my tongue.

A great university friend of Caron's, Matthew Byam Shaw, wrote the following:

Dear Gloria,
I was so profoundly grateful to be present at Caron's truly extraordinary service at Hever. Having not seen her

properly for so many years, I felt reconnected to her life and family. It was like a surge of electricity and what an intensely emotional and fitting celebration of Caron's life. Desperately sad but also utterly uplifting, it captured the essence of Caron's extraordinary qualities perfectly. It was very important to hear of Caron's recent life depicted so beautifully by Russ, and of course I was in the dark about much of it. But it greatly touched those of us who have been absent from Caron's life to see, hear and be with her again. I swear I heard Caron's laugh, clear as a bell, throughout the service.

Caron had a deep bearing on me, which I have always hugely appreciated. Her curiosity, vitality and class were utterly beguiling and have been indelibly printed on all of us who were fortunate enough to have had her as a friend. She energised all of us around her to broaden our horizons and look beyond our everyday experience. She had a big impact on a hell of a lot of us, and I wish we could speak to her now.

In the middle of all that, it must have been so horrible for Caron and all of you who were close to her. I am so glad that she had such an amazing, fulfilling spiritual journey over the last seven years. I am so glad that she found the incomparable Russ to share her life with and that they had two such beautiful boys. I am so glad she had the best of loving brothers in Michael and Paul, and I am so glad that she had you at her core to love and balance her. I hope that you are letting Stephen look after you. I am thinking of you all.

With much love,

Matt x

Another university friend, Robin McCallum, wrote:

Dear Gloria,

I distinctly remember the first time that we met. You looking immaculate of course, and me in my granddad's dressing grown, dispatched by Caron to entertain you with tea and chat in the tiny kitchen of our top-floor flat in Bristol while she – overslept and hung-over – sorted out hair and make-up. I have been back to that flat in my head a great deal since 13 April and it always makes me smile.

In the winter everything froze and Caron and I shuffled around swathed in eiderdowns and legwarmers, making endless slices of toast, washed down with mug after mug of tea. In the summer we would escape through a skylight on to the roof, where we would sunbathe and eat ice lollies and talk and laugh until our jaws ached. In many ways, I felt protective, very protective of Caron, having been able to rescue her from the grisly accommodation she had originally been allocated at Bristol. I was delighted when my cocktail of paracetamol and hot-water bottle was regularly welcomed by her as a cure-all. But she looked after me too and was the only person to call me 'wee lamb'. I cherish that because with those two words she made me feel loved, and that was one of her defining qualities.

I can only begin to guess at how you must be feeling. Siobhan and I returned home last night and held our children closer than we ever had before. The separation that you have had to endure in recent years while Caron has been on her journey must have been difficult to bear, and although I know that your relationship was able to transcend physical distance, there are times when only the sight or touch of a person will do. How perfect then, in a situation that was anything but perfect, that Caron returned home to you for her last few hours and that you were able to be with her in every way possible.

Now we are all left to deal with the emptiness, but you are not alone, surrounded as you are by your exceptional family, wonderful friends and, beyond them, the people who were part of the rich fabric of Caron's life and who, speaking for myself at least, offer you love, support and a vast reservoir of memories of today onwards as we struggle to come to terms with what has happened.

Thank you for Caron,

With my love,

Robin

You can imagine how much those letters mean to me, and I still read them often and get as much comfort from them as when I first received them. It was wonderful to know that Caron's life and, in its own way, her funeral had touched her friends so deeply.

While others felt strangely uplifted at the end of the service, I was clinging on for dear life. My emotions were all over the place and sometimes it was all I could do just to hold the boys' hands and feel the warmth in their fingers. Each time I looked at the coffin, I was plunged further into disbelief and despair. Charlie and Gabriel kept saying, 'Please don't cry, Nana. Please don't cry any more,' but I couldn't stop. That is why I suppose I don't remember a great deal of the day. The enormity of it is really too much to take in, so much of it just flies by you. It was all happening to somebody else.

That cosmic split I'd first experienced in the garden seven

years ago, when I'd learnt of Caron's illness, had occurred again with screeching finality when she died. On 20 April at 2 p.m., the day of her funeral, I vacated the premises completely. I was sitting on a pew at St Peter's Church, but my mind and soul were elsewhere. Sometimes it felt like I was hovering just above, watching the proceedings, immune, but then, and this is the weird bit, I would also feel completely immersed in it. Tears would pour down my face; then suddenly, perversely, my cheeks still wet, I'd find myself laughing. Charlie and Gabriel have their mother's sense of humour in all its wicked abundance. During the service they'd take it in turns to pipe up and correct or contradict their father. Towards the end, when Russ invited people back to Hever Castle, announcing that there would be refreshments there, Gabriel shouted out, 'Is there going to be any Fanta?' It was clear to everyone in church that day that there was nothing Russ wouldn't give his sons, if only he was able. We smiled at a little boy's single-minded concern; after all, he'd been sitting there for over an hour by then. I recalled again the insightful doctor's words: *Watch, the children will lead you.* Perhaps he wasn't completely right when he said 'lead', but they certainly distracted us long enough to bring us back to the present. Thanks to Charlie and Gabriel, in the middle of this terribly sad occasion everyone could laugh again. They broke the spell of gloom, a welcome relief, even if it was for just a moment or two.

Little did I know that the service provided a sort of faint blueprint for what was to come. The out-of-body experience, that sense of sheer disbelief and of being frozen, remain with you, to a greater and lesser degree, for ever. The sensation protects you from being swallowed up by this black hole. Eventually you absorb that part of your grief-stricken soul into the 'new you'; you learn to live with the frozen bit, the missing piece, and in doing so allow yourself to be distracted temporarily. It is while you are distracted that you can laugh, sing, smile, talk and eat along with everybody else, but when the distraction is over, you're back there again, staring at a coffin in utter disbelief, split in half with pain, a world away from those around you. I'm sorry to say it never goes away. I have witnessed too many things to forget: my daughter dying, her body being lowered into the ground in a casket. Of course it never goes away. Four years later those things still feel as if they happened yesterday, and I know now that they always will. You can't erase only the memories you want. Would I give up all the others in order not to have those ones? Would I turn the stork away? I say again, No.

We didn't exclude people from accompanying us to the graveyard at St Peter's, but mostly everyone held back. It was very respectful, and I give thanks for that. Everything, in fact, was done beautifully, but my God, watching Caron's coffin being lowered into the ground caused actual physical pain. I have heard of mothers' attempts to throw themselves into the open ground, and I understand this desire completely. I know now that it was not just Caron we were interring, but our life too, the life I had envisaged. Until my dying day I will never forget watching the little boys solemnly throwing flowers into their mother's grave. My heart had been ripped open by losing Caron; watching those little boys doing that ripped it out.

Everything that happened after that is even more of a blur. I obviously left Caron at some point, but I can't remember doing so. Did I turn my back on her? Did I back out of the graveyard? Did someone help me out? Surely I didn't have the strength left to walk away. Graves are so hard; it takes a very long time to see beyond the earth that separates you and your loved one. It takes a very long time before they become the emblem of a life lived and not just proof that a life has ended. As much as many glean comfort from visiting a graveside, I believe that there are very few of us who haven't dreaded visiting the grave of a loved one at one stage or another. Even with my parents, who are buried in Northern Ireland, I find I much prefer to pay homage near to the house they lived in and recall all the fun we had there as a family, than go to Seagoe Graveyard. Many of the letters I received talked of the ongoing battle to muster the strength to visit the grave, because doing so would bring the violence of loss thundering back and restart the mourning process all over again.

A few months after Caron's funeral, Eamonn Holmes and the *Daily Mail* put me in touch with a lady whose daughter, Olivia, had died suddenly when she was only fifteen. I rang Olivia's mother, Carol Chase, and we struck up a friendship. She told me that at first it was thought that Olivia had drowned in the family swimming pool, but in fact it emerged she had suffered a sudden cardiac death where the electrical impulses to the heart simply stop in otherwise healthy fit young teenagers, often during exercise. Olivia had been swimming quite actively for half an hour. It was a shocking death that threw Olivia's mother, Carol Chase, completely out of orbit. Carol was as desperate as I was during this time to latch on to someone who understood what she was feeling. Like Caron, Olivia was absolutely beautiful, kind, talented, generous and vital to her family.

Olivia was buried on a hot summer's day in June. After an incredible service in which Olivia's friends, belying their youth, spoke with compassion and warmth of the very special girl they had tragically lost, the family followed Olivia's casket to the graveside, only to discover that it was still in the process of being dug. The whole family had to stand, wait and watch as two shirtless boys dug the remainder of the grave in which their beloved child would lie. To this day Carol can still hear the sounds of the spades as they dug the earth. When she returned home and removed her shoes she found that her toes and nails were bleeding from where she had clenched them tightly in her shoes during this ordeal. It defies belief. Dealing with a grave is hard enough without such an extra anguish. We were more fortunate, I suppose.

Over the months I became good friends with Carol. For the two years after Olivia's death she confided her feelings in her diary, some of which she has incredibly kindly allowed me to reproduce in this book. It is an amazing collection of writing, because it shows all the pain and confusion first hand, with no hindsight, the huge fluctuations of feelings that mirror what I and many others, I am sure, have every day as we struggle to come to terms with all that we have lost. In one entry she wrote, 'The trouble is, I still have this enormous need as a mother to keep caring for Olivia. We've had freezing weather and thunderstorms, so going to Ripley [her grave] is a nightmare. I so feel I'm letting Olivia down. I don't believe I've ever let her down before.' For a long time Carol couldn't bear the sound of rain on the roof or against the window. At night she would push in earplugs to block out the sound. Having to watch the grave being dug had made it all too real. When Olivia was little, she didn't like the dark. How do any of us leave our children alone in a graveyard?

I got a letter in those early days from Marigold in Colchester. Her son, Richard, was killed just eight weeks after his wedding by a lorry driver on the A14. He was only twenty-two years old.

My advice to you is to take each day as it comes and to give in to your bad days. Let it all out and then you'll

79

appreciate your slightly better days, but in my experience it does get worse before it gets better. Let your family and friends help you when you want it, but also have days to yourself. You will be emotionally exhausted after trying to put on a brave face for the world. You will get stronger and the confidence will come back eventually, and one day you will smile again.

She was right: it was getting worse and worse by the minute, and now I was going to have to leave Caron in the graveyard. Could there be anything worse than that? Somehow I stumbled to the wake at Hever Castle, in a stunned but frenzied silence.

At the castle all about me was noise: a haze of faces and a wall of noise. Some of it was very nice – people I knew really loved and cared for Caron, trying to express their own acute loss – but it was a blur. In the midst of this confusion and panic, I still found myself managing to put on the mask: I recall being worried that certain people were being looked after, particularly my darling sister, Lena, who had come over from Ireland. I really wanted her to be OK because she didn't know that many people. Is it only now that I find myself amazed that I could actually go on functioning on all these levels, or did I feel that then?

All you want to do is go home and lie down and pray for the whole thing to go away. Instead you're faced with a gathering, which in due course feels very much like a party, though for a time I never got further than the door. I remember getting locked talking to someone I didn't have the energy to face. Everyone wants to speak to you to say how sorry they are, and you want to thank them for coming, for their support. People were coming and going all the time, stopping to share their memories, interrupting to say goodbye, sharing previously unknown memories I was desperate to remember but find hard to recall now. It was totally and utterly exhausting and all a blur. What I do remember is that when eventually I made it through the room, I felt spurred on to thank everyone for their support and love of Caron. Would any words come out? After a few heartfelt sentences Gabriel once again broke the seriousness of the moment by piping up and saying, 'Watch out, she's going to cry again!'

I will never forget the bin men turning up to the house a few days after Caron had died with a card signed by all of them. They rang the bell to hand-deliver it and tell us to our faces how very, very sorry they were for our loss. It was an act of kindness that I fully appreciated at the time and to this day. I have another friend who has still not managed to put a gentle hand on my shoulder and tell me how sorry he is, though I know he adored Caron; instead he mumbled something along the lines of not being 'very good at saying this sort of stuff'. I know people have different ways of dealing with a situation like this, but to the bereaved, I feel it is really important to say something. If the bin men who'd never met Caron can find the words, then a man who knew her well should be able to.

Maybe it doesn't matter that I don't remember what everyone said that day; what is important is that they came, they took my hand, they tried to find the words to convey their feelings and sympathies, and that is what counts. It is important that they were there.

Eventually we returned home, flattened, wrung out, desperate for sleep. Did it come? I don't know. I doubt it. I slept very little over that period. Occasionally I fell asleep quickly through exhaustion, but just as quickly I would wake again, my brain would start up, and I'd relive it all, over and over again. At first she was ill but alive. Then she was gone but yet still here. Now the funeral was over and we were truly left alone. I have said many times that it was a privilege to be with Caron in her final hours, and I do still find it strangely comforting that Caron died at home, but on the other hand I have to live with the knowledge that she died in the house I still live in and it took some time to get beyond that point. To be honest, it disturbed me for a little while. I was trying very hard to cope with the death, trying hard to be led by the boys, trying hard to focus on the future, but every time I walked into my home, every time I went up the stairs, I would pause and look at the bedroom door and I would think, Caron died in there. I can still see Caron's casket leaving through the front door. I know other mothers experience the same thing. It is just another double-edged sword, to add to all the others.

We all ask ourselves the same question: how do we reconcile all the beautiful memories – Caron at the kitchen table, Olivia on the floor watching TV in front of the fire – with all the bad ones? How do you tidy an unmade bed that a child never returned to? What do you do with your child's clothes when they still smell of them? You don't. You leave things as they were. I am not alone when I take Caron's clothes out of the wardrobe and smell them. It is hard, but I wouldn't want to lose that connection. Eventually they become a tool to put in your survival kit.

In the end, I suppose what wins through is the privilege, the positive and the thanks. Yes, it is hard that she died here, but if she hadn't died here, where might she have been? Australia? Unthinkable. A hotel room in Switzerland before the boys had got here? A foreign hospital? The car on the way home? Didn't Russ set himself all those little tasks to get her across the border and through the Channel Tunnel alive? She was so close to death, though we didn't know it. It really doesn't bear thinking about. Because she died here, we could keep her here. We could still talk to her, say goodbye slowly. And so, in its own terrible way, the seven-year fight had an incredible ending for her. She came home to be with us all. Was precognition why Caron came home? Did she know something we didn't? I don't know. What I do know is that the fact she died at home meant that we had done everything we'd promised. She didn't have to go to a hospice. She didn't die in a hospital. I had been able to keep my word. There was some small comfort in that because it was what she wanted. That was a tiny chink of light to look towards when the darkness enveloped me as I lay in bed on the evening after the funeral. Yes, I had kept my first promise. Now all I had to do was look after the children and I would fulfil the second promise I had made to my daughter. This poem was always pinned above Caron's death and subsequently engraved on her headstone:

Your children are not your children.
They are the sons and daughters of life's longing for itself.
They come through you but not from you
And though they are with you, yet they belong not to you.

You may give them your love, but not your thoughts,
For they have their own thoughts.
You may house their bodies but not their souls,
For their souls dwell in the house of tomorrow,
Which you cannot visit, not even in your dreams.
You may strive to be like them, but seek not to make them
  like you,
For life goes not backward nor tarries with yesterday.

Gloria Hunniford

You are the bows from which your children
As living arrows are sent forth.
The archer sees the mark upon the path of the infinitive,
And He bends you with His might
That His arrows may go swift and far.
Let our bending in the archer's hand be for gladness;
For even as He loves the arrow that flies,
So He loves also the bow that is stable.

'On Children', Kahlil Gibran, inscribed
on Caron's gravestone

5

My Selfish Grief

I will not forget you . . . I have carved you on the palm of my hand.

Isaiah 49:15–16

Rochester, Kent

Dear Ms Hunniford,

I do hope you don't mind me writing to you. It is not something I normally do; it's just that I too lost a daughter, a year ago, at the age of just twenty-nine years old, from exactly the same deadly disease. She developed breast cancer at the age of twenty-five and had a mastectomy. She fought so desperately for four years. My daughter, like yours, was beautiful, so full of life, and until the last couple of months lived life to the full. She made her illness so easy for the rest of us to bear because of her cheerfulness, lack of self-pity, optimism and sense of fun, even when things were not going too well. She was in a great deal of pain, but she still came out fighting.

I just wanted you to know that you are not alone and it is not until you lose a child that you fully understand what people go through. Time does not heal and nothing can make up for your loss, but although I still think of my daughter every minute of the day, I have a granddaughter through my younger daughter who brings much joy into my life.

I still wait for the phone calls, the door going, etc., and can hardly believe I will not see my darling daughter again. I have the consolation that I will meet up with her again, as our bond was so strong, as I am sure yours was as well.

Yvonne

The period of 'doing' ends and the rest of your life begins. It is awful. From the moment we'd touched down in the UK from Switzerland we'd been running around like headless chickens. Shopping, making beds, cooking, booking doctors, the panic of Caron's death, planning the funeral, the logistics, the security, the phone calls, the people, the visitors and the 'big day' had all forced momentum into my inert body. I was a snowball racing downhill, gathering velocity and volume, trying to escape the inescapable fact that Caron was dead. Then suddenly it was over, the last guests went home, and there wasn't anything else to do but face it. I just had to be. But 'being' is impossible when the truth inflicts such excruciating pain.

Marion from Bedfordshire wrote shortly after the funeral. She had seen the letter I had written to Caron, which Russ read out at the funeral, as it was published in the *Daily Express*. Her daughter, Mandy, died aged only thirty-three from leukaemia, leaving behind twin sons.

I cried so much as I read your letter. You said everything I feel in my heart, and it is the very first time I have been able to accept someone else does know the agony I feel. It will be three years on August bank holiday Monday, a date that will haunt me for ever. I do wish I could say to you time heals, but up to now I am unable to feel that. I wonder how I can go on living without her.

Caron and me on her christening day, Christmas 1962.

Caron coming tops, as always!

Mother
and Child
Contest 1965

Sponsored by
The "SUNDAY
INDEPENDENT"
Winner Grand Final :—
Mrs. GLORIA KEATING
and daughter CARON (2)
18 Marnabrae Park,
Lisburn, Co. Antrim.

Caron and her brothers, Michael and Paul, outside their rented cottage in Wales, when Caron presented *Summer Scene*.

Caron's dad, Don, during one of his many visits to her home in Barnes, in London.

Bringing in the New Year in the South of France with her brother, Pau

Blue Peter days with Yvette Fielding and Mark Curry,
Caron's big break into national television.

Caron with that
coveted *Blue Peter*
badge.

Publicity shot for BBC's *Family Affairs*, which we all presente together. It was Michael's first and la: foray into TV!

A special moment on the morning of Caron's wedding when she was given her grandmother's five-stone diamond engagement ring, which I now wear.

Wedded bliss, a treasured moment of pure joy.

Never a dull moment – a spontaneous sing-song even during the wedding pictures.

An early photo-shoot for Charlie.

Gabriel's christening day

Charlie seeing his new baby brother, Gabriel, for the first time.

A bittersweet time, shortly after her dad's funeral. Caron cradling newborn Gabriel.

Gabriel suitably unimpressed with his first shoot for *Hello!*

Another all-singing, all-dancing birthday for Charlie. Including Hugh Wooldridge, the theatre producer, behind me, and Caron's greatest friends Cathy and John Comerford, far right, who have raised tens of thousands of pounds for Caron's Foundation.

One of our many tea drinking and gossip afternoons.

A mother's touch and boundless laughter with Charlie and Gabriel.

This was exactly what I was feeling. How could I go on living without her?

County Monaghan, May 2004

Dear Gloria,

My heart goes out to you, having lost your beautiful daughter and best friend, and I know you will never get over her death. I will pray for you every day of my life. I lost two sisters to breast cancer, Gillian at forty-one, Gemma at forty-nine.

I had to tell my mother that Gemma was dying. She was roaring and crying and shouting, 'Not another daughter. My two little girls, why take them from me?' Gloria, I can still hear her to this day crying and crying and crying.

Dorothy

I spoke to one woman whose mother had died of cancer twenty years ago, when she was thirteen. Her mother was only supposed to be alive until this girl was five and a half years old, so she had fought hard. In the end she had to wear a neck brace and was confined to a wheelchair because her bones were so weak. She described her grief, 'It's like your arm has been chopped off. It's like something physical has happened to you, but nobody can see it. Sometimes you want to scream, "Don't you realise that half my body is missing?"'

She's right. I felt it too: the early stage of grief is really physical. It's like being hit in the stomach with a bat, it's like being winded, but of course that doesn't come close. It's more like falling from a fourth-floor window and somehow managing to survive. Sometimes you can hardly move because it aches so much. The pain is very real.

When the girl's mother died, one of her friends gave her some almond-scented bubble bath. People kept saying to her, 'Have a hot bath. Relax. It'll help,' so she decided to try it. She ran a hot bath, poured in the bubble bath and climbed in. Instead of being relieved by the sensation of relaxing in hot water, as she lowered herself into it she experienced a violent physical shock and leapt back out, bent double with pain. It was grief and it consumed her. Still now, all these years later, she can't get into a hot bath. Instead she runs the water when she's in the bath, because the wave of release that she experiences when she sinks into a deep, hot bath still takes her back to that moment and freaks her out. She hates it.

I can totally sympathise with her. You really don't want to do anything that causes relaxation because if you relax, it will allow the emotions to catch up with you. You don't want to relax; you don't want to switch off; you don't want to be quiet; you don't want to be calm; you just want to bolt, go, run away. For the same reason I think people find it hard to be alone in the beginning: when you're alone, all those dark thoughts creep in and take over – the horrible thoughts about graves and coffins and mounds of earth, of mortal beings and immortal souls. You wonder, wonder, wonder, Where has my child gone? The death of a child is so enormous that it cannot be explained. It's like trying to visualise infinity: it is outside your normal range of understanding. I would wander from room to room whispering under my breath, 'Where are you, Caron? Where are you?' I can still to this day imagine Caron walking through the door, and back then this made more sense to me than the fact that I was never going to hear her voice again or see her in the flesh. That is why night-time is so hard. While the world sleeps, you are left alone to face the enormity of what has happened. Night-time is one long hot bath.

Dear Gloria,
My heart goes out to you at this terrible time, and may
God, or someone, help you to come to terms with it all,
which I'm sure you will in time. We don't expect to bury
our children, do we?
Keep busy, my dear, and talk to Caron. I'm sure she
will help you in her own way to cope.
You are in my prayers and thoughts,
A grieving mother

Grief swallows you up, breaks you into a million pieces, then spits you out to mourn. You land with a terrifying jolt and realise the circus has left town and once again you are alone. Let me clarify by saying that I was very rarely actually physically alone during this time. For starters, we had Russ and the boys staying with us, and they, as always, were our main concern. I had Stephen with me all the time. My sons, Michael and Paul, and good friends kept the visits up, but mentally I was in a lonely place, mentally I was alone, and this is what I want to convey. Russ was watching the boys; Michael had to return to his life in London – though he came up and down all the time, he couldn't press the 'pause' button for ever – and Paul had a business, a wife and two small boys who needed him. Life did not, could not, stop, and yet for me a part of it had. Not only did it feel that I was the only one in the family to be feeling this indescribable desolation, there were times when I felt I was the only person this had ever happened to. Nobody else in the world could have felt what I was feeling because my pain was so deep. Nobody could feel like this; not my husband or my sons or even my son-in-law had gone to the place I had gone to. Of course I now know this was not the case, but at the time it is what it felt like. No one but me had given birth to Caron, and her father, Don, had died years before. I was alone. I was desperate, desperate to talk to somebody who could grasp the enormity of what was happening to me.

My advice now to anyone who is trapped in the clutches of grief is to find someone to talk to who really understands what it is like. Having someone to share this with is imperative for survival. Choose wisely, though, who to let in. Some will help, but not everyone can. In my case I wanted to talk to another woman who'd buried her adult daughter. I became almost obsessed with it.

Carol Barnes, the former newsreader, who very sadly died this year, was the person I sought out. I knew her reasonably well to talk to, and because her daughter had been killed in Australia just a few months before Caron's death, I somehow felt that we had a link. In fact, there were no similarities between what we'd both experienced except for the brutal fact that both our girls were dead. Carol's daughter had been killed in a terrible, traumatic freefalling accident, miles from home, fighting to pull the cord on her two parachutes until the end, so Carol's grief and my own actually had very little in common. But I wasn't thinking about that at the time. I just felt that I had to talk to someone who knew how I was feeling at that precise moment, so I picked up the phone and called her. It was awful. We were both in a terrible place, raw, exposed, in the absolute eye of the storm. We couldn't help one another at all; it was the blind leading the blind; we were both drowning. It was far too soon. We ended the conversation saying we'd meet up, but we never did. When I say pick carefully who you talk to, I mean it.

I'm not suggesting you have to find someone whose story is exactly like yours. Some people you just connect with, and some you don't. I know from the letters that many people, like me, need to seek out other bereaved parents. They need to be understood. Grief is associated with a vast range of emotions, and since they are constantly shifting, finding someone who is in the same place as you is not always easy. It is, however, worth persevering, because you only need one or two who can share the heavy burden of ongoing grief for ever. Some people have to deal with acute anger and bitterness, which if offloaded onto another grieving parent, can add to the trauma. Everyone grieves differently; you just have to find a way that suits you.

I do feel that finding another woman, another mother, to talk to is a good idea, as women tend to grieve differently from men. We are inclined to verbalise, ex-ternalise our feelings; men more often than not do the opposite. This does not mean they are feeling it less, but they deal with it differently. Their 'selfish grief' is often to lock it away, in a private place, and keep busy. Not talking about someone does not mean they are not think-ing about that person, but it can feel like that. Of course, these are sweeping generalisations, but I find them more often than not to be true.

After writing *Next to You*, I received a letter in which a woman told me she had marked up six places in the book, presented it to her husband and said, 'Read this, because this is how I feel and you have never understood.' Grieving women have a need to be listened to, so find someone who will pay your deceased child the compliment of doing that, uncondi-tionally, for as long as it takes.

Trish from Devon wrote to me. Her son, Toby, had died of cancer aged thirty-four.

*I can offer no words to make things better for you –
everyone has to deal with this awfulness in their own way.
My 'crying time' is when I'm alone in my car and I play
the records that we recorded from his collection. I couldn't
listen to them in the first few months, but now it's almost
a release.*

She was right: the sad truth of the matter is that there are no
words to make things better.

In hindsight, I realise now that although I was searching for
help, answers and understanding, in actual fact I didn't want
advice right then. There was none, anyway. There are no rules
about this level of grief. No dos and don'ts, no rights and
wrongs. Whatever gets you through the day is enough. I think
what you're really looking for during that time is someone on
whom you can unburden yourself. The process of talking
about your loved one is essential for keeping the madness at
bay. It's comforting, cathartic; it keeps your loved one alive.
Every day I talk about Caron in some way.

Many, many people who wrote gave me their phone number with the supporting words 'if you ever need to talk, one
broken-hearted mum to another'. Sometimes I did just pick up
the phone, but I also had my wonderful friend Merrel Thomas, whom I trust completely and who in those early days
said, 'You can call me anytime, day or night,' and she meant it.
I could tell her anything, offload anything, and though I never
did call her at 4 a.m., just knowing that I *could* helped
enormously. I cannot thank her enough for that. All these
thoughts and feelings are building up constantly, and if they
have nowhere to go, you'll crack. It's like letting steam out of a
pressure cooker: for a small window of time, there is a little
relief and then the pressure starts to build again. When it gets

excruciating, you need to let some steam out . . . On and on it goes. It could be every few minutes, hourly, daily or every second. As I said, there are no rules.

I was lucky I had Stephen at home 24/7. Although he loved Caron deeply of course, like the daughter he never had, he was able to devote his energy to taking care of me, perhaps because he wasn't her father. He wasn't drowning, so he could hold me up. He was and still is always willing to listen. I didn't want answers and I didn't want well-thought but ill-placed platitudes; I just wanted to unburden, release some steam. I think I am fortunate in that I can talk openly to Paul and Michael; at times it is just enough to verbalise my feelings – to actually say the words – and get it out of my system.

Carol Chase, Olivia's mother, became another person with whom I could share my grief, and she hers. Not long after I first got in touch with her, she sent me the following letter:

Dear Gloria,

Thank you so much for phoning me on Sunday evening. Since Olivia's burial, when we had to sit waiting for her grave to be dug before we could bury her, I have been so desperately low. I've tried so hard on the surface to be strong for our other children, but the effort is at times too much.

I wanted to let you know how your call lifted my spirits – just to share it all with someone who really does understand. I thank you so much for that.

This morning I awoke in the early hours and was totally engulfed by the enormity of it all. How will I ever live the rest of my life without seeing my beautiful daughter again? It's just too much to take in. I adored her so completely. She and I were like 'peas in a pod', as so

*many friends have commented to me, and there is
absolutely nothing that can help. What other situations
have we had to face in our lives where there is nothing at
all we can do to change things?*

*Today is a bleak day, but yesterday wasn't quite so bad
and that is how it goes. I try to read or watch
Wimbledon, anything to distract me, but nothing goes in.
My head is full of Olivia. Like a video replaying over and
over – what if . . . ? So now I have to start the journey of
coping, and I am determined to do it. I'm going to try and
help other people who find themselves in the situation
we're in. It will be a time before I'm capable, and how I
will go about it I have no idea, but I am determined to try
and make some good of this terrible tragedy.*

*We must be thankful for such wonderful daughters – we
were truly blessed and, as you so rightly said, 'touched by
an angel'. Many people never have that, but how very
hard it is to lose them.*

Wishing you very much love and strength,
Carol Chase

Grief really is very selfish. By that I mean it is all-consuming.
For a time you simply can't get further than your broken heart
and soul, and you definitely can't take on board anyone else's
grief. It's very me, me, me. You can't think of others because
that's going beyond what has happened, and you can't go
beyond it because that would mean leaving it behind. The one
thing you absolutely do not want to do is leave it behind,
because *that* means placing your child in the past. More than
anything else in the world, you don't want that. Like picturing
the casket underground, moving on from your loved one is too
terrifying to contemplate. If releasing the steam means your

brain stays intact, then talk, talk and talk some more. It is survival, basic survival. It is a way of protecting yourself. Of course, talking is my area of work expertise. Not everyone wants to be a consummate talker, but everyone has something as a release – writing, painting, walking, meditating, swimming – that expends the energy that was once taken up by loving the person you've lost.

Beryl from Lincolnshire wrote to me about her daughter who died. Karen was 'one moment cutting her hedge; next she was on the ground unconscious . . . I hope you don't mind me writing to you, but something made me do it. I found it helps if sometimes I write a letter to Karen telling her how I feel. It might help you too.' I was open to any suggestions, because very early on I realised that this kind of loss could take you under.

A woman in Bath wrote about the death of her only son, 'The first two years of grief are such hell. I became an alcoholic. Went to a treatment centre for ten weeks. Thank God.' I can totally understand why. You are in a pit. You can't get out. You're trying to crawl your way up the sides, but you just fall back down over and over again. You need other people to pull you out, or at least hold on to the rope while you very slowly drag yourself back up.

I remember talking to Carol, and although I was still in the depths of my own despair, I realised that I had more things to be thankful for than I was remembering – things I could put in my tool kit, things that would, over time, help on the monumental climb out of the pit. Unlike Carol, I hadn't had to deal with a sudden death. Unbeknown to me, I had started on this journey of grief long before my daughter actually died, and so although we had both recently buried our girls, I was further along this path than I realised, further from the bottom of the pit than I felt. When you've seen someone deteriorate through a long illness, it is sometimes hard to remember anything beyond the disease. I do of course remember Caron as a fabulous young girl, a free spirit, hair blowing in the wind, but a huge chunk of my memories is taken up by her last seven years, when everything was put under the microscope and brought sharply into focus. Time slowed right down, and although there were many atrocious hospital visits, more and more blows, less and less hope, when I look back on her time in Australia, I honestly don't think any other time of my life can compete for the number of laughs, sing-songs and get-to-gethers. We had so much fun and yet she was ill.

I still marvel at Caron's strength. She was always ready for a party, always ready for a sing-song, always ready for people, always ready to enjoy the day. She was extraordinary. Where that comes from I don't know, but I take great comfort from it because I know that even in the depth of her illness, especially towards the end, she lived every second. We lived it with her, never more so than during those final days in Switzerland, so despite the pain and fear, they are imprinted indelibly in my mind and are more precious to me than anything: the shopping trips, the apple strudel in the mountains, quiet nights in the hotel watching movies, trips to the cinema and the excitement of the children coming to visit. I have so many special moments to savour. As I said, time slowed down, everything was magnified, everything made more precious. Those memories are in my tool kit. In the beginning they hurt, they felt like a burden, but now they help.

Unlike mine, Carol's loss literally came out of the blue. She left their house in Surrey to close down their second home for the summer. It was a Monday. She flew in the afternoon. She spoke to both her daughters that evening. She spoke to Olivia twice on the Tuesday, once because she had a headache and she was asking about getting a tablet, then again about cooking her lunch. At seven forty-five that evening there was a phone call to tell Carol that Olivia was dead. It was her other daughter, Georgina, who made the call. Georgina and her father, Clive, had found Olivia on the bottom of the pool in front of the steps in only three feet of water. Clive and Georgina had tried to resuscitate her; the cleaner had called the ambulance; the ambulance had come and taken Olivia away. Clive and Georgina had followed the ambulance. In his desperation, Clive had a crash and seriously damaged the car. Carol could have lost all three of them. They tried to resuscitate Olivia for forty-five minutes. Georgina passed the phone to the surgeon, who simply said to Carol, 'So sorry. We did everything we could, but she's gone.' Carol was all alone. Like me, she froze. She remembers walking around the house saying, 'Olivia's dead. Olivia's dead,' but it wasn't real. She remembers being on her knees on the floor in the empty house and feeling these arms encircling and holding her between the sobs. She recalls a remarkable stillness. Carol went to bed and managed to sleep for about two hours. Then came that moment of waking, that awful moment of recognition: it was a new day and Olivia wasn't part of it anymore. Even to this day, when she starts to wake up and consciousness begins to creep in from deep sleep, she still feels like someone is stabbing her in the stomach. Four years on she'll feel that shooting pain, open her eyes and say, 'Olivia's gone.'

Whereas I reel thinking about losing Caron suddenly like that, or in a car crash, Carol takes the opposite view. She says, 'At least I didn't see Olivia suffer.' A good friend of hers had a son who had battled leukaemia for eighteen months and died just six months before Olivia. They went through bone-marrow transplants and all the ups and downs that I know cancer brings. There is a memorial to both these young people in the school grounds. Carol and her friend have found great strength from one another, despite the different circumstances. The truth is that whether anticipated or not, we have all lost a part of ourselves. It is interesting to me how we find ways to help us out of the pit. Both I and Carol's friend think, At least we had time to say goodbye, whereas Carol consoles herself with, At least I never saw my child in pain and couldn't ease it. Both Carol and I comfort ourselves with this knowledge, though we could easily make the pit darker and deeper if our attitudes were reversed. Carol could say, 'At least you got to say goodbye to Caron!' and I might retort, 'Well, at least you never had to see your daughter suffer!' We wouldn't be much help to one another then. Don't get me wrong, I have sometimes wanted to scream those words at the world, but anger doesn't ease grief; it cements and solidifies it in your soul. Carrying that sort of heavy load makes the climb all the harder and all the slower. Anger makes it easier to give up and fall back into the pit and stay there. I didn't want to stay there.

Halesworth, Suffolk

Dear Gloria,

When I saw your sad face in the paper today, I just had to write and tell you I know how you are feeling.

I too lost my daughter, seventeen months ago, and asked myself how I could bear this pain of losing a wonderful daughter. A wonderful lady in our village wrote to me telling me she had lost her daughter nine years ago. She came and visited me, and it was a comfort to me to talk to somebody who could understand my pain. Her words of wisdom were, 'It gets easier, but you never get over it and you learn to live with it.'

As time goes on, you talk to many people this has happened to and I myself hang on to some of their words, which gets me through the bad times. An old neighbour from where I lived before lost her daughter at nineteen years of age and her words were, 'Get a new project and remember you cannot alter the situation' – you can do nothing about it.

My daughter was like your Caron, a lovely girl, caring, considerate, clever, and we were such a happy family. My only other daughter said to me, 'Mum, we were such a happy, loving family and it seems as if someone said, "They're too happy, I will stop it," and they did.'

We as a family, like you, watched my daughter become ill and endure her illness and death. This is the saddest and worst thing to happen to you, and you, like us, are so unlucky to have to go through such a thing. My Clare was thirty-five years old when they discovered ovarian cancer in May and she died in November.

I find talking to those who have lost their children very beneficial.

Our lives may be wide apart, but we both know what each other is going through, but for me, with a little bit more experience, that lovely lady was right: it does get a little bit easier.

Cynthia

As I said, I have purposefully tried not to go down the angry route, but anger is a huge part of grief. Who do I have to be angry at? God? Possibly, at times. But Caron herself had been on a spiritual journey that led her to the Buddhist monks in Australia. She met the Rinpoche, equivalent of a bishop, I suppose, who since the age of four had dedicated his life to spirituality, healing and helping people. His soul was pure and yet he'd had a lifetime of health problems. He too was ill. He put his hand on Caron and through a translator told her no divine being had singled either of them out. She had tormented herself over the previous seven years with asking whether she'd done something to 'deserve' this illness or hadn't done something she ought to have. It was a huge relief for her, and it is a relief for me now. I don't like to think of illness and death in those personal terms. Don't comfort me that her place is with God. It isn't. It's here with me and Russ and the boys. Don't tell me God takes the best ones for Himself. In those brutal early days it really doesn't help. It is the way the cards are dealt.

Although we don't know why Caron got cancer and I will never come to terms with it because she had rarely been sick as a child, had a great immune system and lived healthily, I have no choice but to accept it. She got struck down; it was just the roll of the dice. I am not an angry person, though I have been to the bottom of that pit; it is a terrible place full of confusion, desperation, sorrow, pain and everything else I can think of, but anger wasn't the predominant emotion for me. Ironically it is now that I have to deal with anger; it is now, four years down the line, that I have to stay vigilant and keep the anger at bay. But I am angry, angry because of all the things *she's* missing out on, like watching her boys grow up: Charlie's football prizes, Gabriel's gymnastics, their first disco and some of those crazy gelled hairstyles, and of course the clothes shopping, which she would have loved.

Having said all that, of course I was angry at the time. I was livid. Incensed and enraged at the unfairness of it all. But having no one to be angry at, I transformed that anger into other things and projected it onto something more tangible than mutated cells.

Ann from County Antrim wrote to me. Her sister, Dee, had
died of breast cancer aged forty-four.

*I felt I had to express my absolute sorrow over the death of
your beloved and beautiful Caron. I also feel furious that
the tentacles of this dammed, despicable disease were able
to consume yet another young life. I find it very hard to
accept when we all know that there are some people who
still have the privilege of life who really don't deserve it.*

Those thoughts do cross your mind. Why Caron's life? Why
not a murderer or a paedophile? For me, like so many before
me, it was the 'What if . . . ?' that haunted me. I fixated on
certain aspects: did the travelling and then the bed bath set
something off? How is it possible that she went from eating
and talking to dying? I went over it again and again, round and
round in my mind. What happened? Did something happen?
Can't I direct all this misery somewhere else? The letters that
came pouring in from the public asking questions, detailing
lawsuits and making accusations at hospital staff made me
realise that what many of us are trying to do is find some
explanation, someone to blame, somewhere to place the
burden of responsibility, because otherwise you're left with
just a random sequence of events, chance, which means that
your loved one died for no reason at all. So while on the one
hand I knew no one was to blame for Caron's death, on the
other I flailed about for a while, trying to find an explanation
where there was none. I suppose I was trying to make sense of
something that makes no sense at all. Every doctor from 2002
onwards told Russ that they were staggered Caron was still
with us. On my good days I reason that of course the bed
bath had nothing to do with Caron's death; it made her

comfortable, clean, refreshed after her long journey and gave her dignity. Caron simply got home and let go. Trouble is, I don't only have good days.

What if there is someone to blame, directly or indirectly? What if your child was murdered by a drink-driver, killed because someone forgot to check their tyre pressure, blown up by a terrorist, stabbed by another child whose parents didn't bother to parent? What if someone made a mistake at the hospital and mixed up the drugs? Then there was the case on Father's Day 2008, when a man who had lost his job feared he would have to hand over his house to his estranged wife and lose access to his children, so he picked up his son and daughter, drove his Land Rover out into the country, attached a hose to the exhaust pipe and fed it through the window, killing himself and his two children. How do you ever deal with that? Where does the strength come from?

What if it wasn't deliberate and your partner simply took their eye off your child, as we all do, and the child died? I once talked to a woman about her son's death. He was in his baby walker when she went upstairs to get ready for a dinner engagement, leaving her husband in charge. He was watching football. The little boy managed to get himself outside in his baby walker, wheeled over the edge of the swimming pool and fell in. By the time her husband noticed him gone, the little boy had drowned. It is unspeakably awful. The mother never said, 'I blame you,' and the father never said, 'You blame me,' but it broke up the marriage in the end. Now, years later, her new husband copes with her misery days but I suppose he doesn't fully understand, because he hasn't lost a child. Instead she and I talk, because the pressure is always building up, and as I know well, bottling things up is very dangerous.

Parents of murdered children take this grief to another level.

I can comfort myself with the knowledge that although Caron suffered on and off for seven years and was scared, particularly terrified about not seeing the boys grow up, at the end there was some peace, little pain and she wasn't alone. This is sadly not the case for parents of murdered children. I read about Stephen Lawrence's mother, still fighting for justice, still as raw as when she was first told about her son's death back in 1993. There has been no closure for her and she has had to carry the very real burden of knowledge that her son suffered and was in pain before he died. She has to live with that day in, day out. It is still all-consuming.

Even when there is legal resolve, as in the case of Sarah Payne, not even a life sentence can negate the loss. When the perpetrator is put behind bars, the wound is yours to heal. I find myself watching Margaret Mizen with inspiration and awe. In May 2008 her son, Jimmy Mizen, a sweet, innocent boy, was stabbed in a bakery for refusing to fight and died in the arms of his brother. She is determined not to let the bitterness and anger in because she knows they will ruin her family. I find her attitude incredible and so very brave. She said, 'Don't feel sorry for me. I have wonderful memories of my son. Feel sorry for the other boy's mother – what happy memories does she have?' I read an interview where she said, 'People keep asking me, "Why are you not angry?" but there's so much anger in this world. It's anger that killed my son.' It's phenomenal, really.

It reminds me of a letter I got in the early stages from a woman telling me that God only gives us as much as we can bear. I have faith, still, but don't tell me God punishes those who are capable of forgiveness. Mrs Mizen is an inspiration to us all, but did her son really have to die for strangers, like me, to be inspired? I don't know. It's a big question, one of many, and I found some answers in the letters and advice that kept pouring in during those first weeks.

Overall my memory of that time is this constant terrible feeling that I didn't know how to go on. I had lost my sparkle, my *joie de vivre*, and I know now that everyone, particularly my sons, worried for a long time that I would for ever be only a shadow of my former self. Had the fun-loving Gloria disappeared for good? Sometimes I didn't know who I was. I was an unknown quantity. I was shattered, as if there was nothing inside to give to anyone else.

This time is terrible for siblings because their parents are broken right when they need them most. My other children were grown up, so they might not have needed me in the way young children need their mother, minute by minute, but the last thing they wanted was to lose the mother they had known. I said to Michael more than once, 'I'm never going to have joyful days again. Life will never be carefree again. Life will *never* be what it was.' What a terrible thing to say. Michael tells me now that when I said this, it was horrible and deeply upsetting for him. He wanted to say, 'Hang on, Paul and I are also your children. Yes, Caron was this great light, yes, she was a second mother to me, and yes, she was your precious daughter, but we *will* have happy times again. They'll be different of course, but we will have those joyous days. You still have two sons and four grandchildren.' He desperately wanted me to be the woman I was before, for us to be able to go out and have the giggles and the fun and the carefree times we'd always had, but I couldn't see a way back there. I was overwhelmed just thinking about that possibility. To break a bone is tiring, as it takes energy to mend. To break your soul is completely exhausting, though, as you know you will never mend. All you can do is heal, but that healing will take a lifetime. Knowing that, Michael would just put his arms round me and hold me.

Florence from Londonderry sent me the following poem with a note: 'I lost an only son many years ago in a road accident and to this day I still feel the pain.'

> *There is always a face before me,*
> *A voice I would love to hear,*
> *A smile I will always remember*
> *Of the one I loved so dear.*
> *We cannot bring the old times back,*
> *When we were all together,*
> *But those we loved don't go away;*
> *They walk with us for ever.*

'Always a Face Before
Me', Anon

What turned out to be one of the most powerful pieces of advice I received arrived a matter of weeks after Caron died. It came from an elderly woman in Wales. She said:

> *I'd like to tell you it gets better, but it doesn't – you have to learn to live around it and through it, because there is no way you can ever replace the loss of a child, nor would you want to. The easy part of grief is to sit in a quiet room, looking at photographs and weep, but remember if you weep from now till the day you die, it won't change anything and it won't bring Caron back.*

When I first received that letter, very early on, I remember reeling from those words. They looked so bald on the page. I wanted to ball the letter up in my fist and throw it at something. What do you mean I will always feel like this? She went on to say, 'I truly know how you feel. I too lost a child – my son. It is now twenty-two years since he passed on. I still think of him every single day.' Twenty-two years? Am I condemned to this pain for the rest of my life? I had been waiting for the day when I woke up and didn't feel like I'd been hit in the stomach with a bat as the realisation struck once again: Caron was dead. I was waiting for the words of comfort that would actually bring some comfort. I was waiting to be able to look at my family and not only see who was missing. I was waiting for Caron to come back. Each time I read it, and I went back to it often, I wanted to scrunch that letter up and throw it away, but as it turned out, it was one of the first letters I placed in my tool kit. All of the kind words I'd read so far expressed sympathy and understanding and a love of Caron that had helped me through those dark, dark days at the bottom of the pit. This letter made me realise that the pit wasn't going anywhere; I had to learn to live around it. But if I was ever going to be able to do that, I had to first climb out of the pit. I wasn't going to miraculously find myself standing on open ground; no, the only way out of this pit was to climb, and the only person who could do that was me.

Though I didn't realise it for a long time, that woman had handed me a lifeline. I only started to mend at the very moment when I realised I would never be fixed. The pain of losing Caron was always going to be with me. It seems blunt writing it here, and it felt harsh and unsympathetic reading her words back then, but I know now that it is the truth. I had to learn to live with the pain, and that meant returning to the land of the living. I didn't want to. I had no choice. If I didn't, it would do my courageous child a terrible insult. She had fought so hard and would have done anything for a few more breaths, so what kind of mother would I be to throw what breath I had left away? But it was going to be far harder than I thought.

Tony from Limpsfield sent a card:

Above all others I fully understand all those feelings of despair and desolation that now enshroud each day, having lost my own daughter to this awful, indiscriminating disease.

As I well know, there are no words that can ever take away the pain that you feel now, but trust in the knowledge that you are now on a journey that does eventually lead to a much more comfortable place, a place that enables us to honour our feelings and to also reconcile our lives and then become worthy of all those precious memories we so cherish. I know that you will find that place – in time.

I have this day contacted the Carmelite Convent in Ware to ask that Caron be included in the sisters' prayers, as well as thoughts for all the family.

Thank you for your prayers. I needed them. I needed them all.

6

An Alien World

When I must leave you
For a little while,
Please do not grieve
And shed wild tears

And hug your sorrow to you
Through the years,
But start out bravely
With a smile.

And for my sake
And in my name
Live on and do
All things the same.

Feed not your loneliness
On empty days,
But fill each waking hour
In useful ways.

Reach out your hand in comfort
And in cheer,
And I, in turn, will comfort you
And hold you near.

Always With You

And never, never
Be afraid to die
For I am waiting for you
In the sky.

'When I Must Leave You', Helen Steiner Rice,
sent by Joy Coisgrove, whose son, Gary, died aged
twenty-seven, and she enclosed a beautiful white
feather, which I have kept

To incorporate this loss into my life, I had to return to the
world. I may have looked the same, sounded the same, dressed
the same, but I was completely different. It seemed astonishing
to me that anyone could not understand that. When I looked
in the mirror, I saw a stranger. Isn't that what everyone else
saw? One of the hardest things to accept when you have been
altered by grief is that the world goes on. It has to. In fact, it
seems like it's happening in technicolour: everyone in the
outside world is happy, but you can't relate to it. It is totally
divorced from your own reality, so when you step into it, you
find yourself in this alien land. I was first made aware of that
the morning after Caron died. While my very being crumbled
and turned to dust, all around me there was activity and noise.
People were eating and the fridge had to be restocked. Russ
and the children were living with us, so despite their own grief,
there were signs of life all around us, and in our case a
continuity of that ponderousness we'd had when Caron
was ill. We were always worrying about what to do next, only
this time our concerns were for the children.

The world definitely seems an alien place. You have all of
this tragedy on one side, the uncontrollable sobbing, the pain
and anguish, then over here, on the other side, you have

normality. Or a semblance of normality, anyway. The boys
were living in the second, so after Caron died, so were we. We
stayed at home for the remainder of April. Sometimes the boys
were quiet, playing on the computer; other times they were
leaping about with their cousins, seemingly untouched by
what was going on. Looking after the children became the
prime worry for both Russ and me; it distracted us long
enough to survive another day and cross it off. But we were
a whisper away from falling apart. Looking back, I realise we
were all watching each other. Stephen, Michael and Paul were
watching Russ and me, and we were watching the boys.

All our energy went on trying to make sure the boys were
OK and occupied. 'Promise me you'll look after my boys' was
a mantra I repeated over and over in my head. Russ and I were
completely on the same page on this. We talked endlessly
about all the different scenarios for the boys. He decided very
early on he wasn't going back to Australia. At first Russ said he
was going to remain near us in Kent. He went as far as looking
at houses and found some he really liked. I was delighted
because it meant we could be hands-on. I didn't want the boys
going anywhere, though I knew that was impractical, as they
had to go to school. School was a big part of our discussions.
Their education to that point had been very disrupted anyway,
and in Australia they'd been to a Rudolf Steiner school, which
they'd adored but which veered away from prescribed teaching. Russ didn't want them slipping too far behind. All these
things took up the endless days that stretched out before me
with no Caron to fill them.

That time in Sevenoaks seemed to go on and on for a long
time, but when I looked at my diary recently, I was staggered
to see that it was only a matter of days before we packed our
bags and flew to Portugal on holiday. I remember Russ saying,

'We need to get the boys out of here,' and I fully agreed that a change of scene would be good for them and all of us. On 26 April we flew to Portugal – less than two weeks after Caron had died! Airports are packed with happy people, off on adventures, meeting loved ones, saying goodbyes that weren't permanent. It was turmoil for me. All those people carrying on as if nothing had happened. Was it too soon? For me, possibly, but what did we know? Our main concern was the boys. We were making it up as we went along, but it felt like a good idea at the time. Cliff Richard very kindly offered his house in Portugal. We bought the boys these little motorbikes – actually they were motorised cycles – and I have visions of them riding them round and round the garden enjoying the buzz.

We stayed roughly a week and filled our days playing tennis. The boys went bungee-jumping. Keep doing, keep going, do, do, do, go, go, go. We were endlessly looking for things that would be new for them, not only to keep them busy, but to give them things to be happy about. It was all Russ and I talked about. What next? I was happy to see them happy, and I smiled when they smiled, but I wasn't really smiling and I wasn't really happy. I still had a great need to talk about Caron, but I tempered that need around the children. I didn't want to drag them back to that place when they appeared happy, and when they were sad, it seemed kinder to focus on what we had ahead of us, rather than what we had lost.

It was a strange time. I began to think that pure happiness was something that belonged to the past. It belonged to other people. All around me on the streets of Portugal were happy, colourful people on holiday, smiling in the sun. Everybody was happy, or so it felt to me. The pain and the pleasure didn't seem to cancel each other out; they ran concurrently. I was split again. How many more times could I separate myself and stay standing? I wondered. Many times, it turned out.

For the time being, that was generally how we coped. We were all watching each other with fear and trepidation, but mostly we were watching the boys and taking comfort when they smiled. Very soon after returning from Portugal, the notion of returning to Cornwall entered the deliberations. I would have had them live with me for ever if I could, but of course that wasn't practical. They couldn't go on drifting from one 'event' to another. One of the benefits of my daughter's fraught dash to Australia when confronted with the information that the cancer had spread back in December 2001 was that all of the family's things were still in Fowey in Cornwall. Everything was there in their gorgeous family house by the sea: the children's toys, Caron's clothes, her books, the quirky collections she'd built up over the years. Everything was just as it had been when they left. Because Caron and Russ's plans were so fluid, and the Australia thing had never been a decisive, permanent move, the house had just been locked up and left. Russ reached the conclusion that he should take the boys back to Cornwall, although he was very apprehensive about it. We all agreed it was the best thing to do. There had to be some form of closure, and that was taking the boys home.

On 12 May we drove in two cars down to Cornwall. You have no idea how difficult it was going back into their home, Menlo – the embodiment of Russ and Caron's dreams and idyllic life by the sea. Everything looked the same, but Caron wasn't there. When we had visited, Caron was always at the door with a huge smile and hugs of welcome. Now, as we walked down the path and in through the door, we were hit over and over by thousands of vivid memories. Was she just behind the door? Was she waiting in the next room? Was she down on the beach? Was she on her way back from the shops? How Russ coped I don't know, because just stepping into the house made me quiver with fear, but once again that 'something else' descended and carried me forward, so over the threshold I went.

On 18 May we went into Truro to buy new school uniforms. Caron had only been gone for a month and yet life was picking up an unstoppable speed. The next day the boys started back at Fowey Primary School, the one they'd been at before going to Byron Bay. The summer term had already started, but we thought it was better for them to start now than miss another term and then nervously wait all summer for the autumn term. As it turned out, it was almost as if they'd never left. They just picked up life there. It was a wonderful, embracing school, and they were back among all the friends they'd known from before. The mythical home that they'd talked about so much in Australia had once again been made real. The boys were home. People welcomed them back with open arms, and Russ had support when he needed it most. I must say Russ's parents, Eve and Dave, were absolutely brilliant at that time, as was his brother, Craig. They all rallied round and held him up. His concern of course was for the boys; he was just desperate to see them happy. However, there were other things he had to do too. Most importantly he had to go back to work. He'd put his career on hold for long enough. Slowly, tentatively, he returned to his work in show-business management, shifting himself back in, seeing people here and there while managing never to be away from the boys for too long.

It was a very difficult time. Not only was he dealing with his own exhausting personal grief, he was now trying to care for the boys on his own, to be both parents. He needed to start earning again, yet felt guilty about leaving them. Work was in London, sometimes he'd drive up and back in a day, which was ridiculously tiring. He worked hard to get his career back on track, but there was always the guilt, the worry, the concern about being away from his sons. This on top of what had been a tumultuous, emotional rollercoaster for certainly the previous two years, if not the previous seven; it is a wonder the man did not fall apart. I know why he didn't: he is a father, a great father, the sole parent. You'd do anything for your children, and he did. Eventually he hired a really lovely nanny called Laura, a local girl from Fowey, and the hectic daily drive to and from London eased.

Stephen and I have a small house down in Cornwall, but at that time, we never stayed there, as we always went to stay with Russ and the boys at Menlo. We helped get them settled into school. Then Russ's parents arrived and on 23 May and we drove home to Sevenoaks. Walking back through the front door to an empty house was so very hard. It was a relief in some respects, because I was so tired, tired of putting on a brave face, but the quiet scared me. Where had everyone gone? I would sit on my bed clutching something of Caron's and weep at this new loss. The boys had been my focus. Now they were gone. The emptiness and loneliness came flooding in immediately and I realised that I'd made no progress at all.

At these times I returned to the letters to fill the void, and I began to see that loss comes in many forms and many disguises, and could happen over and over again. I had lost Caron. Now the boys and Russ were back in Cornwall. What on earth was I going to do with myself? I reread one of the letters I'd found so helpful: 'Keep busy, my dear, and talk to Caron. I'm sure she will help you in her own way to cope.' So many people were struggling like me: 'In Erin's honour we try to be brave and gracious, as she was, but most days it is impossible. People say things get easier, but as yet I have not experienced this and take each day as it comes.'

The world seemed a brash, noisy, uncompassionate place, a place where good friends could see me and fail to mention my daughter's name. I received a note from a woman called Celeste Abrahams, who had lost her twin sister. She simply said, 'Soon may the pain be easier to bear.' When? When was it going to get easier to bear? I asked myself, because at that moment it felt like it was getting worse.

Was the world an alien place, or was I now the alien in a normal world? Either way, I felt that the earth's axis had shifted and everything I had known was altered. I still had a desperate need to talk about Caron, but I knew that some people just can't deal with death. Perhaps it is because a child dying, however old, is too terrible to contemplate and therefore people shy away from it. In my experience, shying away from the fact leaves a bad taste in the mouth. It doesn't matter how little you say, or what you say really, what matters is that you try. It always means a great deal to me when I see someone just make an attempt to convey their sympathy. You want the name of the person you've lost to be spoken out loud; you do want to talk about them; you do want to remember the good times even if it means more tears.

It never goes away. You can't remind me my child died. I know. I will always know. So please mention her name. When people don't, you feel far, far removed, and walking among aliens is not a nice feeling. I will change the subject if I think I can't handle it, but I never do.

It is not uncommon to find yourself reassessing friends after a traumatic loss. Some people just leave you be because they can't cope. Though this did not happen so much to me, I have spoken to a lot of people to whom it did. In the long run maybe it doesn't matter that you lose acquaintances, because good friends really come to the fore, but in the beginning, when you are needy and raw with grief, and you stop in the street and catch people's eye only for them to look away, it can feel terrible. A friend of mine lost his wife and sought solace in the company of others in his local pub, but after a while he realised that he was sitting more and more on a bar stool on his own. His mates had just got tired of talking about it. I had something different happen to me. A really good friend from Northern Ireland called up to offer her condolences but for some reason what she was saying and the somewhat glib way she said it just weren't helping. There was nothing wrong with it, but the words just weren't what I needed to hear at that moment. I didn't want to talk to her for a while. In the end it was nothing to do with her; it was to do with me. I simply wasn't in the right space.

Of course, because grief is so confusing and conflicting, sometimes it is a relief when a person looks away. It might be one of those days when you actually can't take any more on. After all, do you really want to start chatting in the supermarket only to end up in tears? Frankly, coming out and doing the weekly shop is bad enough without that added pressure. You make people feel uncomfortable. You are aware of that, so then you find yourself expending precious energy trying to comfort others. The whole thing is a rollercoaster. Shopping is a huge hurdle to someone in the grip of grief. It is mundane, but you can't avoid it for ever.

Carol Chase found herself in M&S, where everything Olivia had loved leapt off the shelf. She walked down each aisle thinking, Oh my God, I will never buy these again. I feel the same when I see the special rice milk that Caron drank. It will always feel odd to hold a melon in my hand. Michael still only buys the wheat-free spelt bread that Caron ate. Olivia, being a young fifteen-year-old girl, loved M&S toffee yoghurts. Carol doesn't know whether they still make them, because she can't bring herself to look in that area of the chiller cabinet.

I saw the boys as much as I could now they were in Cornwall. We went down there for Stephen's birthday, on 4 June, and Russ organised a quiet dinner at the house. Russ found something really personal of Caron's to give to Stephen, which was so thoughtful, and all our local friends were there. I will never forget sitting on the terrace of their house at Menlo, looking down into Ready Money Cove below. Charlie, soon to have a birthday himself, was sitting on my knee when Russ made a speech. There was this extraordinary moment when Russ said, 'Caron is with us tonight,' and Charlie sat up with a jolt – for that tiny instant he thought that Caron had come back. That moment will stay with me as long as I live, because a second later he realised that it was only her 'spirit' Russ was talking about, that it was just an expression, it wasn't real. He was quiet and didn't talk a great deal about anything at that time. The boys were both having a lovely time, as best they could, but they were no more getting over it than I was. For a split second that little child had thought his mum was back, and like me, it would have surprised him less than coming to terms with not being able to see her again. I have never spoken about it with him, but I can still feel the tremor rip through him . . . God, how I wished it were true.

Socialising is very difficult in those early days of your loss. On 9 June that year, it was Paul's fortieth birthday. Paul wasn't going to have a birthday party, but we all said, 'You've got to. You must.' Caron's death didn't mean Paul couldn't have a birthday. I encouraged it and said, 'Caron always loved a party. She loved birthdays. You must celebrate it,' though deep inside I was dreading it. It came as a wonderful surprise to me that somehow I could isolate the evening and enjoy it for what it was: the year my son Paul turned forty. He had all his friends in the garden at his home. It was a very hot evening; it was noisy and fun. Sandy, his wife, had even organised a flamboyant belly-dancer. First, I managed my expectations; then I forced my way through it; then, despite what I was feeling inside, I found myself enjoying it. Was I inching my way back? I'm not sure there is a way back. It's more that I was finding a new way. The way to a place where I could enjoy the moment *and* miss Caron.

But it came at a cost. I arrived home afterwards and literally collapsed in a heap. I was consumed with the thought that Caron should have been there to help celebrate her brother's birthday, and I couldn't help recalling that amazing night of her fortieth in Australia. The photograph on the front cover of this book was taken on that night. Russ had decked out the house they went on to buy, Taylors, in fairy lights and made up numerous sets of angel wings for everyone to wear. Caron looked so vibrant, so stunning, so amazing, dancing away without a care in the world in fabulous long, black lace trousers with a deep slash up either side, showing off her wonderful legs. It was the last time I saw her dance at a birthday she was not supposed to reach. Yes, I cried when I got home, because despite everything I had to be thankful for, there was still, and is still, so much to cry about.

I can understand why people in this situation become reclusive: it's safe at home. At home, we don't have to connect with the supermarket and the foods that remind us of our missing loved ones. We don't have to look at people who are happy and loving life or, worse, not appreciating it. We don't have to face life.

Sometime in June, I was asked to a charity dinner for the Jill

Dando Memorial Fund – they asked me to make a speech about Jill, whom I adored, and I was still trying to come to terms with her tragic murder. I got up on stage and started trying to speak but crumbled. I couldn't keep it together. I never write down the things I am going to say at such events because I think these sentiments have to come from the heart, but my heart was still in pieces and I couldn't find anything there. It was broken. So was I. It was too soon for me to do something like that. The truth is, for a long time you're exhausted; constantly living with such pain is tiring. You need energy to socialise, you need strength to stand up in front of a crowd and talk, and I had very little of either to spare. However, that night another big piece of the puzzle moved into place because I ended up sitting beside a lovely couple, Judy and John Halewood, who had come down from Liverpool. Judy had successfully dealt with breast cancer and we formed an immediate bond, both feeling we were meant to meet. That evening during the auction John bid for and won a wooden bridge for the garden, which he then generously gave to Stephen and myself in memory of Caron. I look at that bridge from my kitchen window every day and feel grateful that John and Judy have since become such deep friends and a great source of strength and support.

There is so much to cope with in this alien world. Dealing with your loved one's possessions is an odd and difficult part of all this. There is a danger that you will rush into action because you are in the grip of madness and don't really know what you're doing. My pal Rod literally cleared out his partner's clothes immediately, only keeping a belt and a sweater, a decision he later regretted. I suppose at the time, though, it must feel cleansing. It's not dissimilar to when I tried to give Jackie some of Caron's clothes the day after she had died. After all, Caron used to borrow some of Jackie's jackets when she worked in television and I just wanted to see flesh and blood inside Caron's lifeless clothes. Fortunately Jackie didn't take them, and afterwards I wondered for a long time what on earth I had been trying to do. It was madness.

What I have learnt through it all, and what I think is terribly important, is to give those possessions dignity. This is what I have tried to do. There is nothing worse than bundling everything up and giving or throwing it away. Obviously some things you have to throw away, but even that is very, very hard. For instance, I kept some of Caron's socks – I mean, what was I going to do with her socks? – because I just couldn't throw all of them away. A lot of her stuff I keep in a drawer, even though I would never be able to fit into anything. But you never know. One day the boys will grow up. One day they might have daughters. One day one of those daughters might have a flair for fashion. Her sons certainly do.

The summer continued and the weather got warmer, but I was still a block of ice inside. Then Russ and the boys came up to London for half-term, the week of 17 June, probably so Russ could have a break from the commute and we would lay on the entertainment with Paul's children, the boys' cousins, Jake and Beau. We were lurching from one thing to the next. Meanwhile Michael and Paul were dealing with their own grief, in their own way. Michael, being single at the time, found it hard. I was probably of little use to him at the time, and I understand that after a while a lot of your regular friends get bored listening to the same sad story over and over. A really, really great friend will of course sit and listen for as long as it takes, which they should, but it takes a long time and there is always this nagging feeling that they don't really understand your pain, that they're bored. You don't want to be that moping person any more either, so like me, Michael would force himself to go out and be jolly and throw himself on the mercy of the alien world. Of course what happens then is you are told, 'Wow, you're coping so well,' and you're back to the beginning again. Can't you see a piece of me is missing? Can't you see what's going on inside? And you realise, once again, that you are in this strange place, where no one understands you and no one speaks your language. It is very disorientating, and what I didn't realise was that the alien world was going to get stranger.

7

The Mask of Survival

In idle conversation
You ask me about
My children.
You are an acquaintance.
I do not know you well
And so I don a masque.
I speak happily of joys,
Light-heartedly of mischief,
But I do not speak
Of death.

I do not want to see
The shadow of uncertainty
Pass your face
And feel the
Awkward silence that falls
Like a curtain between us.
I do not want to say,
'It's OK, that was a long time ago.'
It will never be quite 'OK',
And sometimes it seems
As if it happened yesterday.

Always With You

And so I take my masque
Along with me through life
Like a perpetual Halloween night,
To hide just a bit from people
And to preserve my strength.
For mourning is tiring,
And each time I recount
That day of death,
I am a little wearied.
I would much rather speak
Of the joys in his life
Than the sorrows of his death
To strangers who absently ask
Of children.

Yet tragedy is more universal
Than ever I had known
Before it touched my life.
And so many times I wonder
Who else looks out
From behind a masque.

'Masques', Karen Nelson

When you find yourself in the black hole and you're hanging on by your fingernails and trying to scratch your way out, realisation hits you quite early on that you might not get out of this hole, that you might never get to the top and never manage to climb out. You look around and realise you might be scratching away for ever. That is no life at all.

Gwyneth from Newport wrote about her twenty-two-year-old nephew, who died of cancer:

*My sister went into a dark place. No one could get
through to her, and it went on for nearly three years. And
one day we were having coffee and she said, 'How do I go
on?' and I said to her what my brother had said to me:
'You have to get up off your knees and move on or you go
down and down.'*

I had to find a way to get off my knees. I had to find a way to get
out of this dark place. I have thought and thought about where I
went to in those first months, and though I call it my selfish grief,
because it is so self-centred, the truth is at the time I genuinely
didn't have the capability or capacity to deal with anybody else's
suffering. It was all I could do to cope with my own pain, and I
wasn't even managing to do that very well. I couldn't take other
people's grief on board. The knock-on effect of that is enormous, especially if you have lost a young child and have other
young children to care for. Eventually, though, there comes a
time when you look at your husband, wife, other children and
you say to yourself, I have to rejoin the living.

While you're in the frozen cube, in limbo, wallowing in your
own pain, you become sort of untouchable. Nothing helps and
you can help no one. All you are really capable of is going
through the motions, and only barely. A huge amount of that
early grief is tied up with a degree of self-pity for what you've
lost. If I'm being honest with myself, that's what I was grieving
for in the beginning: the beautiful child *I'd* lost. Now I also
mourn what she has lost. At the time I acknowledged that if I
wanted to survive this myself and have some sort of life left, if I
wanted to be a partner to my husband, a mother to my sons,
then I needed to do something. It was a defining moment. I
had a choice to make, a decision to start to thaw and join the
warm-blooded race.

Years earlier I had stood in my kitchen weeping about what might happen to Caron because she had cancer. The worry and fear were consuming me. I remember vividly thinking, I can't go on worrying this much twenty-four hours a day because I'll be of no use to Caron. So following Caron's lead, I had to force myself to accept what was happening at that moment and let the future reveal itself in time. It took a massive mental effort to don the mask of positivity for Caron. Now that the worst had happened and Caron had died, I had to summon up that mental strength again.

Caron wrote a lot in her diaries about digging deep within herself to block out fear:

Thoughts are very powerful things – if we let them be. Like emotions, they come and go. We have hundreds and hundreds of thoughts a day. They come and go, and often · when we start to notice what's happening, we just let the mind run away. But in this we have *choice*. There is a split second before the thought takes form when we can decide whether or not to let it in, and then if we do, we have a further choice as to whether or not we let it through. Do we entertain it? Place it down? Lay a table for it and let it grow and grow in stature, size and importance? Sadly we often do.

I believe it is essential if you have a strong mind given to obsessive thoughts to train and discipline it. It's too easy to let it run wild and out of control, leaving you in pain and despair.

I had received so many letters at this point that I knew many others have gone through what we'd gone through, and worse, and had survived. I had letters from people who'd lost not just one but two or sometimes three people they loved. I knew that if they could cope and survive, so could I. Though it didn't take my pain away, it gave me that extra courage. It wasn't the thought that they had suffered more that helped; it was the knowledge they had been to the depths of that dark place and survived. So, for the sake of my sanity, I tried valiantly to put on the mask and return to work.

For me, and I imagine a lot of people in this situation, it is vital to rediscover a purpose in life. When someone key in your life dies, it is very easy to feel like there is no point in going on. No wonder depression rears its ugly head. No wonder so many people are prescribed medication. But in my experience no amount of blanking out the pain will make it go away. At some point you have to confront it, and you have to learn to live with it. It simply doesn't go away.

Work may not be the panacea for everyone, but for me, it was all I had ever known. An Ulster work ethic was instilled in me as I grew up, and I worked from the age of eight as a semi-professional singer. We were taught always to be busy. Mum would say, 'You'll have years ahead of you to sit in an armchair – go and do something.' For me, work has always been a mainstay. Whatever dilemma I have had in my life – the death of my parents, my divorce, worries about the children – work has always been where I have found a sense of normality, of solidarity. It has forced me to concentrate on something else, or somebody else. It has diverted my mind and therefore stopped whatever problem I am facing from being all-consuming. Work provides a different path, changes the landscape, introduces me to new situations and new thoughts.

I received many letters with lots of different advice, but the ones telling me to get busy struck the loudest chord with me. One letter in particular helped me so much: 'Get yourself back to normal life as soon as you can. I am a great believer in daily routine. I really think it helps, and of course talking about your child helps.' Those words came from May, in County Down. I applied them to my own life and included them in *Next to You*, the book I would eventually write about Caron's struggle and what she had learned about dealing with cancer. After reading the book, May wrote to me again. 'I still get dark days,' she said, 'but I have thawed out more. It just takes time and it will come.'

A year later I was sent a letter from octogenarian Muriel, who lived in Bath. Her daughter, Jane, had died of cancer. Muriel herself had also lost a little boy years before, her husband had died, *and* she had got a DVT after a bad fall. She wrote beautifully of the daughter she'd lost, 'Jane was so gifted, a brilliant teacher, head of economics at Badminton School, married to a bishop, mother of two lovely daughters, but most of all she was the most perfect, loving daughter I could have wished for.' You would have thought that such suffering was enough to make this elderly lady give up the fight, but no. What did she do? 'I heavily support your advice to develop an interest of some kind. I took an Open University course when I was eighty-three (got seventy-two per cent) and am enrolling for another one soon.' She also sent a cheque to the Caron Keating Foundation, which I had by then set up. It was my turn to be inspired.

Doreen from Hampshire also wrote me a powerful letter. Not only had her daughter, Suzanne, died of breast cancer, aged thirty-two, that same year her mother had also died of cancer, aged seventy-nine. Both tragedies were set off, she thinks, by accidents. Her mother was knocked down by a car; her daughter jarred her back badly in a charity parachute jump. Doreen wrote:

I know, as you do, we will never get over losing a child, but as people say, life has to go on. I did not think I would be able to go back to work [as a Marie Curie nurse], but one day my son said, 'Suzanne would tell you to get your backside into gear and get back to work,' or words to that effect. It will be three years this year, and no, it does not get any better and some days are worse than others, but we have to get on with life.

When Suzanne died, a beautiful butterfly came into her bedroom and I like to believe she has wings and freedom.

I was so impressed by Doreen's letter on so many levels that I wrote back. Not only had she lost both these important women in her life, but her career as a Marie Curie nurse, which meant caring for cancer patients in their own homes, would take her right back to the place from which she was probably trying to escape: facing the ravages of cancer. I was so pleased her son had got her back to work – for one, there are so many people who need her expertise. She was a brave woman and I admired her.

These letters helped me reach the top of the black hole and work out what I had to do to stop falling back, down and down. Though sometimes, when I am tired and alone, that still seems like a strangely tempting thought. I knew by now that there was no way I was ever going to be able to leave that black hole behind – I would never be able to fill it in – but I also came to understand that I wouldn't want to. Many bereaved parents spend their lives gingerly skirting around it, but all those letters were right: the schism remains, of course it does, because what should be in place isn't, and never will be. That is why I call it the mask of survival. I have to wear a mask, but what you see isn't really who I am.

Margaret from Birmingham wrote to me in that first terrible year. Her daughter, Joanne Elise, had died of a brain tumour.

I just felt that I needed to write to you because I know exactly how you are feeling. Yes, my heart is broken also and my life will never be the same again. The smile on my face is not real. I feel as if someone is pushing me along.

Joanne Elise was like a breath of spring; the whole house would come alive when she came in.

Meanwhile Carol Chase, whose daughter had died so tragically at the age of fifteen, was continuing to write her diary to Olivia, something she would contribute to for the next two years as she searched for answers. Where had her daughter gone? Why had this happened? How could she go on? She too had so much still to say to Olivia and realised, as I had, that the other people around her couldn't absorb it all either, so, like many others, she was writing it down. She was consumed with pain but afraid of leaving it behind. There is a time when 'moving away' from your pain can feel terribly disloyal, but in fact the mask is not really about moving away; it's just a moment to press 'pause'. The grief doesn't leave you, but the mask enables you to put it in a box for a while. Carol struggled with this:

Happiness is asleep, hibernating, until we can in some way start to recover. I can't at this stage feel it could ever be otherwise, and part of me doesn't want to ever feel differently – I don't want anything about you to diminish in any way, and perhaps that, in some way, must include my pain in losing you. The most personal pain there could ever be. Olivia, I want you to know that a mother's love

never dies. You died, your beautiful soul has moved on,
but my love is so clear and rich and for ever enduring. I
truly want you to know that. I'm sure you do.
All my love,
Mummy xxx

The pages of her diary got the real version; for everyone else, there was a mask.

And so, with my mask fixed firmly in place, I went back to a bit of my old routine. Back to what I've done since I was eight – work. Now, when I look back through my own diary, I am astonished that I returned to work on 1 June, a mere six weeks after Caron had passed away. However, I probably couldn't even have considered accepting a work commitment had the offer come from any programme other than *This Morning*. It was a safe place for me, as both Caron and I had worked there, and the editor said, 'If you feel at any point, right up to the second before we go on air, that you can't cope, we have a standby.' Plus Ross Kelly, whom I'd known for years, had been chosen as co-presenter, and I knew that if panic set in, he would be able to handle it.

Nevertheless, finding the physical and mental strength to return to work often seemed beyond me. Sometimes getting out of bed and putting on the slap was hard enough, never mind going to work. It seemed like a monumental undertaking at the time, but I am glad I did it so early. I think it helped me rejoin life. It was what I knew, it was what I had always been, and I felt in my heart that Caron wouldn't want me sitting in the black hole for ever, weeping.

Every time I doubted I would be able to cope with returning to work, the letter from the woman in Wales who'd lost her son so many years before came back to my mind: 'I'd like to tell you it gets better, but it doesn't . . . If you weep from now till the day you die, it won't change anything and it won't bring Caron back.' She was right. What choice did I have? What choice do I still have? You don't make the decision to don your mask and put everything behind you just once; you make the decision to get back out there umpteen times a day for, well, I imagine for the rest of your life. Even now, after four years, when the house is quiet I still find myself looking at photos and getting angry because I think, Why isn't she here to share this? All manner of life goes on and she is missing out on it. I ask myself furiously, Why isn't she here so I can fill a Christmas stocking for her? Why isn't she here to hear her son compose songs and stand up and sing? Why isn't she here to blow out the candles of her birthday cake? I could easily sit and weep, but what is the point? That woman was right: nothing I can do is going to bring her back.

A vital chunk has been taken out of your life and you know that things will never be the same because that person is no longer there. So for me, keeping out of the black hole became about how I could pick up the pieces and somehow try to knit them all together again.

I had so much going for me, I realise that – sons and grandsons to love, Stephen, who barely left my side, a career to go back to and keep me busy. I fully accept that to some my situation might look easy. If you don't have a focus, if your career is over, if you are alone and don't have a partner, or if, unimaginable to me, you have no other surviving children – no one at home or no one to wake in the middle of the night (not that you ever do, but at least you could) – it would be harder still. But even though I had so much to be grateful for, finding those positives and holding on to them was extremely hard and seemed almost impossible at the time. Whatever your situation may be, it requires enormous strength to think otherwise, and the one thing you don't have in the beginning is strength. That takes time and an awful lot of effort and support.

As I said earlier, work isn't the answer for everybody and a lot of people questioned whether I should be going back so quickly. It is odd the things you are criticised for when you are grieving. I have said it before and I will say it again, there are no rights or wrongs, except perhaps relying on alcohol or drugs, because they don't help in the end, and it is up to the individual to find whatever works to help them out of the hole. For me, it was that Ulster work ethic, a great leveller. It's a lynchpin. For others, it is writing. For a lot of people, it's gardening or sewing. Why did I go back? Because it gave me a structure, it gave me something to get up for, a reason to get dressed and put on some make-up. If you're not going anywhere and you don't want to see anyone or do anything, it is all too easy to think, What's the point? Before you know it, you've slid back down the wall of that hole and have to start clawing your way up all over again.

It may sound too simple to say, 'Keep busy,' but the reality is, the more time you spend reflecting on your loss, the more consuming it gets. You're so inside yourself, inside your own head and heart and what you're missing, inside what you're suffering that you feel you aren't capable of giving space to anything else. If, however, you can get to that point of finding something to occupy you, old or new, it can give your tormented mind respite. So the advice is, keep busy, fill your head with something else, whatever it is – looking after your grandchildren, writing, painting, playing golf, charity work – find something and somebody else to take you away from this all-consuming grief. Like Caron, I needed to find something that would give me something else to think about other than the pain and fear:

Art work out of the cupboard. Painting. Can I do it? Will
I be good enough? Does it really matter so long as I enjoy
it? That's enough. What am I worried about? Worried
about being judged or being watched? Concentrate on the
recognition of something that makes your heart sing. To
live and love in harmony, doing what I love, surrounded
by those I love – with my passion for life and God on
high. What do you love to do? Paint, write, see my
children, friends, laugh, love being on the beach with the
sun on my skin, lie in the sand, lie in bed with my
husband, loving each other, amused, music, playing my
drum.

Let myself melt with the gladness and joy of that
moment.

To me, work was a relief, but most of all it gave my life
structure. There is of course a fine line between keeping busy
and running away from grief, because grief is not something
you can outrun. It is OK to let the tears fall – for me, it was
vital – but the fact is that in the end buckets of tears won't
bring your loved one back.

The other thing that death teaches you is to re-evaluate your
life, to live and appreciate every second and understand what a
miracle life is. It can make you love more deeply and create
stronger bonds than ever. It is a difficult place to be in, because
though you now realise how very short and precious life is, you
are at that point incapable of doing much more than curling
up on the sofa and wishing it all away. That is why donning the
mask and getting out there is so important. Because otherwise
the cancer, the drink-driver, the heart attack, the asthma
attack, the epileptic fit, or whatever terrible blight has fallen
on your family, will claim another life. And that would be a

terrible, terrible waste, since we each have something to give and a lot to gain from our time on earth. As one woman wrote, 'What will I say to my child when I see him again in heaven and he asks me, "What have you done since I left?"' I think about that a lot too. Caron so firmly believed in angels and had faith to the end. I have her in my mind always, and it is she who gave me the strength to get out of bed, put on the slap and get myself back to the studio.

On the Friday before I was due to start work, the production team at *This Morning* brought me in for a special programme about Caron, presented by Phillip Schofield and Fern Britton. It was a very clever move. Not only was the studio a comfortable place for me, but everyone there knew Caron because she had worked on the programme too, so I felt very safe with them and felt they understood. Phil had known Caron for years and years, and they'd dated before Russ and Caron got together, and that comforted me because, like the letters, I knew I could share the pain. I remember being quite self-conscious about whether people were waiting for me to break down, but in the end I wasn't the only one who cried, so it didn't matter so much. The programme was extremely emotional. We all wept, including Phil and Fern, most of the production team and even some of the cameramen. It was so raw, just six weeks after Caron had died, that it was really hard to watch the clips they played. Seeing her moving about, talking, smiling, laughing and singing tore me open, but it was also very cathartic. These people loved Caron too, so it was OK – I didn't have to move on without her; I could take her with me; we all could. It also allowed me to talk about her in the context of the studio – the lights, the cables, the cameras – which meant, come Monday, I was able to return as a presenter, as I had already addressed the subject of Caron's death.

In spite of all the support from the team at *This Morning*, I still really wasn't sure I was going to be able to do it. My mind was in real turmoil driving down to the studio on the Monday morning, but I did and I was really quite pleased with myself. In my diary I wrote, 'First day back at work. Despite the odds, really enjoyed *This Morning*.' However, I have to admit I was still just doing my job. I never actually had to leave that cold place. I was going through the motions, rather than truly rejoining the living. I was still in the same mould I'd always been in. To really break out of the ice block was going to take something unexpected or much, much more time.

If nothing else, however, being back at work was a welcome break from the never-ending gloom. It introduced different things to think about. It allowed me to read about other people for research, concentrate on their lives, focus on fresh subjects and escape from the all-consuming burden of grief. I maintain that it doesn't matter what you fill your head with as long as you fill your head with something other than your loss. It was a relief to realise that I could go on *This Morning* and do two hours straight live television and not weep or consciously think about Caron. I was staggered to discover that despite myself, for the first time since Caron had died, my head was filled with something other than thoughts of having lost her, though the idea that I might be leaving her behind, if only for a couple of hours, was also scary. In truth, my grief never went away, but I was able to push it aside. The fact that I was able to do that gave me hope that I wouldn't be disabled for ever, that in time I might defrost and really join the warm-blooded people who laughed so easily.

Still in the throes of selfish grief, what I never anticipated, never even considered, was that my appearance on *This Morning* would help anyone other than myself. Over three years after *This Morning* broadcast its tribute to Caron, the production team received an email from a woman called Sandra, which they kindly forwarded to me.

I know that in the past you have had Gloria Hunniford on your show, talking about her daughter Caron's battle with breast cancer. I watched the programme about Caron and her battle. I too was diagnosed with breast cancer, just before Caron lost her battle.

Despite my husband asking me not to watch the programme, as I too was fighting my own battle with breast cancer, I watched and sobbed. She was so brave and fought so hard; it is so unfair. Gloria's last words on the programme were that her daughter, Caron, would have been forty-one years old on 5 October. Those words were so significant to me: I too was celebrating my forty-first birthday on 5 October.

To me, it was as if these words were a personal message to me to make me fight as hard as I possibly could, for myself and my family. I have three children; the youngest was just two years old.

I had my first lump removed and the results were not good. The cancer had travelled and I needed more surgery. I then went on to have chemo and radiotherapy. In the middle of my treatment there were complications. It transpired that I had multiple pulmonary emboli. Part of the embolism broke off and managed to lodge just by my right atrium. This resulted in me having open-heart surgery.

Six major operations later, thankfully I can now say that I am winning my battle (fingers crossed). It may sound silly, but I actually believe those last words of that programme really were a personal message to me. They gave me the courage and strength to fight my way through the treatment and come out the other side.

I will always be grateful to Caron and Gloria for giving me the strength to fight. I believe that Caron was my guardian angel. I know that Caron strongly believed in angels and it was something that was special to her.

On 5 October (our forty-fifth birthday), I did something as a special tribute to Caron, which I would like Gloria to know about.

If you could possibly pass this email on to Gloria Hunniford, I would be eternally grateful.

I do hope this is possible.

Many thanks,

Sandra

Well, it was possible and I got that email. Although it was sent years later, it just goes to show how very powerful sharing Caron's story was. Perhaps life didn't have to be about going through the motions. Perhaps there was a way out of this sorrowful state.

Nothing was clear to me then, but it was soon to become so. For a few hours a day I was, if not happy, then at least not miserable. I enjoyed the comfort and company of work. It gave everyone around me a break, not least Stephen. I will never forget dragging myself home after that first morning in the studio, wrung out, tired through and worried once again about whether it was too soon or indeed the right thing to do. Now Caron's story is widely known, but back then it was a very personal, private, secret story of one woman's battle with cancer. I knew Caron would want to be remembered, but I was still reeling and uncertain how I could ensure that when the rest of the world seemed so keen to move on. I pushed open the front door and saw, there on the stair, a single white feather – the first of many. I asked my daily, sceptical at first, but she told me the staircase and landing had just been vacuumed. She'd seen no white feather. I picked it up and held it in my hand. Was it my daughter telling me it was OK to go back to work, that I was doing the right thing and she was behind me all the way (or in front of me, as I generally think)? Was the white feather simply out of a pillow, or was it Caron's calling card? It really doesn't matter, and we'll never know either way. As far as I am concerned, the feather was from Caron, and that's what matters.

I'd like to point out that in actual fact Sandra, the lady who had drawn such strength from Caron's story, had misheard me: it wasn't going to be Caron's forty-first birthday on 5 October 2004; it was going to be her forty-second. Perhaps it was an easy mistake to make, perhaps not. Does it matter? No. At least they shared the same birthday. Again, what matters is that a young mother facing her own terrifying ordeal was given the strength to fight, was handed something positive when the negative was threatening to invade. That feather did the same for me and I knew then I had done the right thing in going back to work.

Though I was pretty good at putting on the mask at work, the truth was that at home all of it fell apart – more so than ever, because for those few hours of thinking about something else, the pressure was building up again, so when I walked in the front door, the lid came off and the pain swamped me once more. When it manifested itself like that, it completely took over and there was nothing else but pain. The outside world was getting the best of me; to my family, I was still in pieces.

It was then I was given the second tool to put in my tool kit, in the form of a story from footballer Bob Wilson's wife, Megs.

Their young, wonderful daughter, Anna, had also sadly succumbed to cancer in her thirties and Megs had found a way to bring purpose back to their family life by starting a foundation in her daughter's name, the Willow Foundation. One day Megs was rushing out of the door to do something for the foundation, which was taking up her every waking hour, when her son intercepted her in the hall and said, 'Stop, Mum, stop. I am your child too.'

When Megs told me that, it struck a chord and the image of her son grabbing his mother's arm and pleading for her to make room for the living had a really profound effect on me. The way she so brilliantly described it to me meant I could actually visualise it from every point of view, physically, mentally and spiritually. I have no doubt she told me that story for a reason – no doubt at all. I thought of course, Here I am, wrapped up in what I have lost, and although I know my sons are in pain too, I haven't really understood the depth of their feeling. On top of that, I realised they were having to see me disappear, broken. It was a wake-up call. It wasn't just me who had lost a loved one. Paul and Michael had lost a very special sibling, and Michael had lost his second mother, his best friend. Although I had always recognised that they'd lost Caron too, I hadn't fully taken on board their feelings – I just hadn't been able to. Megs was right: I had other children who needed me. The mask of survival changed. It wasn't just to get me out of bed; it was to give something of myself back to the people around me who needed me. I've read countless letters from people who were not able to do this, and were it not for Megs Wilson, I might not have recognised my mistake so early on. There are women out there whose sole surviving child has decided to emigrate because they have been unable to carry the burden of their mother's grief, unable to cope with a mother who is of no use. There are so many terrible, sad stories of lives being destroyed long after the funeral. I didn't want to let this happen to my family.

Up until that point, I had been moping around the house without really making an extra effort to see my sons or look after them. After all, they were watching me to see how I was coping, and I remember doing exactly the same thing, trying to be strong for my mother after my dad had died. Part of it is also the difference between sons and daughters, though of course not always. Girls tend to come home to their mother and in time bring their own children; boys are often more independent. We are lucky to be a very close Irish family and I never had to look too far to find the boys. I have numerous vivid memories of all of them in the garden, a noisy table, eating, talking and laughing together. I know they wanted those times again, so I had to be that mother; they needed me to be. If I hadn't come out of it, they would have lost their mother and their sister. It took me a while before I could understand that, and more time again before I could walk Michael and Paul's path and Stephen's, as well as my own.

I think I manage that now, and I channel my energy into seeing as much of Paul and Michael as I can, but much of the time I'm conscious that the wound will never heal. My sons don't want me for ever to be associated with grief and loss, so for them I smile and laugh and enjoy the moment, but truthfully, I am changed. Changed to my core. Incorporating Caron's loss into who I am now is a very important thing for me. I say to many people, 'It's impossible to conceive a baby, carry that baby for nine months, give birth and then lose that baby and be the same person.' Of course I'm changed. I can't leave her behind. She is as much my child as they are, and I have as much a need to have a relationship with her as I do with them. I'm sure at times they would like the carefree mum they knew back, but to a point she has gone. People want me to get over it, but that is asking the impossible. I am it and it is me. Talking about Caron, missing her, crying for her, talking to her, thinking about her can keep my child 'alive' – not alive in the usual sense of the word, but a living memory, someone with whom I can continue to have a relationship. Today, I think I might have finally, almost come to terms with the awful fact that my child is dead and is not coming back, and I think for the moment that is enough. You can't ask any parent who has buried a child to banish them as well.

Someone told me that the mother of a deceased child has as much need to talk about that child as a mother whose child is living, so let us have our memories and talk about those departed. It doesn't necessarily mean we're being morbid, gloomy or depressed, or that we can't smile too; it just means our children aren't forgotten, which is everything to us. And so I decided I needed to wear the mask I'd been wearing for Caron for seven years for my grandsons, my sons and my husband. It fell off over and over again and I would weep and weep and weep, but there were also times it stayed on. I got back to work; I built some structure into my life; I forced warmth into my veins. The task that lay ahead of me now was finding a way of living that allowed me to move on from this place and take Caron with me.

Two years later I got a letter from an incredible woman called Vicky Harper. Her twin daughters were killed, and this terrible tragedy was in the papers. Having read *Next to You*, she sent me a copy of her own book, *Double Take*. It was a staggering journey of heartbreak, anger and ultimately survival. In her letter she wrote:

Like you, I was confronted early on by the fact that things do not really ever get better. The vicar at the church where the twins sang introduced us after six weeks to a couple who had lost their son some years before. My first question to their mother, Trish, was, 'When does it get easier?' Like you, I was hurt by her reply and felt it insensitive. She told me that it never got any easier but that after five and a half years she was teaching and singing with the children and realised she was happy. I have always been eternally grateful to her since for her honesty, something which I pass on when asked the same question. Some people react as you and I did, but I believe that in the end it is right to be honest.

It is better to know what you are up against, otherwise how on earth will you be able to fight what lies ahead and understand what you'll need in order to fight it? Knowing that it doesn't get better doesn't make it easier; it just makes you realise you're not alone and you're not going mad. It is a long and lonely path, and eventually you leave everyone behind you. No one wants you to grieve for ever, so you pretend you aren't, but it is a lie. It's always there; you just don't allow anyone who doesn't totally understand what you've been through to see it.

I still get letters asking me to ring, and sometimes I pick up the phone, as I did back then, and call. I rang a woman called Deirdre, whose beautiful daughter had also been killed by cancer, on her daughter's birthday because her sister had written and asked me to call: 'I feel it would be of more benefit to her than all the counselling available.' I totally understand that sentiment. You are just longing to talk to someone who understands your pain, because under the mask it is still there.

8

Finding the Positive

This is my oath as I am born:
To strive for peace or be forlorn
To leave this world proud of my name
And a better place than when I came.

W. G. Royce

In late August 2004 I pulled out of the daily crate of post one of the most impacting and constructive letters I was to receive. Ultimately, it threw me a lifeline.

Dear Gloria,
It is 1.48 a.m. on Wednesday, 25 August, and again I find God is using my quiet time to interrupt my sleep. I am being driven, quite strongly, to write to you again.
I now better understand that I will not get peace and rest until I capture, on paper, the words being given to me to convey. I now find it easier to simply give in to the direction I am being led in. What helped was obviously your confirmation that my last letter made a connection with you, even if in some small way.
Having a faith is a large part of who I am. I am therefore not afraid of pushing past the normal and expected behaviour to reach beyond what is on the surface.

It comes easily, flowing with no thought required, just an instrument to make the necessary link.

This all feels so right. Caron is so much in my head, particularly at this time of the early morning. Why and how is not important or frightening any more; it is simply how it is. The connection is made.

The next chapter is still important. You must stop and listen to what needs to be done. Think about how Caron's life is to be carried forward and used to make sense of her early passing in some way. Place your faith, love, energy and skills to move Caron into another dimension for all to reach and touch the essence of her spirit.

The world continues to search for a purpose, but you have a key to unlock the treasure, the treasure that Caron brought with her into this world. It is not lost; she is not lost – you must believe this. It is not a coincidence that you are in the limelight. Caron is also known and loved – these events have been lined up purposely. The wider world can see and connect to what they know; it will just give the next chapter validity and credibility.

The difference that can be made is huge. Caron's courage, kindness and days of pain will not be forgotten or lost for one second, as there is too much to lose.

As difficult as this is, the next chapter awaits. You need to start work. This is a great opportunity to honour Caron, to move forward in a positive way, in the right direction, to make sense of something that on the surface makes no sense at all.

Look deeper, feel deeper, search deeper. You will be given the answers and the direction. Our loved ones are gifts from God. They come to us, even if for only a short while, to share essential messages with us. Think and remember.

*There is nothing to waste here. Caron can teach us and she
was sent for a purpose – to share messages of truth. Her
faith was in place and is important now. Take quiet time to
reflect and interpret her message. Others need to hear the
things that she is still trying to convey.*

*Caron is not lost to you. Her soul is bigger than death
– death is never the end. To stay healthy and focused, you
must work with the loss and not against it. Caron needs
to know this is how it will progress, otherwise her passing
is for no reason, and that can't be. It is not the truth. In
your heart I believe you understand this. I hope whatever
I have taken down makes sense to you.*

With much love,
God bless,
Ann

What words: I needed 'to make sense of something that on the
surface makes no sense at all'. I had reached a place in my
grieving where I realised I had to try and find my way back to
Caron. Trying to get over it and move on were false starts. In
some respects I had to go back to the beginning. I had mistakenly
thought we were all on this healing journey together. Now I
realised I was on my own path, and everyone else was on theirs.
There were many pointers given to me as to how to find my way
back to Caron, but it wasn't immediately obvious to me where to
look. Overall I seemed to be getting two types of letters. The first
were from people sharing their pain. They'd sign off with
prayers and tender thoughts. I could tell that writing had been
part of a cathartic process, and I got the impression that some of
the senders had never been able to tell their story, perhaps
because talking about death makes others feel uncomfortable,
and writing their story was a much-needed way to release steam

from the pressure cooker. I treasured those in the beginning because they let me know I was not alone. The second sort of letter, however, provided essential clues to managing the future without Caron. They'd offer helpful pointers: 'In time you'll remember the good and not the bad', 'Get busy, return to normal life', 'Talk to her.' The letter I have just included, though, stood out from the others. I received it at a time when my already shattered world was again being shaken up.

As a mother, I needed to keep the memory of Caron alive. It was imperative to remember her well. I just didn't know that was what I needed to do. It's trial and error; you find these things out as you go along. This letter gave me the clue. What I took from it was, because Caron was in the public eye and I still was, I had the means of raising money in her name and I had to do this in order to carry her name and spirit forward. To 'make sense of something' that made 'no sense at all', you have to do something positive. Finding the positive out of all this pain was vital to being able to put some order back into my life. Ann had written, 'Her soul is bigger than death – death is never the end.' That was music to my ears. There was a way I could keep the memory of Caron alive, turn a negative into a positive and keep busy.

I said to Russ and the rest of the family that I would like to start a foundation in Caron's name and they immediately agreed. We set about organising a big launch night. The date we chose was 4 October, the day before Caron's forty-second birthday. Had I not had such an event to plan, Caron's first birthday without her might have pulled me under. Instead I focused on making some good come out of all that we had lost. There wasn't going to be any dancing – I wasn't ready for dancing yet – but we planned a big auction and a proper sit-down black-tie dinner.

Taking what May from Northern Ireland had advised me, suddenly I had the key. I could do something profoundly constructive against this barrage of negativity and something I knew Caron would be proud of. Now I truly had a reason to get up in the morning; it would be a counterbalance to the loss.

We decided the event had to be smart and upmarket, so we chose the Savoy in London as a venue. We took on a great girl called Diana, who had organised a lot of events for the BBC and who helps do things for charity in her spare time. As well as great organisational skills, she has a fantastic database, so we started sending out information packs and invitations. We invited the press for the launch and I was really pleased when all the papers booked tables. All Caron's friends did too.

The launch was an incredible night and I felt very close to Caron, her spirit and everything she had encapsulated in her shortened life. I was able to stand up in front of all her friends and colleagues and talk about our aspirations for the foundation. Despite the nerves and apprehension, her friends made it into a wonderful event. The indomitable duos Richard and Judy, Ant and Dec, and Phil and Fern also ensured it was a memorable evening, auctioning off their own items and making everyone laugh. We raised £90,000 for cancer charities. It was a magnificent launch for the Caron Keating Foundation, and the event also turned out to be a celebration of Caron's life.

Was that the beginning of the healing? I don't know. It was certainly the beginning of something very positive. It seemed the right thing to do, and the foundation went from strength to strength. I know that Caron would be proud of it, just as we are very proud of what is now being done in her name to help cancer charities of all kinds, not just breast cancer. To see Caron Keating treatment rooms being opened in various parts of the country brings me enormous pleasure. I think she'd be bowled over by it, surprised and humbled, as I am. Only recently I opened a letter from someone who had sent me all their funeral donations. A business friend of Paul's sent us £15,000 from a golf day he'd organised. Then a week later he sent us another £15,000, which had been raised the previous year but had never been passed on to a charity.

The foundation also has a huge added bonus, in that I can share it with Caron's sons. I take great joy in bringing them to some of the happy occasions I am able to attend thanks to the work of the foundation. It would be impossible to take them to everything, as there is so much, and I wouldn't take them to the very serious events because I think they are too young to hear about how Caron coped with her cancer, but I delight in spending time with them and sharing the successes of the foundation. Hard Rock Café have a month-long event called Rocktober during which they collect for charity. Last October, on the final night, the boys came with me on stage along with Marti Pellow and Wet Wet Wet to receive a cheque for a staggering £45,000, which Hard Rock had raised for the foundation. It shows the boys how much their mother was loved and respected, and that she is remembered. It also teaches them the importance of giving to others and shows them that some people need help. Another joyous event we attend together is Strictly Tea Dancing at the Langham Hotel – a Sunday afternoon full of music and dancing, sticky buns and a lot of fun.

I love bringing the boys along and seeing them accepting a cheque on behalf of their mum. I think people take pleasure in seeing the continuation of life. They, after all, are the most enduring aspect to come out of Caron and Russ's life together. Not long after the launch, when the wound was still so fresh, I saw that Charlie had written about the foundation in his school exercise book. He had been asked to write about a charity day that he would plan. He wanted to invite a huge list of major sports personalities and give all the money to the Caron Keating Foundation. It was then I knew he understood what we as a family were trying to do. That really blew me away. It was all going in, in a good way. He knows that if he wants to talk about his mother and her fight, he can, and the foundation is there if he wants to get involved more as he gets older.

As Stephen often says, charity work gives me pride. It also gives me much more. It gives me a fraction of my daughter back, which I can then take with me, and that makes the future a little less frightening. All bereaved people want is for their loved ones not to be forgotten. It may be slightly easier for me because I have access to the public through my job, but you can do it too.

Dear Russ, Gloria, Stephen, Gabriel and Charlie,

When it was announced that Caron had died, I felt compelled to write to you but didn't, and then when Caron's story was aired on Tonight with Trevor McDonald, *I had the same feeling again. I told my grandparents and my mum that I had this urge to write and they all said that they felt exactly the same. So here I am.*

You see, we have a very similar story to tell. My auntie Ruth died of breast cancer about eighteen months ago. She was forty-two. She left a husband and four children, the youngest of whom was six years old at the time of her death. She battled bravely and courageously for almost five and a half years; she never gave up. She wrote her own eulogy and in that she told us all that she hadn't given up even then. She said that her spirit was strong but that her body was too weak for her to carry on. She said goodbye to all of her children and her husband, and she thanked her parents and brothers and sisters for the cherished life they had given and shared with her. She was truly astounding.

After she died, we felt that we had to do something. We heard of a charity called Genesis that was raising money to build Europe's first ever breast-cancer prevention centre. In Ruth's name we began to fund-raise with the hope of having a room named after her. We have raised £54,000 so far. I think that our fund-raising was the only thing that kept us going in the months after she died.

We all still feel her loss so deeply. We were a close family before Ruth died and we're probably even closer now. I don't think any of us will ever get over losing her, and the sad thing is, I know so many families that feel exactly the same way about the loss of a loved one.

My thoughts and prayers are with all of you and with Caron.

With love,
Vikki

She sounds like an amazing woman, and to raise that sort of money is a very honourable mark of respect. I agree with the family: fund-raising was also a major part of keeping me going.

This feeling is in no way uncommon. Calum's Cabin was set up after Calum, a boy of twelve, was diagnosed with an inoperable brain tumour. He himself was raising money for charity between bouts of radiotherapy and chemo. When he died, he left behind his twin sister, Jenna, and his parents, who immediately threw themselves into continuing to raise money for charity. Their aim is to build a holiday cabin on the Isle of Bute to give families dealing with cancer a break.

The Rosie Crane Trust was set up in Somerset after Rosie,

aged twenty-three, died of leukaemia. It was set up by her mother to provide a much-needed ear to bereaved parents.

Neil and Rachel from Buckingham lost their son, Jake, when he was only six, two terrible, heartbreaking days after being rushed into Great Ormond Street Intensive-Care Unit. They set up the Forget Me Not Fund in support of leukaemia research and, in a letter to me, wrote, 'The intensive-care-unit staff were wonderful and helped us immensely through these traumatic two days, and indeed through the weeks and months that have followed. The pain of losing Jake is unforgiving, and by raising money it helps us cope with our loss.'

There were many, many more letters of this nature. Some were struggling, finding it hard to reach their goals. It is no small undertaking. The Charity Commission has many rules and regulations. You have to register as a charity before you do anything else, and then the commission oversees that the charity is sticking to the principles for which it was set up. Of course this needs to be done – you don't want money for good causes to disappear – but it can seem daunting. My advice is to persevere. The commission is there to protect us and the people who give so generously. Continue the fight our children started.

10 December 2004

Dear Gloria,

I just wanted to introduce myself before the evening at Eton College next week. In a nutshell I will tell you our story, and I know you will completely understand my reason for wanting to write.

I am bringing Rosie's Rainbow Choir to sing. The choir is part of Rosie's Rainbow Fund, a newly registered charity, which I set up last year following the death of my eleven-year-old daughter, Rosie, in May 2003. Rosie was a talented, kind and wonderful little girl who loved to perform. Although she was so young, she had already written and staged a full-length musical and appeared many times in theatre and on TV. She was a full-time pupil at Redroofs Theatre School in Maidenhead, our family business.

It was Rosie's wish while she was in hospital that she would raise money for other sick children. Sadly she was unable to do this herself and so we are doing this for her through our fund. We raise money for research into childhood respiratory diseases, and among several other aims, we fund a music therapist, who is now placed by Rosie's fund at the John Radcliffe Hospital in Oxford, where Rosie was a patient.

As one bereaved mum to another, I know you will only too well understand my need to keep Rosie's spirit and memory alive, and I do this through the work of Rosie's Rainbow Fund. My older daughter, Ellie, who is now sixteen, is singing in the choir. She also composes and performs. At the end of last year she composed and recorded a CD called Rainbow's Light, *which was taken up by SGO Music and produced by Chris Eaton, who writes for Cliff Richard. All proceeds from the CD are going to the Child Bereavement Trust.*

I wonder whether it would be at all possible for you to tell the audience a little about Rosie and what we do. It would be perfect to do this before our first song, 'You Paint the Rainbow', which has been specially composed by our musical director with lyrics by Michael and myself. I know you will identify with the words!

With very best wishes,
Carolyn

The principle of the Caron Keating Foundation is to help as many smaller 'cancer' projects as we can. They can be anywhere in the country and vary from a drop-in counselling service for patients and their families, a lymphoedema clinic, physiotherapists, helping children with bone cancer, supplying specific pieces of high-speed diagnostic machinery and setting up treatment rooms for complementary therapies, right through to providing at-home hospice treatment and funding the hospices themselves. Because we are a small family-run organisation with no administrative costs, apart from Mary Clifford-Day, our fabulous part-time secretary, and Vicky Tibbitts, who deals with our grant requests, we can have a direct impact on many situations. As a result, we give to a huge number of people. It's very rewarding. The foundation is my baby; I administer it – it's a privilege – and it gives me a great deal of positivity. If something positive hadn't come out of Caron's illness and the pain of losing her, I honestly don't know where I'd be. A lot of life would be idle, meaningless. It gives me a good feeling when I write a cheque knowing that we're helping other, smaller organisations, knowing we're targeting a scheme that our donation will really make a difference to.

We look for projects where we can meet the people behind them and see the impact of our help. For example, we went to Northern Ireland and met a radiographer who scans young girls for breast cancer. We gave the Royal Marsden Hospital in London £25,000 for a lung project, and donated £5,000 to a London counselling project called Cyana. It was wonderful to meet some of the patients who use that service. One lady, who was in the process of having some complementary treatment, said that the centre was a lifesaver for her because it was a place where she could either have a laugh with somebody or find a shoulder to cry on if that was what she needed on the day.

I also hadn't anticipated what a source of strength I would find in meeting the people behind the projects. They are humble, everyday people who give so much of their energy and time to help others and yet don't ask for thanks. That alone reaffirms my faith. It brings light into the blackness. On top of that, I have met people who are in the same position as us. We are united in our grief, if only for a little while, and take strength from one another. It is very life-affirming and, particularly in the early days, I needed that.

The letter that I received from Ann back in August 2004 was so right. I can safely say that having the foundation has been the single most important factor in coping with Caron's death. Not everyone can do what we have – I'm not suggesting that. The mammoth work of Vikki's family, or those other families who have put so much into raising money, can seem too big a mountain to climb, too big a hurdle. Your contribution really doesn't have to be anywhere near that ambitious. In every town there is a voluntary outlet that needs people. See a neighbour who is sick or help out in an Oxfam or heart-foundation shop. Do anything, anything to redress the balance. It might be your local church, a hospice, hospital, school or library. Go and find whatever it is that creates a resonance with you.

Like everyone in this position, I have asked myself a million times, What was all that about? What was I supposed to learn? What was that meant to teach me? What is my life about now? For me, helping others is a simple, positive way of dealing with all those questions. The truth is, I am no philosopher; I can't sit and allow those endless questions to turn over and over in my mind. Why? Why? Why? Caron did enough of that to herself. This is what she wrote.

I have spent many, many hours trying to figure out why and how it happened. It's often one of those things we ask ourselves – 'Why this', 'Why me?' I found myself thinking of other people who had stuff to cope with and thinking, Well, I didn't cope any less well than them. Why should this happen to me? The simple truth is, often we don't know. We can have a few ideas why, but there are some things that are plain and simple mysteries and it's a waste of energy trying to figure it out. One thing I do know is that it comes with an onslaught of fear. Unfortunately all fear is ultimately a fear of death – some of us have been forced to face it sooner than we'd anticipated.

Even when you think you have an answer, the loss sends you tumbling back into turmoil and the questions start again. I will probably never know the reason why Caron died, and if I ever do, I will never really be able to comprehend it. What I do know is that the positive aspect of the foundation offers a counterbalance, which stops me sliding back down to the bottom of the pit. Right now I feel that I have to fund-raise and campaign because I have the voice and the profile to do it and Caron's story still has resonance. Because of those two things, I *can* raise this money and help many people. Knowing that, how could I not?

The foundation is always in the process of assessing requests from the thousands of cancer projects that need help, and at least twice a year, along with my doctor colleague, Richard Husband, and the family, we decide how the money is to be spent. The joy I get out of it is a welcome break from the emptiness I sometimes feel. It is a two-way thing, I know: the foundation benefits from Caron's profile and my own, and I benefit from it because I get to talk about Caron. I am allowed to stand up in front of people and talk about my beloved girl, and that, along with putting something back, helps me to survive. I go to a lot of functions, and though 'enjoy' isn't the right word, I do find it satisfying to explain to people how important it is to look after themselves and have cancer checks regularly. I often tell them about Caron's positive thinking. Of course, in the end you could argue that it didn't work out for her, but you'd be wrong in many ways, because she did manage to buy herself extra time and considering what she was going through, she had a full life, with an amazing quality to it. She had a happy home, and the boys, I hope, will remember only the singing and laughing and all that love, because that is what Caron's positivity gave them.

This year, 2008, is proving particularly busy for the foundation. The Society of Women Artists recently hosted a special evening for the foundation at the Mall Gallery in London. Six of their artists donated paintings to be auctioned off that night, and the gallery even gave 10 per cent of what was sold overall, resulting in a donation of many thousands of pounds. Ironically, a print of Caron's last painting, which was completed in Australia during one of her much-loved art classes, sold for the highest price. The painting is a self-portrait in which she is standing with one arm across her breast. She would have loved a painting of hers being exhibited, and therein lies the double-edged sword: I wish she'd been there to see it.

Also this year, her dedicated friend Cathy Comerford has organised the Pink Power Walk in the Richmond and Barnes area. She has done it every year since Caron died, and it raises tens of thousands of pounds for the foundation. This year over 400 women completed their marathon, including some of the Hodder girls involved in this book. So well done to them and well done to Cathy. I must say I love getting together with

Cathy and Caron's other friends, Yaz and Fiona. We have some raucous times and it brings all my memories to life. I see for myself why Caron loved their company, and I in turn love what they do in their bid to help the foundation.

Even Paul's sons, Jake and Beau, are now involved. Their school, Shrewsbury House in Surrey, had a sponsored walk and raised £30,000, which is an amazing feat for anyone, let alone young boys. It was a joy to go along to their morning assembly to accept the cheque and explain to the boys what a difference they have made in raising money in this way.

Later this year, after this book has gone to print, there will be another golf day, organised by Paul's friends at Sennheiser, and a ladies' lunch is planned in Buckinghamshire. In September, we will take part in a ball supported by Cliff Richard at Wentworth Golf Club. The Hard Rock Café are doing Rocktober again, and staggeringly Number 10 have offered us an event in November. The singer Daniel O'Donnell has generously given us an evening at the Waterfront in Belfast in December.

In May 2009 'The Night of a Thousand Voices' is to celebrate its tenth anniversary at the Albert Hall, in aid of our foundation. It is spiritually uplifting to hear that magnificent volume of sound, as close as you can get to angelic on this earth. In a previous year the evening raised the largest single contribution for the foundation, an astonishing £100,000.

All these things add up to a lasting tribute to Caron. Anything that is a force for good is worth doing, but sometimes we just do things in Caron's name. We have created an award through the Variety Club of Great Britain for new young talent, which in its first year went to Fern Cotton, now doing very well on both sides of the Atlantic, and last year to Lee Mead, the star of *Joseph*. The other glorious thing that happened was that Harkness Brothers, the famous rose-growers, developed a rose named after Caron and launched it in the Cancer Research Garden at the 2005 Chelsea Flower Show. It's an exquisite, full-blown peach rose, and as you can imagine, they get a great deal of TLC in my flower bed at home.

Of course, I would like to go to every event and I would love to be there in person every time we hand over a cheque, but unfortunately I can't be everywhere. I try, but already I've worn out two drivers.

It comes down to this. When you are faced with unexpected death, you can go one of two ways. Anger, rage and self-pity are real, powerful emotions and are very, very common, but they will make you bitter for the rest of your life. In the end they add to your pain; they don't ease it. The alternative is to find a way to become more spiritual, and hope that some good will come of something so terrible. This can, in some way, ease the pain, but it takes time, energy, will and self-discipline. It's a bit like swimming against a rip tide. Just when you think you don't have the strength to fight the ocean any more and it would be easier to allow yourself to be pulled under, there will be a buoy to hold on to. You can catch your breath, relieve your stiff and aching muscles, and find the strength to swim on and keep your head above water. Then you launch yourself back out into the rip tide, until eventually, gradually, imperceptibly even, you find yourself in calmer waters. It is a long, harrowing and exhausting swim, but the buoys help. My buoy is the foundation. It is my sons. It is the boys and my husband. But sorrow is never far below the surface and can pull me under at any time, into that churning, powerful water.

Sometimes the place to rest and take strength comes from therapy or counselling, maybe healing, acupuncture, yoga or a long walk. It doesn't really matter what it is, but we all need to give ourselves a release from this terrible pain, an hour's peace.

I am not surprised that most charities are set up by people who, like me, are dealing with the aftermath of illness and death. We have a focus, a common cause: finding a cure for disease. Those who've lost their loved ones in avoidable accidents or crimes have a longer road to travel, though I know many join up to campaign against the wrong that has befallen their child – like Mothers Against Drink-Driving (MADD) in the States, like Sarah's Law, which led to a register of convicted paedophiles, like the McCanns and their attempt to get a cross-border alert system in place when children go missing. They are all doing the same thing: finding some way to make a positive out of a hideous negative.

I was at the 2008 Children of Courage Awards and listened to a striking British man, who'd lost his son to a stabbing, talk from the heart about the terrible waste of life. I observed the audience as they watched this pained father talk stunningly, eloquently and passionately about how he plans to take his son's name to every school and every youth group he possibly can and talk to young kids about the futility of knife crime. His son's death had transformed this ordinary man into someone extraordinary and the room was collectively moved to tears. You could hear in his voice that he was on a mission. He was driven, driven, driven, to stop this from happening to another child. He had turned his anger and sorrow into a force for good, and in doing so had found his reason to go on.

Sometimes I ask myself why I drive myself into the ground racing around trying to meet all the various obligations of the foundation, as well as work and trying to be a good granny and a supportive mother. Why can't I just relax and be thankful for what I have? Well, I am thankful, more than thankful. I feel utterly blessed that I have my sons, that I have Stephen, that I have a busy life, that I have my grandsons, but I also have something missing. I can't ask anyone to fill that gap for me; it puts too much pressure on our relationships. It's not their job; their lives should not be defined by Caron's death. So I have to fill that void another way – I do that with the foundation and sharing my deepest feelings and fears in books like this.

Whether you have surviving children, a job, a hobby or not, it is important to find something to occupy you, and hopefully in doing so, you will find a way to fill part of the void. If you have watched a loved one die, the process of getting involved and putting something back is very healing. It helps to repay mentally what your loved one gained from the care leading up to their death. But what's important is giving back to the community in whatever way that may be. Caron was helped so much by so many people – from the doctors to the staff in the café who made her juices. If you can give back on behalf of your loved one, then it helps. You don't even have to give back directly to the people who helped you; just pass on the help to someone who has given you purpose.

I got a letter from a woman called Frances from Surrey. Her son, David, was twenty-four when he died. After being diagnosed with cancer at eighteen, he carried on with great dignity at university, became an investment banker, played rugby, was active and brave, but was then hit by secondaries and passed away.

You are their mum and you can't let this happen, and then you sit and hold them as they take their last breath and all you can say is, 'I am so sorry.' I would love to be of some help to mothers of young adults who have to endure what we have gone through. There is help for mothers of young children, but once they have reached eighteen, then you really are on your own, but to us, they are still our babies. I

*do believe that some good must come from the loss of our
wonderful children of whom we were so proud.*

Rachel from Doncaster put it perfectly: 'As Caron's mum,
you want to shout from the rooftops, "I had the best daughter
in the world!" I can and do empathise with these emotions,
and as a family, we have also turned to fund-raising as a
positive step forward.'

I am immensely proud to say that the Caron Keating
Foundation has raised in excess of £2 million in just a few
years – not bad for a small family-run foundation. We couldn't
have done it without the help and support of thousands of
people from all over the country. Thanks to them, the foundation is my salvation.

*The wings of my angel have spread and flown
To where peace replaces pain,
But she will live for ever on
Till I see her again.*

*Her life so sweet and gentle,
Taken in its prime,
Will help to serve others now
And be remembered for all time.*

*Her heart that fought so many fights
Until it took its pause
Is beating now for those in need
And for a worthy cause.*

'Brave Heart', W. G. Royce,
written in memory of Caron

9

Those Unspeakable Firsts

Let there be purpose in this suffering
Or else our crazy world has gone all wrong,
And pray that death is not an end but a beginning,
Now one so beautiful and loved has quietly gone.

Let us draw strength from helping one another
And through compassion may our grief commence to heal.
May we have courage as we step towards the future
And not be overwhelmed by pain that we still feel.

Let us remember happy times we spent together
And in that memory see gentleness and love,
And know for every smile and act of kindness
White feathers float down slowly from above.

Sharon Stanton Keep

As one prophetic letter said, grief is like standing with your back to the sea: the waves continue to crash over you when you least expect it. As well as the waves you least expect – it could be a phrase that reminds you of your loss, a song, a toffee yoghurt – there are other, bigger things that can wipe you out altogether: those unspeakable firsts. As Michael says, it feels as if there are a million of them. Just when you think you've

162

managed to make some headway in your climb out of the black hole, a date comes along that seems to undo all the progress, taking you right back to the beginning. There are birthdays, anniversaries, Christmas, New Year's Eve, Valentine's Day, Mother's Day, the children's birthdays, the first anniversary of the death itself and even the days leading up to it. On these occasions all your positive thinking fails you, the mask slips off, the tears flow, and you are back in a place that is beyond pain, beyond agony. In truth it is not just the firsts; it's the seconds . . . and the thirds . . . and the fourths. I can try to focus on all the good the foundation is doing to help others in her name, and I can see it as a memorial to Caron, but there are days when I can't find it in me to celebrate her life, much as I try. Instead I mourn all that we have lost.

As I mentioned earlier, for the sake of Stephen and Paul we more or less coped with their birthdays, which came very soon after Caron's death, on 4 June and 9 June respectively. It was hard, don't get me wrong, but not impossible. The first real challenge for all of us was Charlie's tenth birthday, on 25 July. It was horrendous. I was racked with worries about how we would cope. Caron was always so involved in her sons' birthdays – she would make cakes, choose a theme, put on a big event – but this was worse because Charlie and Caron had already planned the celebration together when they were in Australia. Since the family were due to be back in Cornwall for the summer, they had chosen to hold the party in Alldays Field, high up on the cliff, overlooking the sea, for one of their spectacular birthday picnics, cricket and laughter. Well, that was enough to send me over the edge. Where was Caron? Where the hell was she? Why wasn't she going to be there?

On the big day I watched Charlie closely. He got his presents, maybe a little more than usual, and to be honest he seemed really great. I was so pleased he was having a good time of course, but it made me feel very isolated and a little bit afraid. If I stayed focused on Caron, did that mean being left behind? Children are amazing, as they really are able to live in the moment and get involved in whatever is going on, and if that means having fun at a birthday party, then that is what they will do.

I, on the other hand, found it very, very hard. How I managed not to simply stand up and scream at the top of my lungs seems a miracle to me. Caron herself had stood on those clifftops many times and raged, screaming into the ether about this hideous, indiscriminate disease. That day, as the party started, I was screaming with her. I was there laughing and chatting with all the local people she had introduced me to, yet she wasn't there. I couldn't begin to fathom how we could be having a birthday party at the traditional venue of Alldays Field without Caron. Or was she there? It was raining that day, but at three o'clock, when everyone started to arrive in earnest, the clouds parted and the sun came out. It was as if she'd raised the blind. Just when you reach the lowest, darkest place, I am amazed how often you are thrown a lifeline. Knowing where to look and how to recognise it becomes a quest. The sun shone for three hours while the cricket match was played, the children ate, people laughed and candles were lit.

Charlie looked happy. I recalled some words his uncle Michael had said to him the day his mother died and wondered whether they were somehow easing his private pain. Michael had taken the two boys to the window the evening Caron died, put his arms round them both and looked outside. It was a perversely beautiful evening and the sun beamed down through the clouds into the garden. They could feel the warmth of the rays through the window. 'Every time you feel the warmth of the sun on your face, Mummy is with you,' said Michael. Well, the sun had certainly come out for Charlie.

There were loads of lovely people there – school pals, neighbours, Caron's girlfriends. So many people turned out because they wanted to be there for Russ and the boys, and to remember their days with Caron. There was no doubt they had a great wave of support down there. Everyone had brought something and I suspect everyone had made a special effort, so it turned out to be a really magnificent picnic. It was wonderful.

Most of Charlie's subsequent birthdays have been spent there, in Alldays Field. I like to think he wants to do that because that was what he did with Caron. It's tradition. I like it because it is a link to the past. I now know I can't drag her memory around like a hefty weight. I don't want to drag the boys down either. Having said that, I do have a desperate, no, desperate is the wrong word, absolute want to keep her memory alive, and that is the knife-edge I perpetually walk. That's why I always like to make chocolate Rice Krispie cakes and nanny's special marshmallow cakes, because that was what Caron did. To make nanny's cakes, you get those little cake cases, pour melted chocolate in the bottom, then put a single marshmallow in. The chocolate will pool round it. Then finally you put a dab of chocolate on the top and something on top of that, like a Smartie or a jelly sweet, and allow the chocolate to harden. They look amazing. They are so easy to make, but they're lovely and of course there is always the bowl and spoon to lick afterwards and cries of 'I want to sink the marshmallows in the chocolate.' I've been making them since my children were small, Caron continued the tradition, and now the boys and I make them together. So the tradition is upheld and that encourages me.

As summer turned to autumn, we crept stealthily towards Caron's first birthday without her. She would have been, should have been forty-two. Every year it is the same. She would be, should be forty-five, then forty-six. Everything she had missed out on since the day she died came back to haunt me. Finally it was 5 October. I awoke to that familiar frozen feeling, numb to my core. The day before, we had launched the foundation, with all the accompanying pizzazz and noise, which though a very positive thing to do and with a magnificent result, was shockingly difficult and totally unreal. The following morning was worse. It was so bad that to be honest I haven't got words to describe it. On her actual birthday night we had a quiet dinner for her at home. We sat in the dining room where she'd sat so many times and each person got a candle and a glass angel. The usual gang were there – Stephen, her brothers, Russ, Johnny and Cathy Comerford, Richard and Judy – and we lit our candles at the same time and sent her our love. Like Charlie's birthday, I found it all too much. Grief got the better of me and I couldn't stop reliving giving birth to this beautiful baby forty-two years before and recalling all the joy she had brought our entire family. I never dreamt for one second that I would not see her life unfurl.

In the last week of August we had filmed *Tonight with Trevor McDonald: Caron's Courage* and it had been aired on 4 October, in conjunction with the launch of the foundation. As it coincided with Caron's birthday, I was in a desperate, desperate place, as bad if not worse than the week Caron died, because I was not as numb and there weren't so many people around to help absorb the shock and soak up the tears. Thanks to the documentary, though, people I'd never met once again handed me the lifelines I needed to struggle on through these drowning days. The documentary revealed snippets of Caron's story and I could tell from the surge in letters that flooded through the door that it had struck a significant chord.

Audrey from County Down sent me a letter. Her son, Gary, had cystic fibrosis but ended up dying of aggressive cancer, aged twenty-one. He died in his mother's arms at home.

> *Dear Gloria,*
>
> *I just felt I had to write to you, first of all to offer my deepest sympathy on the loss of your beautiful daughter. I admire you so much and I think what you are doing by setting up the Caron Keating Foundation is truly wonderful and worthwhile.*
>
> *I was in hospital having an MRI scan on 20 April . . . I will never forget the heartache to be seen on your face. I cried as I felt so sorry for you and your family, but little did I know three months later I would be saying farewell to my darling son.*
>
> *Be strong, Gloria. Caron would be so proud of you.*

It sounds daft to say you found reassurance from people you've never met, but I was reassured. There were many difficult days around that time, with people questioning what I was doing and why, and I felt so bereft and alone. I couldn't seem to rise in any way above my loss.

Then, that same month, I received an extraordinary letter from a woman called Jill, in Tunbridge Wells. She had been diagnosed with breast cancer in the spring of 1997, when her son was only nineteen months old. She had been re-diagnosed with secondaries in her bones on New Year's Eve 2002. She wrote, 'I am now terminal.' It looked so very final on the page and I wondered what I could do for this woman, who was surely seeking advice. As I read on, however, I was stopped in my tracks. 'I am now terminal. Even worse, though – like you, Gloria, I have lost the most precious thing in the whole world: a child.' I soon understood she was not writing to me for advice – she was writing in order to share with me her full understanding of the pain I was in. What I had begun to suspect was there in black and white: losing a child was worse than dying. And that, I suppose, is at the very heart of our loss. We would rather it were us; we would rather take the pain than watch our loved one in pain; we would rather die. Here was this dying woman congratulating us for the foundation, telling me how well I was doing in celebrating my daughter's life. I was profoundly grateful to hear that from someone who truly had the right to comment.

Jill had also managed to raise £5,000 for a small charity called Against Breast Cancer (ABC) and said in her letter that she would like to raise money for the Caron Keating Foundation. Humbling doesn't come close – here she was, dying, but still offering to do volunteer work for the foundation. It was letters like this that saved my life. If I have been in any way an inspiration to others, it's only because people have been an inspiration to me. My thanks go to the faceless many whom I will never meet, whom I know only by their handwriting, who shared their wonderful words and confided their terrible stories, and of course one who I knew very well, who I believe guides me still. Caron. My baby girl.

After *Tonight with Trevor McDonald* was aired, the journey of my loss started another stage as the letters continued to pour in. I found these to be an incredible source of strength and inspiration, because it did feel at times, real or imagined, that I was the only one suffering. My sons would still let me talk and cry whenever I was with them, as too did Stephen, but so often we were all putting on a brave face for one another and I would find myself standing alone in one of the rooms at home, staring at the wall of grief that barricaded me in. Was I the only one feeling this? It felt like it, but of course I wasn't. June from Worthing wrote:

I have just watched the programme about Caron and I just had to tell you how brave and strong you have been to share your story. Like you, I have survived this experience – a mother watching her child die – and you will know this must be the hardest thing any human can endure.

Her son died of colon cancer four weeks after diagnosis – the silent killer.

He will never be gone from our lives, but I just wanted you to know that gradually you learn to live with the gap that they leave. There is nothing that makes it better – no words that help you through – but somehow you learn to put your grief away, and for the children's sake, the light comes back into your life.

My other son – I had only two children – also died young, at twenty-eight, after an asthma attack, so I feel I can say with all honesty that I really do know what you are going through.

I was suddenly in awe, and it gave me the courage I needed to face another day. I supposed I had begun to work out for myself that what June said was right: there were no words that would help and nothing did make it better. Rather than be terrified by this, I realise now it was what I, as a woman brought up with an Ulster work ethic, needed to hear. There was nothing to be done but survive this, and that survival was completely and utterly down to me. No one else was able to do this for me. No one was going to make it better unless they could bring Caron back, and that wasn't going to happen.

June's letter made me think again of the letter I'd received from the woman in Wales just a few weeks after Caron's death, which had seemed so harsh back then: 'I'd like to tell you it gets better, but it doesn't – you have to learn to live around it and through it.' After Caron's first birthday without her, I realised that what these people were telling me was right. It was up to me. I cannot say I was fired up with a sudden zest for life, but I think a very, very small pilot light reignited and gave me enough warmth to crawl on towards Christmas. Christmas . . . I was dreading Christmas.

After the misery of Caron's birthday, the days shortened, it got darker, wetter and colder, and I for one welcomed the grey skies. Sunshine somehow seemed fraudulent. I was battered and bruised, and the thought of Christmas plagued me. Should I write Christmas cards to everyone as normal? How could I? Should I shop for gifts as usual? How could I? I was demented with the word 'Christmas' and all it stood for.

Surrey

We lost our wonderful daughter, Sarah, aged thirty-four, to ovarian cancer last 22 January. I know you understand how we feel.

I was hoping and praying that I would be starting to feel better, but the pain just gets worse. We are dreading Christmas as it always used to be so happy and now there is a hole in our family.

We have done quite a bit for charity as it seems to help a little to help others.

Mr and Mrs Henkun

I think everyone who has lost someone close to them dreads Christmas. It was actually my great friend for thirty-five years Cliff Richard who gave me the most valuable key to dealing with this bitter-sweet time of year. It was really quite amazing because here was a man who has never had children and yet with one sentence he was able to empathise with my pain and give me the tools to fight it. Shortly after the launch of the foundation, he asked me, 'How are you going to cope with Christmas?' Well, I had no answer. I didn't know if I *was* going to cope with Christmas. I couldn't even bear thinking about it. Cliff looked at me and said, 'Did Caron like Christmas?' That was a question I could answer. My daughter loved it. Absolutely loved it. Christmas, like all celebrations in our family, was taken extremely seriously. For Caron, Christmas was huge. 'So why don't you make it bigger and better than ever for Caron and her boys?' said Cliff. In that one simple sentence he gave me the solution – to celebrate on special occasions, rather than commiserate. I've told so many people that story. I know now why it helped. It was because Cliff was clever enough to make it about Caron; he wasn't saying, 'You have to do it for everybody else,' which although true, doesn't always help. He was saying, 'Do it because that was what Caron loved.' It suddenly became clear. Caron loved Christmas, so Christmas we would have. And did we ever.

Instead of one tree, we had five, and lights like Blackpool illuminations – we even had two six-foot, all-singing, all-dancing Santas and decorations in every room. We turned our little patch of Sevenoaks into a mini Las Vegas. We were joined by Paul and Sandy and their sons, Jake and Beau, as well as Russ, the boys and Michael. I am sure Sandy wanted to spend the day with her parents, but instead she kindly asked them to come and stay with us, which they did. Everyone arrived on Christmas Eve, which hadn't been the case for years, and I loved the sight of children everywhere and people in every room. I remember the four little boys in their pyjamas looking out of the window at some lights in the sky, probably planes coming in to Gatwick, and us all pointing and saying, 'Santa Claus is coming. Look, it's the lights on his sleigh.' Then the four of them jumped into bed, because Santa wouldn't bring any toys if they were awake!

That night, though, as I passed by Russ's room, I saw him wrapping up his presents by himself and I ached. I went in to hold the Sellotape for him. I recalled to myself how only the previous year in Australia, despite Caron's pain, all of us had wrapped the boys' presents like we were working on a conveyor belt. Caron had been determined to make it a brilliant Christmas.

On Christmas morning everybody gathered in our bedroom and we opened the stockings and sacks on our bed together, which made it bearable. Children make it bearable.

I know I am fortunate. I know because I have read countless letters from people who've lost their only child or, in some terrible instances, both their children to genetic diseases or in mind-bogglingly stupid car crashes. I'm not sure making special occasions bigger and better works in those cases. In those cases, I often think about what Lord Richard Attenborough has said. As most people know, he lost his granddaughter, daughter and her mother-in-law in the tsunami that struck South-East Asia that fateful Boxing Day, just a day after we had marked our first Christmas without Caron. He said, 'How could you sit down at the family table and do Christmas as you used to with all those people missing?' Instead the family make sure they do something very different. I agree: I would hate to be sitting in Sevenoaks on our own on Christmas Day reminiscing about how it used to be with Caron, Russ and the children.

Carol Chase always bought her daughters miniature decorated real Christmas trees for their bedrooms from M&S. The first Christmas after Olivia died, she stoically went to the shop to buy one for Georgina and one to put on Olivia's grave. She remembers the acute pain of standing in the queue, surrounded by jolly, laughing people, and holding the tree for her daughter's grave, and it felt as if it were killing her. It seems you can die many times over.

I know what she means. We don't have Caron's boys on Christmas Day any more, so we have to make it different. One year we went to France, one year we spent it at home with Paul and his family, and last year we had a very quiet Christmas with some friends in their home in Kent, which was actually lovely because, like Richard Attenborough said, it was *so* different that it almost didn't feel like Christmas and therefore was much less exhausting. I do still always have a Christmas with the boys; I just don't necessarily do it on Christmas Day, but we have the whole shebang – turkey, decorations, presents galore. Yes, I'm pretending it's the actual day, but as long as I get to see them open their presents, I don't mind.

That first Christmas, though, I needed everyone around me, and I needed them on the actual day, and they all came. And thank God, because there were more unforeseen hurdles ahead that day that may well have taken me out if I hadn't had some noisy boys and a lot of presents to distract me. After stockings and breakfast we went to church. We went to the grave, left flowers, lit candles, wished Caron a happy Christmas and then went inside for the service. That was hard. The drive to Hever was still so poignant, still so soon after the one behind the hearse. I could see the pall-bearers struggling under the weight of the coffin; I could see all the faces; I could hear

Russ's eulogy in my head. Yes, going to church was hard, but leaving it was something different altogether.

> *Hampshire, December 2004*
> *We felt we must write to express our extreme sorrow at the*
> *loss of your cherished daughter. Our hearts and thoughts go*
> *out to you all at such a sad time. We can feel your grief with*
> *real understanding. Our beloved daughter, Louise, died last*
> *year following a nine-year battle with breast cancer. She was*
> *just forty. Like your daughter, Caron, she was beautiful,*
> *bright and full of life. We have no words that can offer you*
> *any comfort; the only comfort we found was the fact that all*
> *her anguish and pain has gone.*
> *Gaye and Terry*

Her anguish and pain had left her with her last breath, and so will my anguish and pain leave with mine. Until that moment comes, I will bear it as best I can. Leaving the church that first Christmas, though, I was bereft. It seemed utterly hideous that I was leaving my daughter in the churchyard. I couldn't bear the pain of it; I couldn't even go back down to the grave after the service ended to say goodbye. The memory of the coffin going into the ground was still superimposed in my memory, and remained there for a long time. She is in there. What wouldn't I give to see her just one more time?

I remember coming out of the church. To my left was a grave, cold and alone, a place where there is nothing, yet to me held everything, and to my right, a warm car to take me to home, which was full of food, presents and people. For a moment I couldn't move. I couldn't even look. I turned my back on the graveyard and left. I had to get away from there because standing at the entrance to the church, I felt with terror what it was to fall further and deeper into that dark, never-ending pit of despair. I fled because I thought it unlikely I would ever have the energy to haul myself up from there. If I hadn't left, it is quite possible I would have run down to the bottom of the graveyard and started clawing away at the ground with my bare hands. I just wanted her out of there. The pilot light fluttered and very nearly went out. Instead I went home and let the noise of ripping paper and laughing boys smother the piercing scream that only I could hear.

In another excerpt from her diary, Carol Chase wrote:

> In the next few days I must visit your grave – sorry, darling, I dread it so much, so dark and wintery now. I don't like to think of you there. I remember you and me chatting in bed. We had so many long chats in my bed, cosy times, and for some reason we were talking about death and I remember telling you that if you ever died, I would be at your graveside every single day. Seems such an odd conversation for us to have had, and now I feel I am letting you down. I must remember your grave is one place you have never been.

Carol has spent hours in a quiet meditative state, thinking about and writing to Olivia. Sometimes she receives very powerful thoughts that she believes come from her daughter. She received one such response in answer to her fear of visiting Olivia's grave: 'When you reach by habit for my hand and, finding none, feel sorrow start to steal upon you, be still, close your eyes, breathe, listen for my footfall in your heart. I am not gone, but walking within you.'

Now I can visit Caron's grave and feel, as Carol can, that my beloved one is walking within me. We carry our loves in

175

our hearts. I don't think so much these days about the separation; I seem able to take Caron with me wherever I go, so I don't leave her behind when I get in the car and drive away from the churchyard. That's the one reward after a long-fought battle, and believe me, the fight goes on. A grave can be a hard place to visit, but I am at least able to go there now and see beyond the dreadful day of her funeral. The grave is no more than a symbol. I go there to lay flowers, to light candles, to talk to her, but I also know I can talk to her anywhere and everywhere. I don't have that cold, icy feeling that she is in there and that we leave her when we go home.

A friend in Germany told me that the tradition there is for everyone to light candles on Christmas Eve, scatter them throughout the churchyard and leave them blazing throughout the night. Instead of the cemetery being a dark, dismal place, it is a symbol of everlasting light, hope and love. It is a lovely tradition and one we adopted. That first Christmas was terrible, but now on Christmas Eve when we leave the church after midnight mass, I look down towards the grave and see all the candles lit in her memory and feel warm, rather than chilled to the bone. Somehow the pilot light inside me never did go out completely.

Shortly after Christmas I received another glimmer of light in the form of the following letter:

27 December 2004

Dear Gloria,

I was deeply moved and touched by the Tonight *programme covering Caron's illness and her ultimate death.*

Something you said toward the end struck a chord with me – that you were sick of seeing and hearing yourself cry, that you must find a path forward. In this day and age it seems to me that most people feel the pressure to have a defined path that they take – to be seen to cope with the many curve balls that are thrown their way with strength and independence. I imagine being in the public eye you feel this pressure more than most.

When it comes to such raw and unbearable grief, I don't personally think there is a timeframe to place over this awful experience that can or should be deemed acceptable. You may find your path today, tomorrow or in ten years' time, but what I wanted to say to you is, please don't feel like you aren't coping as you should. You can only use the strength you are given each day to do what you can at any moment. Some days that will be a tremendous amount, and some days, as I'm sure you know, you'll barely have the strength to get out of bed. But you do what you must, and what you can. Caron was an incredibly brave and positive woman – that's what made her so special – but we can't all be that amazing. To continue to cry over this isn't weak; it's OK to feel angry, helpless or even pointless.

Grief is so predictably painful and full of horror, but I know for myself that nobody prepares you for its complexity: the intricate layers of feeling and memories that are released one by one, remembered moments and conversations. It might be the sight of something, a smell or a sound that makes you remember. While time may offer the grace of a scar to heal over the wound, nevertheless a scar remains, and when that scar is scratched – months or years later – that pain returns, but that in itself becomes comforting. It doesn't mean you're looking to the past; it means you won't allow your love for that person to be locked away and forgotten about.

177

When, and only when, the time is right, you will find your path forward, and with it the strength to take you on that journey. The thing that will probably surprise you more than anything is your life will be enriched because of it, and Caron's death will not have been in vain. That's a hard thing to hear or imagine, but the qualities you loved and so admired in her will become part of you.

I do hope that in time life will regain its full colour for you, and the occasional tear you see those colours through will make them all the richer.

With kinds regards and love to you, Russ and your beautiful grandchildren,

David

Sandra from Belfast also wrote to me that December. Her daughter, Tracey, had died, aged thirty-five, of cancer. She was a meeter and greeter at Belfast City Airport. If you are ever passing through, there is a plaque and photo of this much-missed girl in the departure lounge. Her mother raised money for a relatives' room at the cancer centre where Tracey was treated because they had to sleep on the floor for eight nights when Tracey was really sick.

*I am writing to you not as a celebrity but as one mother to another, both of whom have lost beautiful daughters to the b*****d cancer. I am dreading Christmas without her. How do you get through it? I try hard, cry every day; I cry as I write this letter to you.*

I didn't know the answer then, but I can tell you now, Sandra: I do what Cliff told me to do and just about get through.

When Christmas was over, we were totally drained –

drained by trying to keep it together, drained by the energy of the young boys, drained by trying to look like I was getting better for the sake of my sons, drained by everything, so for New Year's we were strangely drawn back to St Paul de Vence, where we had rented a house for many years, in the south of France. It's a medieval area and obviously has a timeless quality. Caron was never happier than when she was in that village.

I've never particularly liked New Year, and I certainly hated the thought of this one; seeing in a new year knowing that there would be no Caron in it was another scary first. The awful conflict between moving on and leaving behind, survival and death, plunged me back into despair.

Seventeen of us found ourselves packed into a gourmet restaurant in the mountain village of Haute-de-Cagnes. It was small and intimate, which helped, and it also had a very classy jazz quartet. Once again, something took over and as the band started to play the only song I know in French, 'J'attendrai', I found myself grabbing the microphone from a much-shocked, very competent singer and proceeding to give her my Northern Irish rendition. To this day the children talk about the night Nana got tipsy and they say the maître d' dreads me walking through the door in case he gets a further rendition. However, it got me through one more of those unspeakable firsts. Was it the wine, or was it another example of the human spirit rising to the moment?

In another letter I received around then, a woman in Surrey wrote to tell me about how she was struggling with her own troubled daughter.

I hope you don't mind me writing to you like this, but I want to say a very big thank you to both you and Caron.

*I myself have never believed in anything, not even religion,
but after hearing your story, I decided to say a silent
prayer to the angels myself. What has followed over the
next two days has made me change my opinion.*

*A feather fell out of the sky and landed in my son's
hand the day of the prayer. The next day a feather landed
on my husband's windscreen. I looked up Caron and
angels and discovered we have the same birthdays. I truly
believe that your Caron is out there and is telling me that
someone is listening and that I'm not alone after all.*

*I wanted both you and Caron to know how very
grateful I am and for giving me faith again both in myself
and my little girl.*

Whether it really was Caron or not doesn't seem important.
That lady felt she was being listened to and understood, and it
helped me enormously to think that in some small way
Caron's life and death meant something to her. So many
people were struggling and I knew even then, while I was in the
thick of it, that few received this enormous amount of exceptional help and guidance from other bereaved parents.

On 28 January 2005 it was Gabriel's birthday. I didn't know
what to do. Anything at home seemed too contrived, and it
wasn't the time of year to go galloping about in Alldays Field.
Instead we decided to do something different and got on the
Eurostar to take the boys to Disneyland Paris. We all went –
Paul, Michael, Russ, Jake, Beau, Charlie, Gabriel, Stephen
and me. It was a wet, dismal day, and we were walking along
the covered platform at Waterloo when right ahead of us we
saw a single white feather gleaming against the dark-grey
concrete. I picked it up and looked at it and fancied I heard
my daughter saying, 'This is a great idea, Mum. I'm coming

with you.' Was it Caron? Does it matter? It made the day a little more bearable for me to think that she was boarding the train too, that she could hear the screams of delight as Charlie and Gabriel were plunged down some terrifying ride that made me sick just watching.

Charlie was now ten, Gabriel was eight, and time was marching inexorably further from Caron's death, ever closer to the anniversary. First, though, we had another few mountains to climb – the anniversary that is hard for every single one of us: Mother's Day. The real killer. And it isn't just a day – the build-up starts earlier and earlier every year. Mother's Day is the last Sunday in March, but the cards come out as soon as the last red heart-shaped balloon is deflated, or so it feels. I will never forget our last Mother's Day, which just the two of us spent in Switzerland, for it was one of the most special days of my life. The painting Caron gave me, of tulips, hangs in my sitting room and rarely a day goes by when I don't think of how, suffering the way she was, she managed to paint it, write a beautiful inscription on the back, wrap it in tissue and pack it in her suitcase, let alone hide it from me and produce it on Mother's Day. I look at that painting and think over and over again, What was this girl made of? I still can't believe she could think only of others when she was on such a journey herself.

It was the only Mother's Day that we had spent on our own since her brother Paul had been born. It was an utterly blissful day. I only learnt recently tulips were her sign. She discovered on her spiritual journey that these powerful flowers were her sign of truth and joy and enlightenment; now they flank her headstone, carved into stone. Was it her way of leaving something for me? I don't know. I've read through all her diaries, but I don't see any references to death in any of them, except one, but only to state emphatically that she did not feel as if she was dying. Was she wearing her own mask, or was she so far down this path of positive thinking that she was managing at least to stay one step ahead of the cancer? She was always so stoic, always so kind. She just seemed to have this incredible resilience and a determination that she was going to be around and carry on as normal.

That first Mother's Day, my sons found a way to navigate the knife-edge we walked that whole year between commiserating, commemorating and celebrating. I am their mother and they wanted to honour the day. I wanted to crawl into bed until the whole ordeal had passed, but they were saying, in their own way, 'We are your children as well, and you are still our mother. We are going to take care of it. You don't have to do anything or think of anything. You just have to be there.' Paul and Michael arrived at our house laden with food and wine, cooked an amazing dinner, served it, cleared it up. Paul had even made two pavlovas, which he hadn't done since he was a teenager. More importantly they kept me company, and excellent company at that. I am blessed with having bright, amusing children, and a sense of humour can make all the difference at times like this. Russ came in the morning and delivered handmade Nana's Day cards from the boys, which I really loved. Because Caron treasured any celebration – Christmas, Mother's Day, Valentine's Day . . . frankly any excuse to dress up and have fun – not one of those days goes by when we don't pay homage to Caron in some way now. We put new flowers on her grave and leave cards from the boys. However hard it is for any of us, we would never let an occasion go by without visiting.

I was not the only mother who held on to the memory of the previous Mother's Day as an aid to get through the first one and subsequent others. The previous year Olivia had given

Always With You

Carol a Mother's Day card in which she'd written, 'Thank you for always being there, for always knowing exactly what to say. Words can't explain how proud and blessed I feel to be your daughter. All my love, today and for ever, Olivia xxx.' Words from a fifteen-year-old that provided a lifeline later on. That first Mother's Day Carol noticed a poem in the newspaper and wrote it out in her journal, wishing, hoping, it could have been sent by her youngest daughter. Once again Olivia's voice answered her wish.

A new morning, Mother's Day. This weekend a poem comes my way.

I'm looking back on childhood years
And my eyes fill with happy tears.
Those times together, you and me,
So clearly in my mind I see.
You've been my oak, my mighty tree,
With branches safely wrapped around me,
My golden thread through tender years
To sew up all my hurt and fears.
My teens – they put you to the test.
I couldn't see that I was blessed.
I wonder if you'll ever know
The love I didn't always show.
A special Mum I have in you,
The love you share, the things you do.
And when I look upon your face,
I feel in the warmth of your embrace
My love today and every day.

Mum, you will find me within yourself. In the warmth of your being, in the beat of your heart. Hear my being by listening inwards to the stillness of your soul. My voice is still there.'

Dear Gloria,

There is no one in the world who can understand your feelings better than I do. I too lost a lovely daughter, at the age of thirty-three. She died of Hodgkin's disease, leaving three small children. Her death changed my whole life. From that day onwards nothing seemed to matter.

Like Caron, she was a loving, friendly girl, and we were very close. I miss her so much, especially on Mother's Day. She used to make such a fuss of me.

That was nineteen years ago and I think of her every day. It does not get easier, Gloria. I think of all these wasted years that we could have spent together. It's not an exaggeration to say that her death spoilt my life for ever.

I miss her so much.

Sincerely,

Margaret

Mother's Day is bad enough, but for me it marks the start of a hideous countdown to losing Caron. I relive those days in Switzerland over and over: the trips to the clinic; dinners in our room at the hotel when Caron was too sore to move; the constant planning of the next thing; Russ being thrust wildly about by the pinball wizard of cancer. Caron's demise seems more acute in my memory than it did at the time. Back then it was another blip she'd bounce back from. Now it seems that it was always more sinister and we simply couldn't allow ourselves to see what was plainly in front of us.

We all know that the anniversary of a loved one's death is a date that resounds cacophonously throughout the year, and as it approaches, the tools we have learnt to survive this agonising limbo desert us. Put simply, 13 April is bloody hard.

My friend Carol Chase had a week alone with her daughter just prior to her shocking premature death. Olivia was home to revise and they spent the week eating together, talking, enjoying one another's company. A gift to a bereaved parent. Time. I know how grateful she must be to have those intense one-on-one memories. I feel the same about Switzerland and Australia. For all the miles apart we were and all the months I was in England without her, we had truly wonderful, memorable times when we went out there. Even so, remembering the lead-up to a death is a very strange experience. You relive it all over again, as painfully as the first time. There is no way round this.

At the beginning I thought I would never have a reason to smile or laugh again. It was undoubtedly the same that first anniversary and all the subsequent ones. You are jettisoned right back to the beginning, literally, mentally, physically and emotionally.

We visited the grave and had a commemoration dinner at home in the evening – just the family and a few close friends. I was back in the block of ice for the days leading up to it and the day itself. That surreal quality seeped back in, the numbness and the intense pain. I had a glass angel for everyone and had brought a candle from Fowey for each of us. We all lit our candles and raised a glass to Caron. Could it really be a year since I had seen her alive? Could it really be a year since I'd heard her voice? Could it really be a year since I'd sliced that melon and cut up those childlike squares of toast? Had I really survived a year without her? I wondered fleetingly whether I would be able to survive even one more day. But I did. The following morning Russ left with the boys at 9 a.m. to move into their new house just outside London. 'Official' mourning was over.

10

The Uninvited Guest

There's always another tomorrow,
However hard the day.
There's always an end to sorrow;
Time wipes our tears away.
There's always a reason for living,
Though sad your heart may be.
There's always another horizon
Beyond the one you see.

'Another Tomorrow', Anon

Mourners are understandably not that great to have around. Sometimes people don't know what to say, where to look, how to sound. While you are in the throes of your selfish grief, your friends will hold your hand and they will listen. For a while. Then you have to learn to stop weeping and stop talking because once the official period of mourning is over – some say a year, some expect it even sooner than that – people get tired of comforting and consoling. They would rather have the jolly you back, a smile, proof that you are 'on the mend' and they can be relieved of duty. Grief is most certainly an uninvited guest that people tire of easily, and if you don't alter your behaviour, you will find people simply stop asking how you are or, worse, stop seeing you altogether. Now *you* have become the uninvited guest.

My son Michael frequently notices that others don't know what to do or say. His situation is slightly different to most, in that his sister was on the front of newspapers, so more often than not people know what has happened to our family before Michael even meets them. Because of that, it means that when he is meeting people for the first time and they are struggling with what to say, he isn't even given the chance to avoid the subject of death. For most people, though, when you meet others for the first time, they will not know about your loss. Friends in this position talk openly of the terror of being asked, 'How many children do you have?' As the poem that I included at the start of Chapter 7 says, when you tell people about your loss you 'see the shadow of uncertainty' pass their face and a silence falls between you. Suddenly death, and in my case cancer, stands between you, and the truth is, it might be one of those rare moments when you just don't want to talk about it.

After Caron died, Michael got texts from people he didn't know that well. Some people might think that is a bit impersonal, but every little tiny message from anybody – be it by text, email, phone or letter – were all appreciated by him. He needed to talk because within the family his prime concern, apart from his own grief, was how I was coping. Because I was of limited use to him at that time, he had to get support from elsewhere. He got phone calls from people in Jordan and Australia, friends and acquaintances he hadn't spoken to for a couple of years, and it was strengthening. People don't know what to say, but as Michael points out, it almost doesn't matter what the message is; it is the attempt that counts. Having said that, there are also times when you can't appreciate what someone is trying to say because it doesn't suit your mood at that moment. Judging what sort of state of mind a bereaved person is in requires a certain amount of sensitivity. Knowing whether it is the right time to make someone laugh, listen or hug is not easy. Maybe it would be better just to ask, 'Do you want to talk about it?' If yes, then listen, if no, then great, let me tell you about my latest crush!

Michael spent much of his energy consoling me, so when others also sought consolation from him, he sometimes felt impatient. There was one woman who came round to pay her condolences when he was at home with friends. She then sat there bawling her eyes out and he found himself in the position of consoling her and thinking to himself, Hey, this is the wrong way round. Come round, be strong, make me laugh, sit, talk about it, let me cry if I want to, but I don't have the energy to console you too.

Salah, Michael's best friend from school since the age of fourteen, was living in St Paulo when Caron died. He rang, distraught for Michael as he knew how very close he was to Caron, and said he was coming to London to be with him and would be there in twelve hours, and he was. Salah is a big, strong, macho guy of few words. At that time, Michael didn't need words; he just needed not to be alone, so Salah was there right when he was most needed. He stayed for a month and I think it got Michael through those hideous, shocking first days. Salah would go and get the groceries, because like me, Michael couldn't think about shopping, and in the evenings he'd sit and drink wine with him and watch telly. For a time Salah was Michael's shock-absorber. We all need one.

Other friends of Michael's came over a lot too and stayed the night to keep him company. Amanda, Danielle and Annette all made adorable silly excuses to drop by. Everyone could see through their stories, but no one commented, and Michael appreciated that they were thinking of him. I have to thank them all because, once he was back in London, on his own, I was anxious about him. It is often too easy for people to think of someone who is grieving, Oh, they probably don't want to be disturbed. Well, maybe we don't always, but the fact that people care and acknowledge your pain and loss helps so much and makes you feel less like the uninvited guest and more like someone who is understood and loved despite being so sad. Eventually Salah had to go home and Michael, being single at the time, went out a lot. He himself says that he would frequently find himself in a bar or a nightclub, pouring his heart and soul out to people he didn't know after a couple of glasses of wine, or more, and then gently being guided home by friends.

Grieving is so hard. You have so much to say, or more accurately, you have a few words you want to say over and over and over again: 'She was so special. She was so funny. She was so brave. It's so unfair. It's so painful. It's so awful. Why? She was so special. She was so funny . . .' On and on you go, asking questions that have no answers. The reality is, it *is* boring after a while, and that's when you need people around you who have experienced the same sort of loss. You need people who understand that your compulsion to talk about your loved one never leaves. Your very, very good friends will always listen, no matter how many times they've heard it before.

Dear Ms Hunniford,

   I so clearly remember seeing the death of your daughter announced on the news in April. I am sure it registered for two reasons: one, because I thought to myself, I don't think I could cope if I lost one of my daughters, and two, because I had always felt that you two were very close and tried to imagine how you must have been feeling. I also saw the programme where you very bravely spoke about your daughter and the years of illness leading up to her death. I was moved by this too, because so many people treat death as a taboo – something that doesn't belong to us and will never happen, but of course it does; it is the one certainty in life. But parents never expect to outlive their children – it isn't the natural order of things – and in our case we lost a longed-for grandchild as well.

Never did I ever think or imagine that, at the end of the following month of May, our youngest daughter would die very suddenly in an accident. She had only been married fifteen months, to a very dear man, a Spanish Basque, and was living in the Basque country. They were expecting their first child on Christmas Day, having in cruel circumstances lost a pregnancy at three months in the February. She loved where she lived and threw herself fully into everything about it – the language, the culture, the people. I too was very close to Sally. It is now just over six months since she died, and rather than feeling an easing of grief, I feel it is getting worse. I am sure this is partly due to the fact so few people will mention her or talk about her – it's so painful that people seem to have an expectation, or need, that you have moved on, got over it in just six months. Either that or they can't bear to see pain. Not that I would ever inflict my pain on others – I just want to mention her name and feel I haven't said something terrible. We loved her dearly and we feel a huge hole in our lives.

I hope you don't mind me writing to you like this, but I felt it would help me if you could at least share a little of what it is like for you – I know you don't know me and may think it odd that I should write to you like this, but as I say, your relationship with your daughter had always seemed over the years to be a close one and I would imagine you are still grieving and hurting a lot.

Of course this letter may never reach you, but I just felt the need to try and communicate with you.

With kind regards,

Wendy

It didn't just reach me; it spoke to me. I don't recall where I got Wendy's number from, but I rang her and we shared our pain. Loneliness is another of those insidious uninvited guests, a direct consequence of people not understanding the many layers of pain the death of a child can penetrate and produce. We are wounded to our core. We change. The new us is probably a shadow of the old one and no doubt not as fun to be around. The new version cries; the new version is unpredictable; the new version is a brutal reminder that life can change in the blink of an eye, and sometimes we don't want to be reminded of that. As Wendy says, death is 'something that doesn't belong to us' – we don't like to get too close to it; we don't want to catch it or deal with it; we don't want to be given a problem that has no solution. That makes us uncomfortable, so many of us decide not to acknowledge it, not to invite it in.

A woman once said to me that she felt she was never invited anywhere any more and it had contributed significantly to her depression after her two children were killed in a car crash; it was a vicious circle. This is so often the case when a young child dies and people with children of a similar age simply don't know what to do. Are you invited to the fourth birthday party of your friend's child when your child will never make four? Personally, I would rather be asked to those big occasions and decide for myself whether I am up to going. Not being invited only makes the lonely feel more isolated than ever and more disinclined to strive to rejoin the human race. But the truth is, invitations can dry up and suddenly people avert their eyes. I would say, 'Please offer me a place at your table, offer me a chance to participate in your child's wedding or grandchild's christening, and I will tell you whether I am up to it. Let me decide. Please don't decide for me. If I accept the invitation, I will do my best to don the mask, and when that gets too heavy and starts to slip, I will leave.'

I distinctly remember being questioned by someone not that very long ago. She asked me whether I was 'always going to do this foundation thing'. She made it sound like it was a tedious hobby that had gone on too long. I was rather startled. I was sure that she understood my absolute need to do something like the foundation. Even without the enormous healing power of putting something back, or trying to help others in Caron's position, this is what I do now, alongside my work: I raise money for cancer charities and it keeps me going. As Wendy wrote in her letter to me, 'I just want to mention her name and feel I haven't said something terrible.' Well, that is all we want to do. I am lucky; I have a bigger voice, so I can say it louder, but essentially I'm doing what all bereaved parents want to do: talk about our missing children.

In May 2008 the beautiful actress Natascha McElhone buried her wonderful, talented, generous and good surgeon husband, Martin Kelly, in a very private ceremony, with just their little boys. As private as she is, I noticed with interest that she too felt the need to tell the world what an incredible man her husband was and wrote a piece in the *Mail on Sunday*. Her husband and a colleague had set up a charity called Facing the World, which did wonderful things for children born with terrible disfigurements and changed their lives for the better. What could this man possibly have done to deserve being taken from his loving wife and sons? Nothing. It doesn't work like that. Death is indiscriminate; it is arbitrary. I particularly liked his motto: 'Work hard, expect nothing, celebrate.' I marvel at his wife's ability to say thank you, even at this early stage, for the years they had together, rather than mourn the years of which they have been robbed. I am getting to that place. I am nearly there. I am closer on some days than others, but well, I'm working on it.

Jenny Parnwell is another woman I have befriended through sadness. When her lovely daughter Julie-Anne got ill, she and her two daughters went to live with Jenny in Fowey. Julie-Anne met Russ and Caron in August 2000 at a party, and the following year they got involved in the Fowey Regatta Week Carnival. They all climbed aboard the Barbie Float and bonded over pink glitter. Caron was Rock Chick Barbie, glammed up in pink wig, pink feather boa and pink plastic guitar; Julie-Anne was Hippy Barbie; Russ was Roller Ken on skates. Caron's guitar is still a treasured possession of Jenny's, who went as 'Hormonal' Barbie with a bottle of gin and a large container of HRT tablets! Apparently Jenny had called Russ and Caron beforehand to see if Gabriel and Charlie wanted to be involved in the float, but the boys were busy with their cousins, so Caron and Russ had asked if they could do it instead. It was a great day and tragic to think that both these gorgeous girls were to be stolen from us by cancer.

Julie-Anne had two daughters, Jessica and Chloe. She had divorced their father but had a very amicable arrangement about access to the girls. In June 2000 Julie-Anne was referred to a specialist about a mole beside her right eye.

It was removed in August, and after a biopsy revealed a malignancy, some further tissue was removed that September. She was then declared clear. Later that year, however, Julie-Anne told her mother, Jenny, that she had a lump behind her ear 'like a Mint Imperial'. She went to the doctor immediately and was referred back to her specialist in East Grinstead. He was on holiday, so there was a bit of a delay, by which time Julie-Anne had five lumps. An X-ray followed on 5 November, and a CT scan on 27 November. An appointment on 4 December with the specialist told her the cancer had spread. Two days later they were at the Royal Marsden Hospital in London. The doctors realised that it was so far advanced there was little they could do, but offered her chemotherapy. Sadly on 10 December she was admitted to Princess Royal Hospital in Haywards Heath. Her deterioration was rapid. She and her lovely boyfriend, Steve, were married in the hospital, with her two little girls as bridesmaids, on 15 December. Two days later the family took her home with round-the-clock nursing care, and on Wednesday, 19 December, she died. Steve, her daughters and her mother were with her.

I met Jenny again in Fowey and she told me about Julie-Anne's death. I comforted her without telling her that Caron herself was suffering from cancer. It was difficult. As Caron said, the stories that don't end well always are. Of course when Caron and Russ disappeared to Australia, Jenny suspected something was off-kilter, as she knew how very happy they had been in Fowey. Jenny says now that for some reason she just knew Caron had cancer.

Not long after Mother's Day in that first year of grieving, Jenny sent me the following letter:

Always With You

8 *March 2005*

Dear Gloria,

   I hope you do not mind my writing to you, but you have been much in my thoughts, especially with Mother's Day last weekend. I can imagine that Caron, like Julie-Anne, made it a special day, and I know that this next month, leading up to the first anniversary is going to be absolute hell. The only comfort I can give you is that it will never be quite as painful again. You are quite right to keep so busy. I know that for me it was a good day if I could just get out of bed during that first year. During that time I had a telephone number of a woman at the Compassionate Friends [a charity for bereaved parents and families] whom I could talk to when things got really tough. She recently sent me the enclosed poem, which I thought you might like.

   The grandchildren also kept me sane, despite the fact that I hardly ever saw them, as their father married again and they live in Margate. The new stepmother decided she wanted them to see less of me, and I had a fight for the first two years just for access. Grandparents have no rights in the eyes of the law – you have to prove your worth in court.

   I am sorry I was away at half-term when I gather you were down looking after the boys. Please do call me on your next visit to Fowey and maybe we can get together if you have the time.

   With best wishes to you both,
   Jenny Parnwell

Jenny has taught me a lot about the rights of grandparents and how frequently they lose not only their child to illness and accidents but also access to their grandchildren, often when the surviving parent remarries. I thank God every day that's not one of the problems I've had to face. I see my grandchildren regularly and they are a continuous source of joy and light. The poem she enclosed with her letter is called 'Masques' and is included at the start of Chapter 7. It was written by a member of the highly regarded charity the Compassionate Friends, which I know has helped many in our position. The poet is Karen Nelson from Box Elder County in America, and I sincerely hope she doesn't mind me repeating her beautifully written, understated, understanding words. Like so many of the poems I have been sent, I have read it many times.

Julie-Anne had made a will and had asked her mother to look after the children. The girls' father was too tied up with his new life to want to be involved, and Steve, being a lone stepfather, would have had great difficulty organising child-care. But then Jenny's former son-in-law, Edward, spoke to her and said that he had 'divorced the mother, not the children' and wanted to look after them. Originally she thought about fighting his decision, but having lost their mother, it was not fair to deny them their father. In any event, as so many letters point out, grandparents have no rights if a parent is still living.

Jenny says the hardest thing she has ever done was to pack up their belongings and take the two girls to Kent to start a new life with their father. They were like little plants pulled up by the roots and plonked on to a new bit of earth without any help to settle down. Edward loved them very much, though, and she just hoped and prayed that it would all work out. Unfortunately his girlfriend had not planned for two small grieving girls entering their relationship, and after some spectacular rows, she left. Edward coped very well. As a fireman, the rota system enabled him to spend more time than most fathers with his children. The plan was for them to spend their holidays with their grandparents to give him a break. Jenny had always been a very hands-on granny, and as much as possible, that continued. They laughed and talked about their mummy and how naughty she had been as a little girl. Like I do with the boys, Jenny looks at them and sees Julie-Anne in their eyes, laughter and behaviour, and it provides much more solace than pain.

Then Edward met a single mother with two slightly older girls. The new lady immediately moved in and became 'mum' and Jenny was suddenly 'granny' to two more girls. Things changed. Jenny was devastated when, less than nine months after Julie-Anne's death, Edward and the new lady married and her access to the grandchildren became severely restricted. She went to a firm of solicitors to seek advice, but of course discovered that grandparents had no rights.

Like any of us going through difficult times, Jenny can't imagine how she would have coped without her family, who ensured she kept her sense of perspective and helped in every conceivable way to keep faith in what her daughter would have wished for her girls, whom she believed were also unhappy with the situation. Our daughters are not here, but we are and always in our ear we hear our daughters' pleas to take care of their children on their behalf. It is a difficult line to tread.

Thankfully Jenny finally managed to have a private conversation with Edward and realised just how unhappy he too had become. He was most distressed that his second marriage was not working and that it was having an effect on the girls. He had no idea which way to turn. Things came to a head in December 2007. Following a row on Christmas Day, Jessica and Chloe came to stay in Cornwall for the New Year. They continued to live there until the stepmother and the other two girls had moved out. Her granddaughters and Edward are now back in Kent and life is starting over.

Seven years after Jenny's daughter died, the girls are back to their happy selves, and Edward once again has the full support of his own family and Julie-Anne's in the difficult times that lie ahead. They are a unit again. I am so pleased for Jenny and thank her for sharing her story, because I know she went through absolute hell for four years. I only take this example because of the link between Caron and Julie-Anne, but I have had many, many letters from mothers whose daughters have died and who have had to cope with problems with access and distance. Knowing that Jenny could do nothing but wait must have been like going through another death all over again.

It was becoming more obvious to me that, like the poem Jenny sent me said, I was not the only one donning a mask. None of them invited death in. For most, it is thrust upon us, wielding its shocking force on families and individuals. Then, for a long time afterwards, we have no choice but to heal, because the truth is that the only alternative to healing is to invite death in again, which I couldn't do, since I know full well what havoc it causes. What I find remarkable is that the death itself is only one part of mourning. Maybe 'layer' is a better word. Death is the first page of a book of many pages, chapters and constant false endings. Just when you think you can hold it together no longer, another weight is added to your burden. You reach a peak only to discover it was a false horizon and another steep incline lies ahead.

Dear Gloria,

I am writing because I know you will understand how I am feeling after losing my daughter, Nicola, to ovarian cancer on 27 February 2003. She was only thirty-one years old and so beautiful, just like Caron.

Unfortunately, since Nicola's death, not only have we had to come to terms with losing her, but we have also been fighting a losing battle for visiting rights to our beautiful granddaughter, Charlotte.

Charlotte was only sixteen months old at the time of Nicola's death. Nicola's partner left shortly after Charlotte was born, leaving them living in rented accommodation in Sevenoaks. At the time Nicola was still on maternity leave, but the family gave her as much support as they could and helped her in her decision to buy a house, to give both her and Charlotte some stability.

From the day Charlotte's father left, I became her sole support and the bond between Charlotte and I grew as I helped Nicola to care for her. Nicola became very ill and came home to live with us in August 2002 after her first operation at Pembury Hospital. She and Charlotte lived with us for eight months until her death in February.

It was then that our problems really started and we have been in and out of court since the day after we buried my daughter. Initially the court ruled that Charlotte should remain with us. However, after a residency application from both Charlotte's father and ourselves, the court ruled that Charlotte should live with her sole surviving parent.

Unfortunately Charlotte's father has gone out of his way to ensure we see as little of her as possible and resorted to moving away to Cumbria to put distance between us. Despite a lengthy and costly court process, Charlotte's father continues to break the contact orders from the court, which concerns us greatly. As we have such a strong relationship, Charlotte, who has just turned four, must be wondering what is happening and where we have disappeared to.

Every time this happens and we return to court we leave with less and less contact, which breaks our hearts – I have lost my daughter and now my granddaughter too.

In addition to this, Nicola died without a will, and as Charlotte (her next of kin) is under the age of eighteen, her father has been given a letter of administration to administer my daughter's estate. Sadly we are sure that this is part of the reason he has fought so hard against us for Charlotte.

I have been made to feel so unimportant; as Nicola is no longer with me, I am continually labelled 'a grieving mother' and accused of allowing it to cloud my judgement. We feel that the law has treated us so badly and that things must be changed to prevent other families going through what we have experienced over the last two years. We would like to highlight these issues and wondered if you can help us in any way.

Our thoughts are with you all – I can honestly say I know how you feel.

I look forward to hearing from you.

Regards,

Lynn

This was one of many letters of this kind, from grandparents who have found themselves having to fight in court to see the grandchildren who were once on their doorstep. Solicitors, judges, court officials – these are all uninvited guests and they can cost a huge amount of money.

I know one sad story of a dying woman who entrusted her

younger brother with her estate and asked him to protect it for her three young children. After her death, she also left behind a partner, whom she had never married, and he believed the assets should be in his name and he should be allowed to run his own family in his own way. Believing he was keeping his word to his dead sister, the woman's brother, who was not even thirty, fought the father of the children in court to maintain control of the estate until there was simply nothing left. The children, whom everyone agreed this money had always been for, got nothing and the family was torn apart.

Leah from Cheshire wrote to tell me about her daughter, Judy, who died of breast cancer, though it went to the brain in the end, another seven-year battle lost. Her daughter's husband was also loving and caring, but three months later got together with a friend of Judy's, something her mother found really, really hard.

Another woman told me of her childhood. Aged ten, she went away on a school trip and came back to be told her mother had died. She later learnt that she and her siblings had been shielded from the extent of their mother's multiple sclerosis. Within weeks their father had moved in with his new girlfriend and they found themselves in a new home far away from their maternal grandmother, with a new woman in the kitchen and shortly after that a new sister, and were told not to mention their mother again. Oh, yes, death is just the first page of a book with many twists and turns and, sadly, all too often no happy endings.

I too am another unfortunate mother who has lost her darling daughter to breast cancer. I truly never thought I could survive. It's a daily silent grief only I am aware of. We never get over it; we just get used to it.

During her illness my daughter divorced her husband

*(who had left her for another woman just before it was
confirmed she had breast cancer, though he must have
suspected something with all the doctors and clinics she
visited), so naturally he took the three girls. Do you know,
Gloria, he and his new wife will not allow me to go to
their home? I am not allowed. Whenever the girls come to
Cardiff, of course I do see them, but I want to know their
friends, see where they go to school. I know nothing.
Believe me, it is a second bereavement.*

I am so alone. I am expected just to get on with it.

*Hope I have not bored you. I believe it helped me to
talk to somebody who might understand me.*

Dorothy

Death can bring other uninvited guests too. In the end Carol
Chase had to endure more than the death of her daughter and
watching those bare-chested boys dig her grave. Because
Olivia had died unexpectedly, her death had to be investi-
gated. That meant Olivia's body was taken away and there was
an autopsy. Thinking that Olivia had drowned, the family
spent a long time wondering how it could be that their fit, able
daughter could drown in three feet of water, even though she
was a highly proficient swimmer. Then a letter came through
the front door and it was revealed that Olivia, unbeknown to
anyone, had long QT syndrome, a rare genetic disorder. The
remaining children had to be tested immediately to see if they
were in danger. It is unimaginable; you are struck down by the
death of your young child and then told you are possibly at risk
of losing others. Until the test results came back negative,
Carol was terrified that something was going to happen to
Georgina and her half-brothers.

Death is the ultimate uninvited guest, but as the above

shows, there are others: autopsy reports, inquests, court cases, investigations, suspicion, loss of access, displacement, divorce.

In her diary, Carol Chase wrote:

10 February 2005
Oh, Olivia, I have never, ever known such exhaustion, weighted down, can hardly move, such stress, grief and huge depleting emotion. A week ago today was your inquest. Just felt panic rising up inside me for days before. Would I cope? But I did. Everybody was very kind, all over now. Primary cause of death: 'sudden cardiac arrhythmia.' Secondary cause of death: 'drowning.' Verdict: 'accidental death.' Such a neat little package of words, isn't it? Just summing up the end of a life of such glorious richness, hope and vitality, all ending with the brief summing-up of a coroner – I can't possibly relate it to you, but feel so relieved it's all over.

We all faced uninvited guests of one kind or another. One of the things both Carol and I have in common is that our daughters died at our homes, stayed in our homes and left from our homes to be buried. I could not have done that any other way. I could not have left Caron in a morgue. However, like most aspects of death and grieving, it is a double-edged sword. Sometimes memories of your child dying at home are also like uninvited guests, who do not leave at your bidding, but stay and stay, and play havoc with your mind. For a very long time after Caron died I could see her lying in the bedroom at the top of the stairs. When I walked into the sitting room, I did not see the white, squishy sofas that have always offered such comfort; I saw a coffin draped in lilies, and in the hallway I saw large men in dark suits lift and take my daughter away forever.

Grief is so very private and personal and difficult to share, but there are people who understand. When my wife was told that she only had a few weeks to live, she told me that she wanted to die at home and asked me to look after her. I gave up work, and the task of enabling her to die at home was the greatest privilege I have ever, or will ever experience.

I had hoped that Celia would visit me in my dreams, but this has not happened and I find this quite distressing. My mind, after all, is the only communication channel open. When I read about your beautiful Caron, it gave me the opportunity to grieve a little, so has the opportunity of sharing my own loss with you.

Edward

He's right of course: it is a privilege to nurse a person you love, ease them even if you can't cure them, but sometimes I have to force myself to think of the young, cancer-free Caron, and not a woman, a mother, fighting with staggering strength to stay alive. Olivia Chase died in the house she'd lived in since she was five years of age. Her mother looks out on the lawn and pictures when she taught her little girl to ride her bike. She sees all the precious things that happened since she was five, but Carol also cannot wash up a coffee cup without looking out of the window and seeing the candle that marks the place where life left Olivia. She walks down her sweeping staircase and in her immaculate hallway all she can see is Olivia's coffin being taken away. Those memories play like a loop in your brain, over and over and over. When Paul stays in Sevenoaks, he finds it quite difficult to this day to sleep in Caron's room, the images are too strong, and sometimes I think he'd rather camp in the office instead. It was a privilege to have Caron home, even if it was for less than twenty-four hours, but it came with an edge. I obviously don't talk about it with the younger boys, and they seem to love coming to the house, but I wonder when they tear around the garden what they think when they look up at the window that overlooks the garden. Do they ever think of their mother, lying in there, unable to wake up?

I try not to dwell on such things. I could go over the ifs and buts, the whys and hows for ever and ever, but I am only too aware how very easy it is to make grief all-consuming and therefore be consumed by it. Sometimes I have to curb my inclination to talk about Caron: it's not fair on Stephen, even though he's always prepared to listen. Stephen and I have been married ten years this year. He got to know Caron and the family very quickly. I was by nature a carefree and usually upbeat person. He would act on a whim as quickly and sharply as I did. Caron always used to say how lucky we were to have met one another, two impetuous people likely to go off on some crazy idea or trip on the spur of the moment. That characteristic was vital while Caron fought her cancer or just needed support. When she and Russ moved to Fowey, we bought a little house nearby so that we were on hand if she needed us, but not in the way. When they moved to Australia, Stephen spent weeks and sometimes months away from home, his sons and his business. His gallant staff in Bond Street carried on without him to allow him to stay in Australia with me and the family for anything up to four months. On one occasion Caron needed unscheduled radiotherapy on her spine and I said to Stephen that it was OK for him to return to London to his business. En route to the hospital, as we stopped to buy Caron some fruit at the roadside, he said there was no way he was leaving me there and again I wept buckets of relief. All of that is a testament to my husband and our marriage.

I really want to stress how important your partner's support is when faced with a life-threatening illness or a death. There were times when I have been screaming in my head, Where is that strong, buoyant person I used to be? Just as I couldn't find Caron, I couldn't find myself. Now, though, Stephen and I know that by sharing our worst and most devastating moments, we have grown together in understanding and knowledge. Just as pressure drives couples apart, it can also bring you closer together. If you manage to stick together, the bad times can become like glue and add layers of depth to your relationship. To have a partner who is prepared to accept your daily moods, listen, absorb and comfort all at once is simply pure gold.

Luckily my relationship with Michael and Paul has always been open and fruitful. I enjoy their company; I like them as people and am so proud of them as my sons. I am very fortunate to have strong sounding boards around me, and sometimes that's all you need in the middle of your grief: to be able to voice the words of despair, prevent them from festering in your throat, and then cope with the rest of the day. Little could we have known how events would unfold after the utter joy of Charlie being born, that we would end up being tested as we have. It will be an emotional return to Hever Castle this year to mark our tenth wedding anniversary. It will be a day packed with emotion and poignancy. We will have a small blessing in the church to say thank you for the strength we have gained from each other and then be joined by family and friends to celebrate in the evening. It will be a very different day because Caron is not there.

I am so lucky to have Stephen. I sometimes wonder if God moved the big pieces to allow us to find one another. Some of the letters show how badly people sometimes react to death. Stephen is brilliant with me, but then, you see, he's had training, long ago. Seven years before Caron died, it had already become apparent to him that life would never be quite the same. He was, in a way, more prepared than any of us, as his brother, Johnny, had died, aged twenty-three, at the end of the Second World War. Stephen was the youngest of nine children. Johnny was the eldest and had gone to war aged eighteen and survived. The war ended in June and the family celebrated with the rest of the country: their golden boy, their hero was coming home. Banners were hung across the streets. Tragically, though, Johnny died before he made it home. In September 1945 he was shot by some remaining renegade Asian soldiers hiding out in Malaysia. He went through the Middle East, Burma, India, survived the whole thing, then got shot making breakfast one morning during peacetime.

Johnny was a handsome, intelligent, wonderful boy who loved his baby brother as if he was his own son. Stephen remembers him as a beautiful presence in his life. Stephen saw his mother go from being an effervescent, lively person to a broken woman. He'd come home from school and she'd be sitting at the kitchen table with her head in her hands. This went on for years. Stephen recalls the house falling apart along with his mother. There was no new furniture, no decorations, no care. What was the point? He remembers one of his other brothers saying, 'It should have been me,' and fleeing from the intensity of their loss to Australia, which devastated his mother all over again. Stephen was only about ten at the time and saw his family change overnight. He would listen to his older brothers and sisters discussing what to do and what not to do. His father would say to his mother, 'You have eight other children to care for,' and she'd go wild, because that belittled what she had lost. He would beg her, saying, 'You have to get over this,' but Stephen knew there was no getting over it. Until the end of her life if she saw an oriental face, she'd go mad. The pain always felt like it had happened yesterday.

The telegram informing the family of his death said he had been 'killed in action', but there was no action. Eight British soldiers had been clearing the area of unexploded bombs and shrapnel for the village. It was Johnny's turn to make breakfast and he and the other boy on duty that morning were shot in the back of the head. Stephen can still hear the scream that erupted from his mother when that telegram came. The day Caron died, Stephen heard the same scream.

How does Stephen manage it? He says my moods change on a daily basis. He's wrong, actually: they change hourly, by the minute, every few seconds, so if he thinks it's only daily, I must be doing something right. His analogy is this: you set your sails according to the wind. When you want to go somewhere, which for him is peace and happiness, you put your finger up to see which way the wind is blowing. He wants more than anything to simply stay on course. If you had no aim in sight, it would just be wild all the time, being buffeted in a whirlpool of changing moods and emotion, but he has a goal, so he adjusts the sails slightly depending on whatever maelstrom is coming his way. He actually has a technique for it. He puts his little finger on to his thumb to create a circle and that reminds him to ask himself, Where do we want to go with this? How do I respond to her? How do I react in order to get to where I want to go, which is ultimately peace and happiness? That technique stops him reacting instinctively. If I am being grumpy about something,

Stephen tries not to react. What I'm being grumpy about is usually irrelevant, because what I'm really upset about, as ever, is Caron. Stephen is maybe one of the few people I know who got to know death and tried to understand it when it came knocking on the door. As a result, death is a slightly easier guest to have to stay. It is a wise thing to do, because this guest is going nowhere.

Many times when I walk around the house, I think I should have more photographs of Caron. Then I worry that actually I should have fewer, because we share this house and I can't turn our home into a shrine. There are photos of Caron everywhere, but not huge, dominating ones. I have a montage upstairs on the landing where I see her all the time, but downstairs I worry whether I have too many. Hard to know. I remember in Cornwall, right after Caron died, there was a large photo of her sitting on a little table by the loo. Charlie asked Russ to take it away because it was too much at the time, too close. Nowadays, Charlie and Gabriel treasure the photos of their mum, which sit by their bedside. At the same time, I don't want the boys coming to Sevenoaks and feeling they are constantly being watched. It's an intricate balance that we each constantly try to strike.

May you always have an angel by your side,
Watching out for you in all the things you do,
Reminding you to keep believing in brighter days,
Finding ways for your wishes and dreams to come true,
Giving you hope that is as certain as the sun,
Giving you the strength of serenity as your guide.
May you always have love and comfort and courage,
And may you always have an angel by your side.

Gloria Hunniford

Someone there to catch you if you fall,
Encouraging your dreams,
Inspiring your happiness,
Holding your hand and helping you through it all.
In all of our days, our lives are always changing.
Tears come along as well as smiles.
Along the roads you travel
May the miles be a thousand times more lovely than
    lonely,
May they give you gifts that never, ever end:
Someone wonderful to love and a dear friend in whom
    you can confide.
May you have rainbows after every storm,
May you have hopes to keep you warm,
And may you always have an angel by your side.

'May You Always Have an Angel
by Your Side', Douglas Pagels

II

Living on the Lips of the Living

People never die if they live on the lips of the living.
Wise words given to me by a good friend

The mention of my child's name
May bring tears to my eyes,
But it never fails to bring
Music to my ears.
If you are really my friend,
Let me hear the beautiful music of his name.
It soothes my broken heart
And sings to my soul.

'The Mention of His Name', Anon

It was over a year since my daughter had died. I was busy with work, filling my head with something other than loss, but deep down I felt as bereft as the day Caron had died. How was it possible that all the people who were close to her were able to move on? Why wasn't I? Where was I supposed to go that wasn't a place without her?

Around the time of the anniversary of Caron's death, I was interviewed for an article in the *Daily Mail*. I had been working almost non-stop, appearing on *Songs of Praise* and *This Morning*, and I suppose people were seeing the professional me, the smiling me, and I managed to make people believe that I was getting on with life. You know that expression 'You can fool some of the people some of the time, but not all the people all the time'? Well, I was amazed how many letters now came in from people who made it clear that they had not been fooled for one minute. I was so relieved. 'It was lovely to see you on *This Morning*. You looked radiant, although I know that, like me, underneath it all you have a broken heart.' The woman who wrote that card, Mrs Harris from Norfolk, was absolutely right. Work was a relief, a moment to press 'pause' on the pain, but it was merely a distraction. The pain wasn't going away. In fact, like others had noticed, it was getting worse, changing shape. I felt the passing of the first anniversary keenly. To me, it signalled the end of being able to freely talk about Caron, and that scared me more than ever. To me, it felt the losses were piling up, one on top of another. They were unforeseen losses, losses I had no control over. I got a letter that made me realise my love for my grandchildren is as deep as my love for my children. I missed them.

Dear Gloria,

I read your very moving article about your beautiful daughter, Caron Keating, in today's Daily Mail. *I sobbed as I read it. She was a mirror image of you; the love on both your faces in the photo was very poignant. I can empathise with your situation: one of my beautiful grandsons died of leukaemia four years ago, aged six. His name was Nathan John Jude Kane. He was diagnosed when he was three. He had chemotherapy on and off for three years. He had black hair; then he was bald; then he went blond, then ginger and back to black again. He was my daughter Tracey's youngest son. She also had one who*

212

was eight, Joshua, and her eldest son, Billy, was thirteen. Nathan was in and out of hospital for four years. Her marriage broke up (as most of the parents' did, due to stress and not being able to talk to one another).

He never complained about any treatment he had to have, although he screamed when he saw the nurses in their uniforms, so they usually wore their normal clothes so as not to scare him.

I looked after him with my husband, John, while Tracey had to work. In May 2001 they said he could come home for the weekend. We left him with Tracey and said we would give her time to have him to herself. We had a phone call over the weekend at five o'clock in the morning from Billy asking if we could come quickly, as Nathan wasn't too well. We live in nearby Epping, so it only took us fifteen minutes to get there. When we neared the house, we saw a police car and an ambulance outside. I jumped out of our car before it even stopped and said to my husband, 'He's dead. I know he's dead.' I went hysterical. I screamed and screamed. I'm crying now as I am writing this, as it brings back such terrible memories. I went up to Tracey's bedroom, where he slept with her so she could keep an eye on him, and her face was a terrible sight. The grief on her face was terrible. She was holding on to him tightly and wouldn't let him go.

It is the worst thing that has ever happened to us. I miss him so much, as we all do. My grandson Billy had tried to give him the kiss of life, but to no avail.

I am suffering from acute depression, have developed diabetes, and my health is terrible. I cry at the simplest thing.

*I know that you believe in angels. Nearly every week I
find a white feather in the most unexpected places. We
have made a beautiful garden and dedicated it to our
beautiful boy. Two weeks before he died he said to my
husband and myself, 'Bye, Nanny. Bye, Granddad. See
you in heaven,' when we were going home.*
God bless you and your family.
Lots of love,
Theresa

Another letter that I received at this time that resonated with
me came from Rita in Londonderry:

Dear Gloria,
I have just read Saturday's Daily Mail *and I felt I had
to pen you a few lines. I remember Caron so well on UTV
and also yourself years ago. To make this note as short as
possible, my late husband and I lived in the Stranmillis
area of Belfast. We had just one daughter, Elizabeth
McCracken, who was educated at Methodist College and
was all that one would want in a lovely daughter. She
was musical and sang in St Bart's Church Choir under
the leadership of the late Ronnie Lee. She was married in
St Bart's on 7 June 1976 to Ian McCracken. They made
their home there. We attended the ill-fated dinner of the
Collie Club on 17 February 1978 when twelve people
were involved in the La Mon fire bomb. My husband and
myself attended same as I was secretary of the Irish Collie
Club. Ian and Elizabeth perished along with ten other
people. That was twenty-seven years ago. We never really
lived after this tragedy. I lost my husband eleven years
ago, so I am now alone. I can sympathise with you in the*

Charlie's birthday in Alldays Field in Fowey, Cornwall. A special place where he still celebrates his birthday to this day.

Charlie's fourteenth birthday, 25th July 2008.

'I'm a Barbie Girl . . .'
Getting ready for the
Fowey Regatta float.

Another Regatta week
highlight – here come the
Red Arrows. All four
cousins take to the skies.

Byron Bay in Australia welcomes the family tradition of dressing up.

Marie Antoinette eat your heart out. Caron and Sir Cliff steal the show at a joint 60th birthday party for Stephen and me.

ll the family outside Hever Church, April 2008, to mark Caron's fourth anniversary.

Dark days in Britain replaced with boarding Down Under. Byron Bay really was a tonic.

The morning of Caron's 40th birthday in Australia. What a gift.

It was no wonder that Wategos Bay in Australia gave Caron the space and time she needed to reflect and heal.

Poolside at Taylors in Oz after breakfast, and an early departure for Stephen and me back to England.

Looking radiant on her 40th birthday. Stephen was so pleased to have a celebratory dance.

Another birthday tea for Gabriel. Please note my mother's marshmallow and chocolate treats, which we always make for all the family birthdays.

Despite being poorly, Caro
lived for every minute, whi
even included taking a cabl
car to the top of Mount
Santis with her brother
Michael whilst undergoing
treatment in Switzerland.
She loved the mountains a
far-reaching horizon.

Incredibly poignant
and enlightening days
when the Rinpoche
(a Buddhist leader)
came to visit.

An emotional and
hard goodbye as Paul
leaves Australia to
head home. This is
one of my favourite
photographs, it sits
on my bedside table.

She always was an angel.

One of Caron's paintings which we now use as a symbol for the Caron Keating Foundation.

ternal light during the week the Gyuto Monks chanted for Caron's healing and life.

Carol Chase and her beautiful daughter Olivia. Their story has contributed so much to this book.

A loving and tender moment with my gorgeous daughter in her precious summer house, where she spent so much time writing and healing.

loss of your dear daughter. I do hope you don't mind me
writing to you. I send you my love and commend you,
like myself, to a power greater than us.
  Sincerely,
  Rita

Enclosed with her letter was a page torn out of a magazine from 1978. The article leapt off the page. It was written in what I have to assume is a company or trade magazine expressing sympathy to all employees who had relatives or friends killed or injured in this 'most awful disaster', which struck an area that had already seen some of the most violent years of the conflict. Two other married couples perished along with Elizabeth and Ian, plus seven more women. Outside the function room where people were sitting down to their meal, IRA activists had left the incendiary bomb hanging by meat hooks on the security grille over the hotel windows. Inside, people were burnt alive. Afterwards hopes were expressed that the La Mon atrocity would in some way be a turning point in the horror of the Troubles. Sadly we all know it took many more years and many more lives before the Good Friday Agreement was finally signed. This is not what struck me about the article, however. What hit me was something found in Elizabeth's handbag that somehow managed to survive the fatal fireball. Inside her handbag was a handwritten note. I copy her words here. I realised with a start that I could have been reading from one of my daughter's many journals. It was headed, 'Life.'

The only moment we ever live is the present. It is the only time we have to be happy. Naturally, we have to plan for the future, but too much looking ahead entails fear and apprehension.

The best insurance for a satisfactory future is to handle the present hour properly, do a good job of living now, be effective in your work, your thinking, your helpfulness to other people. The future will turn out to be as good as your present if you keep handling the present moment correctly.

It could almost be penned by Caron's hand, so similar was the message of these two women, who had died twenty-seven years apart, in completely different circumstances and political times. In one of her many diaries, Caron had written, 'In a way, we are so used to dealing with the future by referring to the past. It's the only knowledge we have and we drag it around with us, making it fit with totally different situations, allowing the past to keep reoccurring.' The big lesson was to live in the *now* – in this present moment.

Elizabeth had two other pieces of writing in her handbag the night she died. The first was:

Look to this day,
For it is the very life of life.
In its brief course lie all the verities of your existence:
The glory of action,
The bliss of growth,
The splendour of beauty.
For yesterday is but a dream and tomorrow is only a
vision,
But today well lived makes every yesterday a dreamy
happiness
And every tomorrow a vision of hope.
Look well, therefore, to this day.

'Look to This Day', Sanskrit poem, Anon

And finally:

God hath not promised skies always blue
Flower-strewn pathways all our lives through
God hath not promised sun without rain,
Joy without sorrow, peace without pain.

But he hath promised strength from above,
Unfailing sympathy, undying love.

'What God Hath Promised',
Christian hymn, Annie Johnson Flint

There was clearly something special about Elizabeth. In a different way, Caron too had been on a journey of self-analysis and discovery. She had got angry; she had discovered her faith; she had raged and cried and danced and sang; she had lost some of her ability to walk, but she still went body-surfing with her boys. Her story was worth telling, not just for people who were suffering because of cancer, but to remind everyone, even for a moment, how incredibly precious life is. This was the lesson that Caron had taught me that I so wanted to convey.

The more the world moved on without Caron, the more I wanted to make sure she was not forgotten. The stories of her fight as told on the *Tonight* programme on her birthday and in the *Daily Mail* on the anniversary of her death were only a fraction of what there was to tell. I didn't want people just to know of her secret seven-year battle, but the girl she'd been, what she was to her friends, *Blue Peter* and the shenanigans she got up to in Ireland and Bristol. I recalled one of the letters that had inspired me so much before we set up the Caron Keating Foundation: 'As Caron's mum, you want to shout from the rooftops, "I had the best daughter in the world!" ' I felt like that more than ever now.

The letters continued to fall through the front door and certain things became very clear to me. Firstly, Caron's life story had resonance with people. Secondly, I was the only one who could tell it. After all, Caron's father was already gone and I was the only person alive who knew her story from beginning to end. Finally, and perhaps most importantly, I wanted more than anything for Charlie and Gabriel to know Caron's story. One day the boys would grow up and they might want to know what their cheeky mum had been like as a child and a teenager, what she did at university, how she got into television, what drove her, what she regretted, how much she loved her father, what he did for her, how unbelievably hard she fought to stay alive for them and how very intensely she loved them. Right now, it was all so fresh in my mind, but what if my mind went? What if I got sick? Life is a gossamer thread that can snap at any moment.

Early on after Caron had died, we had been approached by publishers asking us to write a book about her. Russ and I were going to do it together at first. Then, as the months passed, Russ had decided he didn't want to and we had put the idea to bed. But the letters I was now receiving, from people in this same sorry clan, galvanised me into action. A book would allow me the privilege of mourning. I could take off the mask and surrender to the pain. I realised I needed to get Caron's story down as soon as I possibly could. It became a frantic urge in me. Adrenaline and panic frequently surged through me that something would happen before I got it all on paper. I wanted to start work on it straight away, I was desperate to, and yet, and yet . . . was it what she would have wanted? She'd kept her illness a closely guarded secret and here I was about to tell her story. On the other hand, towards the end of her life she so wanted to pass on what she had learned on her journey.

It was a letter I had received some time earlier, on 28 December 2004, that helped me to make the decision once and for all. It came from Mr Fountaine from Rickmansworth, who wrote to me about his amazing daughter, Ruth. Cancer went to Ruth's legs; she lost all her strength, had metal bolts inserted and learnt to walk again in secret to surprise her parents at a big naval ceremony where she was the centre of attention. No one knew she was ill. Two weeks later she died, leaving four children, her husband, parents and many, many affected friends.

Death held no terror for her and she died peacefully on 13 September 2001. Yes, two days after 9/11, and but for her dying, her husband would have been on duty in the Pentagon on that day. Whether her death saved his life no one will ever know.

I believe the Almighty selects carefully those who are to suffer these great tragedies. 'The Lord seeth not as man seeth, for man looketh on the outward appearance, but the Lord looketh upon the heart.' He knows those people and families who have the strength to sustain them through their difficulties and, in due time, turn tragedy into triumph and to the benefit of others.

I believe that the knowledge of how others coped in similar circumstances can help, comfort and give the strength to go on, not for oneself but for the memory of one's loved one and the benefit of others.

The words of that letter resounded in me: 'I believe that the knowledge of how others coped in similar circumstances can help, comfort and give the strength to go on.' Writing a book about Caron would not only give me carte blanche to talk in depth about my courageous daughter's journey, it could possibly help someone else. I should write it 'not for oneself but for the memory of one's loved one and the benefit of others', and in particular for Charlie and Gabriel.

I still had concerns, but eventually the need to tell Caron's story won over my doubts. Like starting the foundation, writing a book about Caron kept her alive. Luckily for me, my extraordinary daughter had provided a story that you couldn't have made up, learnt lessons that were far-reaching and forged a belief system that transcended religion and creed. This was a private story no doubt, but so too was it universal, and timeless. I was actually finishing what she had started: she had been writing two books – one about the quirkiness of her early life growing up in Northern Ireland, and the other about her extraordinary journey through seven years of soul-searching.

From the anniversary of Caron's death right through the summer I worked on *Next to You*. I read through reams and reams of pages she had written while searching the universe for a cure for her disease. Her journals were filled with thought processes, as opposed to being chronicled diaries. She didn't find that cure, but somewhere along the way she picked up the strength to fight on as the cancer spread and it's my belief that she bought herself a few extra years. She was awe-inspiring, humbling, and I was reminded all over again how brave, stoic and positive she had been. How many times have I heard similar stories in the letters I've received of people all over the country who have courageously dealt with this hideous disease?

Only now, looking back on it, I realise what *I* gleaned from going over Caron's story in detail were lessons in strength and endurance during a time when I myself felt weak and unable to go on. You couldn't write that story and not say to yourself, Well, if she can do it, so can I. For example, I went to host a function for a family friend who was raising money for the amazing bone-cancer unit at Stanmore Hospital, where there is a tight team of four doctors and anaesthetists who work on bone cancer on young people. We gave them £20,000 from the Caron Keating Foundation and it gave me the most enormous satisfaction. Though Caron started with breast cancer, eventually it went to the bones, and I had seen for myself what people with bone cancer have to endure. I recall meeting a beautiful teenage girl at the unit who was dependent on a walking frame. She had mustered all the strength she had to get dressed up in her finery for this glamorous fund-raising evening at Claridges. All the time we were talking to her and her mother, we tried to be jolly and positive about when she might improve, and in the back of my head I was thinking, This just shouldn't be. Sadly, I found out only recently that she had lost her fight. I found it very hard. It made me think about all that Caron had gone through, but I took strength from those memories too – because on Gabriel's birthday Caron had thrown away her stick, walked down the path and greeted the other parents as if there was nothing wrong with her. Going over her story while researching the book reminded me how truly amazing the human spirit can be, that it can rise above the most awful levels of pain to do something.

Once again, Caron became my teacher, even though she wasn't even there. I would be led by example. Effectively I suppose what I am doing now is what Caron did. Some people write diaries, like Carol Chase and many, many others. Some read books, find God, go to counselling, have therapy, meditate, sew, paint, pray, whatever it takes to find a way through this path of pain. I simply had to go to my daughter for counsel, as ever. I don't know why I hadn't realised sooner that I still could.

The time spent writing *Next to You*, thinking about Caron, the girl she'd been, her childhood, her friends and the tricks she played on her brothers was an invaluable cathartic process. Russ, Stephen, my sons and many of Caron's friends contributed their happiest memories of Caron, which gave me a piece of Caron I hadn't had before. I loved hearing about the laughs they had at university, being part of her group of girlfriends once more and seeing for myself what my daughter had obviously seen in them – a fun, loyal, happy bunch of girls. However, writing it was not without its difficulties, for although I gleaned much joy from reliving the happy memories, I was thrust again to those moments that pierced my heart.

Writing *Next to You* also gave me a chance to thank some of the people who'd sent me letters in the early days, when I'd been too deranged by grief to focus and respond. It was satisfying finally to be able to address those letters now. They saved my life, gave me clues about how to go on and pushed me in the direction I needed to go, in order to find purpose in my life again: namely launching the foundation and writing Caron's story.

Many people who send letters tell me how much they have to say about their dearly departed; I was able to and I feel fortunate for that. I am glad that I did it. We sometimes, as a nation, find it difficult to express our feelings. Stiff upper lip and all that. Much has been written about the extraordinary outpouring of emotion after Diana, Princess of Wales was killed in that awful, unnecessary car crash. One conclusion is that part of our cultural heritage means we repress a lot. This one young woman's death gave us all permission to experience fully the pain we have been busy suppressing for fear it may overtake us. Though fearful of sounding like a broken record, if I have learnt anything, it is that the pain of losing a loved one never goes away. As I have learnt, refusing to accept a problem rarely leads to a solution. Diana's death let us all grieve for the myriad of things I believe we had not let ourselves fully mourn. In some, small way, the book did the same.

I felt an actual physical release when *Next to You* finally went to print. It was down. No matter what happened to me, should Gabriel and Charlie ever want to know anything about their mother, it was all there. I felt proud of *Next to You*, proud of Caron. I knew from the letters how alone people felt and how thankful they were to find some understanding, albeit remotely, in me. I too in them. Soon it was publishing day. In fact the launch marked what would have been Caron's forty-third birthday and we had a party high up in the Hilton Hotel on Park Lane. It was really lovely that all her friends and everyone who'd contributed and shared their memories of Caron for the book attended. I think everyone was a little apprehensive. I don't think they are any more. As Caron wrote in her journal:

Step into the unknown – live in it – and be prepared to hang out there. We cannot know what's in store for us, and by hanging on to what's familiar we block the new. Until hanging on by our fingertips to the old life, fed up with prising off our fingertips one by one, it simply kicks us into the abyss. As we fall screaming, it prepares a feather mattress for us. Stunned, we wonder why we didn't dive off to begin with. Live life.

There's no waiting game. What is it you want to create right now? How do you want to be? Do it now.

Caron reminded me poignantly, sometimes painfully, that life, in whatever form we were given it, is for living. I couldn't go on hauling the heavy load of the past with me wherever I went. I had to do as she had done, as Russ and the boys were managing to do: I have to live in the now. I had to live. What sort of mother was I if I didn't heed my daughter's words? What sort of memorial did I make if I slumped, defeated, and refused to participate in all that life still had to offer me? As Caron said in her journal, I had a choice about whether I spent 'hour upon hour invaded by fear and terror about what the future might bring or whether I choose to be present in this very second – a second that I will never have again'. Although I didn't know it at the time, Caron's book would help many of those who read it, but it didn't just help them, it helped me. It gave me permission to live. She gave me permission to live.

12

Permission to Live

When I come to the end of the road,
And the sun has set for me,
I want no rites in a gloom-filled room.
Why cry for a soul set free?

Miss me a little but not too long,
And not with your head bowed low;
Remember the love that once we shared,
Miss me but let me go.

For this is a journey we all must take,
And each must go alone.
It is all a part of the Master's plan,
A step on the road to home.

When you are lonely and sick of heart,
Go to the friends we know,
And bury your sorrows in doing good deeds.
Miss me but let me go.

'Miss Me But Let Me Go', Anon

Life never ceases to amaze me. I think that is a good thing. I was
pretty emotionally tired after finishing the book. A year on, the

foundation was running smoothly and was well organised, but life hadn't lightened yet. I must have been nearer the top of the black hole than I thought, because I became aware that lightness was missing in my life, and I don't recall having noticed that before. Everything was so muted and colours remained dull. The climb out happens in such miniscule measures that you barely realise you are moving. I honestly still thought I would never totally enjoy anything ever again. I couldn't understand how others laughed so easily. I used to watch them with a sort of mild bemusement and think, Wow, you can actually do that. I know I had laughed when Michael Ball came over after Caron's death, but I immediately felt guilty and the joy evaporated as quickly as it had appeared. Living without laughter or levity was quite frightening for me. Because my approach had always been jolly, I couldn't recognise the person I had become, and was plagued with the thought that I might never find my way back to her. I must say, for the sake of my children and husband, who'd tried so hard to cheer me up, that there had been fun on the outside, but in all honesty on the inside there was still that dead place, a place I couldn't unlock. Luckily for me, something was about to change.

When I think of my faith, as I often do, I understand God to be in the big picture, moving the key pieces of the puzzle, rather than in the minutiae. This is just a personal interpretation. Mine alone. Was it God moving a key piece of the puzzle into place that brought *Strictly Come Dancing* my way? I doubt it – it seems a bit frivolous for God. No, *Strictly Come Dancing* reeks of another angel's doing, a slightly mischievous one, who was always up for a bit of craic and knew full well how I liked to dance.

When the chance of taking part in the third series of *Strictly Come Dancing* was put to me, my immediate thought was that it was lunacy. How inappropriate for me to go gallivanting around a dance floor after what had happened, let alone at my age! No matter where I turned, though, I couldn't find anyone to tell me *not* to do it – not my agent, not my friends and certainly not my family, who were the keenest of the bunch. Michael was absolutely determined for me to do it. *Next to You* had just been published and I was busy doing the publicity rounds. I know now that he was really worried I was going to become, or had already become, the broken woman, defined by loss: every interview was about Caron. Here was something that was frivolous and fun, and more importantly something completely and utterly different from what had consumed me for a year and a half. Each time he raised the subject I would say to him, 'Don't be daft. It's ridiculous I'm not even thinking about it,' but he would say again and again, 'Why not? It'll be good for you. It'll be fun, a new experience.' Others said the same. The message kept coming back that it would be good for me. I have learnt that if a message keeps being repeated over and over, it's probably worth listening to, and so I did.

And thank goodness. From the moment I started training, in October 2005, I found taking part in the programme to be an utterly joyful and liberating experience. I absolutely loved it because it was so much outside the parameters of what I did and what I'd been doing. You have to smile when you're dancing. In the beginning I forced the smile on to my face, as I hadn't smiled properly for a very long time. The crew and my wonderful dancing partner, Darren Bennett, would be saying, 'Smile, smile, smile,' all the time. 'Show those teeth!' It was nice to use my facial muscles for something other than a grimace of pain, but I still had to make a conscious effort. Soon, though, the smiling came naturally, and after a while whenever I was rehearsing or filming, I found I couldn't stop smiling. What an amazing relief that was to me. What a feeling! For the first time in ages I had a genuine reason to smile. I felt liberated.

It was great physically for me to get up and get moving too, because for eighteen months I'd been moping around. To do something active was fantastic, and it was really full on – we'd be training for two to three hours at a time, really moving. It may only have been adrenaline and serotonin being released, but I think it was more than that. *Strictly Come Dancing* is a really joyful show. The people working on it are fantastic – the crew and the BBC production team. The professional dancers are terrific too, and Darren was beyond brilliant. The poor man was only twenty-eight at the time and had the bad luck of getting the oldie to dance with, but he was so patient and he never made me feel like I couldn't do it. In fact *Strictly Come Dancing* made me feel like I could do anything.

I had some experience of dancing already, as I'd danced my way through school. I was lucky enough to have a Latin teacher who was a ballroom dancing fanatic, and so we had ballroom dancing lessons every lunchtime. I would get on the bicycle, rush the two miles back home, wolf down whatever my mum had made me and rush back in time for ballroom dancing. All the boys would be lined up one side, all the girls on the other. It was a double hit – you learnt to dance and if you were lucky, you got to dance with the boy you liked. Having been a singer from the age of eight, I love anything to do with music. In fact music is very powerful; it really can lift the spirits and feed the soul.

Taking part in *Strictly Come Dancing* gave me a new focus. It gave me licence to laugh and have fun. It was a fantastic thing to do. The camaraderie was marvellous. The first dance I had to do was the waltz. That wasn't too bad, even though it was petrifying, but nevertheless the waltz was my era, so at least I knew how to do it. It was just a question of learning

Darren's routine. The opening night, however, was one of the most nerve-racking things I'd ever done, and when I had to walk on to the dance floor, I was filled with such dread that I didn't think I could put one foot in front of the other, let alone dance. As it turned out, the judges were kind, even encouraging. Maybe the white feather-trimmed gown I wore gave me that shot of luck and helped me glide across the floor.

The real terror and problems, however, set in in week two, when we had to dance the rumba. With a rumba there has got to be a lot of body contact and smouldering looks, but I felt ridiculous doing that with this twenty-eight-year-old. I remember watching Esther Rantzen running her hand down Anton du Beke's body in the previous series and thinking to myself, Stop it – it looks awful. Now it was even worse: Darren was even younger! I kept saying to him, 'I can't do that. My grandchildren will be watching it and saying, "Silly old bat, what does she think she's doing!"' So Darren had to devise a rumba for me that had all the moves but less of the touching.

When it came to performing the rumba live, I remember Bruno Tonioli, one of the judges, saying, 'It was very regal, like you were the Queen; it was a very unusual rumba.' I thought I was definitely going out after that – I had no hope. Arlene Phillips, another judge, said to me, 'Stop thinking about the difference in age. Just go for it. Enjoy the fact that you have a young man and a young man's body to embrace,' but I couldn't. I kept thinking about my grandsons and my husband watching and what sort of relentless teasing I would get when I got home.

The third week was going to be my week because it was the jive – definitely my era, and in fact Stephen and I still enjoy a good old bop now and again. Personally I didn't think my jive with Darren was too bad, but then again we weren't voting and unfortunately we went out. You know what, though, that was fine. Even appearing for three weeks had done me the power of good. It had forced me to smile, then provided the backdrop to turn that smile into a genuinely good feeling. I was elated for weeks afterwards. The fact that I could feel something that close to happiness was a real breakthrough for me. I didn't take it personally that the public didn't vote to keep me in. There comes a time in *Strictly Come Dancing* when the ones who need to go, go.

Of the whole show I think the walk down the stairs to the dance floor was the bit I loved the most, though on that first night it had terrified me. By the end, I would have happily just done the walk down over and over, dressed up to the nines, fluttering in marabou, feeling like the queen bee. That staircase looks so glamorous on the screen, but backstage it's pretty basic, just some scaffolding really and a wooden platform. If you've ever wondered what the dancers talk about while waiting to make their entrance, the chef James Martin used to give me detailed progress reports on his organic vegetables! I loved the show and all the people on it; they were a great bunch to hang out with and exactly what I needed. You can't be glum for very long with people like Darren Gough, Patsy Palmer, James Martin and Zoë Ball around. Colin Jackson was on it as well. Like any athlete, he was absolutely dedicated – he rehearsed eight hours a day and wanted more! Actually, that was the trick: the people who rehearsed the most were the best. It was up to you.

Stephanie Beacham, who appeared in the last series, the fifth, rang me up before she agreed to take part to ask me about whether she should have a turn round the dance floor. I told her, 'It is one of the best things you will ever do, but make sure you have the time to do it.' Looking back, I realise I didn't really – there was so much other work to do. I was busy launching the book, so I was on the road in Northern Ireland. I had a spare hour here, an hour there. Poor Darren had to come to Belfast to teach me. I also had my day job as a presenter and broadcaster. To be honest, I had underestimated how long it would take. In those early days it was rather less serious – if you made any kind of a stab at it, it was OK – now it's more slick, and certainly more competitive. It's so good and the standard is so high that there is no way I'd dream of doing it now. I probably wouldn't be asked anyway.

It was madness trying to cram in some training with such a hectic schedule, but you know, I was still probably in the grips of madness at the time and thought it was perfectly reasonable to squeeze in an hour-long dance lesson in the middle of Northern Ireland with a complete camera crew to boot. With *Strictly Come Dancing* there is no such thing as stealing a quick cha-cha-cha off camera: you've signed a contract that states the camera crew has to come with the dance instructor and cover you at all times. They let you do it in your own area, wherever you may be, but the cameras are *always* rolling. I couldn't do a Colin Jackson, though: after two hours I wasn't able to move and was knackered. I lost a stone in three weeks. It was better than Weightwatchers! I also lost weight because I was afraid of not fitting into my dress each week, but mostly it was because I was on the move. In wardrobe fittings all the young size-eight girls would be saying, 'Can you cut away a bit here and make it a bit shorter there?' while I was saying, 'Could you just add a bit of chiffon here over the arm, or a few more feathers to hide the scar on my shoulder?'

Overall, mentally and physically it was a brilliant thing to do. I still go every year and sit in the audience to watch and marvel, not only at the brave contestants who've worked so hard, but at the person I was before *Strictly Come Dancing* and the person who emerged from it. To a degree, it was a turning point. I say 'to a degree' because of course when the music stops and the lights come up, the bare truth remains. However, while the music played and the disco ball glittered, I felt genuine happiness, and with my hand on my heart I can say I never thought I'd feel like that again. Discovering that I could was a miracle in itself.

Of course, I realise that *Strictly Come Dancing* in isolation was not what had brought about this change. It was the combination of things that had led up to that time, including my invaluable family support, being back at work, time spent alone and with friends, reading letters, calling people, putting something back and the extremely cathartic exercise of writing it all down in *Next to You*. I had finally got to a place where I could smile; the show gave me a reason to.

Reading back over what I've written, it suddenly seems a bit rich for me to advise someone in the same position to walk the same path – to launch a foundation and tackle all the difficulties that come with it, to write a book and appear on a live television show. It suddenly looks a bit easy for me to have picked myself up. The fact that it wasn't is irrelevant. Giving yourself permission to live, laugh and enjoy life again is a very personal, individual part of grieving. I would say that you don't have to be in the public eye to raise money, you don't have to be published to write a story, and you don't need cameras to dance. You just need *something*. It's up to you to find out what that 'something' is. I recall that one of the very first letters I got told me that the strength I needed could be found in the child I'd lost. That was very significant for me. The answer had been there all along; I just needed to know where to look. As Caron's journal said, 'In the end what I discovered was that what I had been looking for had been inside me all along and I'd just forgotten it was there. It's inside all of us; all you have to do to get in touch with it is really listen to yourself. Listen to your heart.'

Many bereaved parents and other bereaved people find that the permission to live comes not from the outside world, but their internal world, the world where they can still coexist with the person that they've lost. Carol Chase went on an extra-ordinary journey of discovery of her own. She read two hundred books on philosophy, including Socrates and Jung, as well as on near-death experiences, religion and spirituality. In order to heal, she had to discover what had happened to her child. Where had she gone? For months she would hold Olivia's photograph and ask, 'You are coming back, aren't you?' She talked to a lot of people who'd had near-death experiences and they all described this feeling of bliss, pure joy, pure love, which gave her huge amounts of comfort because the thought that she hadn't been there with her daughter at the end was terrible for Carol. She couldn't get beyond it. The idea that Olivia had been in pain and alone went against the very essence of being a mother. Carol recorded her quest to learn what it had been like for Olivia in her diary for two years. She went to conferences, lectures, with American university professors, libraries and colleges to hear about the consciousness existing outside the body. She studied astral projections, out-of-body experiences, anything that would give her some understanding, a way to move away from the indescribable fear and pain she was in.

I too received letters telling me about near-death experi-ences and I cannot put into words what a welcome relief such accounts were. Grief is such a complex emotion. Part of you is doubled up with the pain of what you have lost, and another part is thrown about in confusion and chaos because you don't know where your child is. When, since they were born, was this ever the case? An enormous element of your despair is caused by that confusion. I got a letter from a lovely, smiley woman called Eironwy, or Roni, from South Glamorgan who shared her experience with me. She was very keen to assure me that her experience had been authenticated, which was sweet but really quite unnecessary, since the story alone brought me enormous comfort. She was a bereaved mother herself, having lost one son aged four and another aged twenty-six – that was authentic enough for me. People who have experienced such incredible loss very rarely play with others. Below is a précis of the letter she sent:

It was January 1958. Three months earlier I had lost my younger son to Asian influenza (the scourge of 1957) and was now heavily pregnant with my third. During a blizzard that night I went into labour. A midwife was called. Towards the end of the second stage, when the baby is born, I lost touch with what was going on and said light-heartedly to myself, Oh, my lungs have stopped breathing. Unbeknown to me, I had had a post-partum haemorrhage. I felt quite unperturbed about this. I didn't panic or struggle for breath – I didn't need to, for I felt wonderfully well and happy.

All of a sudden I was my lungs. I was no longer composed of a head and trunk and limbs – I was just my lungs, as though my whole self had retreated to my lungs. While on the one hand I was my lungs, I could also observe my lungs.

Suddenly I was diverted from this study of my lungs by the appearance from nowhere of an extraordinarily bright light, just above and behind my head and slightly to the left. My whole being became focused on it, studying it, marvelling at it. There was nothing but the light; it was totally consuming.

It, in turn, drew me into itself, holding me, absorbing me, in deep, white, unimaginably powerful energy. It seemed to be a concentration of me; from its core radiated prism upon prism of pure, soft brilliance – in perfect formation and in no way blinding me.

It stayed completely still; it did not hover or spin; it did not hang or pulsate. It was simply there, soundless, watching, waiting, guarding me like a sentinel; it was as though it was holding me in its arms, but it had no arms – this perfect, unearthly, awesome light. More than that, it somehow conveyed enormous love, in its purest, gentlest and most intense form – such as could never be experienced here on earth. This is the feeling that has stayed with me most for the remainder of my life. This light loved/loves me.

Suddenly, and at speed, I found myself high up and near the ceiling, again to the left and near the open door. I had no bodily form, I had a new form, and again while I was this form, I could also observe this form, which was of an opaque, alive sphere and sort of wobbled slightly. It felt like I was the pure essence of myself – complete, whole, in harmony with everything that had ever been and was to come. This sphere seemed to be the vehicle by which I was to travel somewhere; I actually felt bodily complete too and perfectly at home.

I felt happiness such as I had never felt in all my life before – and peace, though not of the passive kind associated with death. In particular, I felt free and filled with joyful energy. Furthermore I was going on somewhere, and I felt hugely excited in anticipation. I seemed to be looking upwards and away out of the room.

Suddenly I was looking down at the room below me. I noted my body lying spread-eagled on the twin bed. It was of no consequence to me whatsoever except that it registered as ugly, crumpled, deflated, defunct, like something useless, thrown away.

After that, the figure of the midwife came into focus. She was standing at the right-hand side of my body; she had both hands high in the air – loading, testing a hypodermic syringe. Then her arm plunged down, to stick the needle into the outside of my right thigh. Simultaneously I came crashing back into my body at high speed, in a sickening jumble of jolts and bangs and clattering, like a bag of old bones being flung down a long flight of cellar steps.

Everything was black.

I could not believe it. I was furious and dreadfully, dreadfully angry and agitated. I didn't want to be back in my body. I didn't want to be confined in this crude arrangement of head and trunk and limbs. I hated it. I felt totally trapped. Where it was in contact with the paper sheets, my skin felt agonised, as though stung by a million miniscule, scratching thorns. Even worse was my awareness of the external pressure of the force of gravity; I felt pinned down to the bed, leaden.

Then the midwife's tightly clenched fists were pummelling deep into my body, over the region of the womb, bringing bruising pain. Feebly, I tried to push her fists away but to no avail. I moaned in utter misery at the awful sense of defeat.

Then fear entered my mind. The baby – where was the baby? I managed to raise my head and located her, safely tucked up in the Moses basket on the other twin bed at the end of the room. I felt the smile of amazement and joy spread across my face, and then I got on with trying to pull myself together.

The ensuing days were the usual happy and busy ones, devoting time to the new baby, showing her off and generally getting life underway again. At the same time my thoughts continued on another plane – it was like leading a double life. Questions plagued me, but I said nothing to anyone. I played my own devil's advocate, obsessively, secretly.

The light? Where had it come from? What was it?

Whenever I was alone, I lay down on the bed in different positions and switched the electric light on and off and on again, searching the walls and ceiling for some object, some particle that might have caused a reflection. I waited for a glimmer of winter sunlight to slant through the window in the hope that if it struck the handle of the door, it would produce the light. I was wasting my time. I was disappointed. I was miserable. I knew there had been a light and I had to find it.

I accept now that I will not see the light again in this life.

I thank Roni again for her beautifully written account and wish her well with her two daughters and granddaughter. If you go searching out these accounts, then the message that comes back time and time again is that we can exist outside of our bodies and that when we leave them, there is a feeling of indescribable bliss. Like me, Carol listened to the message and let herself hear it and be comforted by it. That is not to say she didn't have many, many dark days – we all did and still do – but then something extraordinary happened.

A few days before Olivia died she and Carol had gone out to the pond in the garden to feed the fish, they were both crouched by the side when Olivia spotted a tiny frog on the surface that wasn't moving, Olivia stirred the water next to it, still no movement, so they scooped out the frog and placed it between them on the patio and watched it for a while, when suddenly it leapt back into the water and they both fell back in surprise, laughing together.

Carol didn't think anything of it until two days after the inquest into Olivia's death when she received a call from Rita Rogers, Princess Diana's medium. Carol had read Rita's book on learning to live again after the loss of a child and had written to her many months before but had received a brief note saying that Rita had been unwell for the last year and was unable to respond. Suddenly she was on the phone saying that she had Olivia with her urging her to call. They spoke for over an hour, Rita refusing any financial donation, and describing in huge detail, the family members, the home, and most importantly for Carol, how Olivia died. Rita started to describe the swimming pool, she described that Olivia had been sitting by the edge of the pool, had tried to stand up "Tell Mum I felt a zig-zag across my chest, tell her I died before I hit the water. Please tell her I didn't drown and I didn't suffer".

These were powerful words to a mother who had been on a journey to understand how the final moments of her daughter's life might have been for her.

Rita then went on to describe in exact detail the story of the frog and the pond and how the frog had leapt back into the water and described this as a shared memory between Olivia and her mother and how they had both laughed together at the time. It dawned on Carol at this moment that Olivia was the only person who knew this story, the only person who could have given this information to Rita Rogers, this was a defining moment when the family truly felt able to believe that Olivia's spirit lived on, it gave them such a huge sense of peace.

Carol had provided no information to Rita when she had written, no cause of death, only that her daughter had died. Was it that story alone that marked Carol's turning point? Probably not. Like me, writing my book and *Strictly Come Dancing* or was it the culmination of a great deal of soul-searching and effort to absorb the loss of our daughters into our lives? I had walked my daughter's journey of self-discovery with her before she died and had rediscovered it by writing about it. Carol had to walk it alone after Olivia died, but we both found that the strength we were looking for had been inside us all along. Our children are here to teach us, if only we let them. Anger, rage and self-pity only make us feel bitter for the rest of our lives and lead inevitably to more pain. It is better to embrace spirituality in the hope that some good will come from something so terrible. Goodness relieves the pain.

And so I scratched and crawled and ultimately danced my way back to the living. By talking constantly about Caron, I had found I was allowed to take her with me, and that made 'moving on' a much less daunting prospect.

Perhaps our loved ones are just up ahead, or just behind. I know the woman whose two children suffered the same genetic illness believes strongly that her children are just over her shoulder, watching, caring for her and urging her on. She'd see them if only she could turn quickly enough. She just never can. Up ahead, within, behind, above – it doesn't really matter. What we survivors have in common, I think, is that we have made our child's death, our loved one's death, a part of our ongoing lives. That in itself was what we needed to do in order to give ourselves permission to join the warm-blooded race and not feel annihilated by guilt and grief that we too, their mothers, were forgetting them or leaving them behind.

13

Same But Different

The deeper sorrow carves into your being, the more joy you can contain.

Kahlil Gibran

I thought that I had received all the letters I was going to receive, for there had been so many, but I was soon to learn that loss has an infinite number of faces. Not long after the publication of *Next to You*, I remember calling up my editor, the intuitive and encouraging Louise Moore, who became such a friend and pillar of support, to ask how the sales were going. She told me they'd sold 75,000 copies that week alone. Totally inexperienced in the world of publishing, I asked her whether that was good or not. She nearly fell off her chair. It wasn't just good; it was incredible. Caron was doing what she'd always wanted to do: pass on what she had learnt. And having made the decision to write the book, I was extremely comforted. I went out on the road to publicise the book and found myself being able to talk and talk and talk about Caron, and this galvanised me to forge forward even on those bad days when every fibre in my body wanted to dive back into the past.

Very soon letters from readers started to flood in. I was absolutely overwhelmed and delighted by the response. I'd been right: Caron's story had struck a chord. More than that, it appeared to be making a difference. Her death was reaching out not just to victims of cancer, but to all sorts of people in all sorts of circumstances. Was it possible that she had not died in vain?

Sharon from Glasgow lost her son in a car crash. Then her mother died from an aneurism, her dad from a heart attack and her daughter-in-law and two grandchildren from carbon-monoxide poisoning. Though I felt her grief keenly, when I started reading her letter, I was perplexed. What was this to do with Caron and cancer? She wrote:

My remaining daughter tells me life is not a rehearsal and you've got to make the most of each and every day. She cannot cope with my grief, so I grieve alone, and yes, there are days you want to scream and are afraid you cannot stop. The pain in your heart becomes so intense you feel it's going to break. I try so hard not to be too protective of my daughter, but every time she goes out of the door I'm afraid that she won't come back, that God will take her too.

Thank you, Gloria, for sharing your grief with us. In doing so, you saved a life. As I read of your wonderful daughter's quest to live throughout all the pain, I asked myself what right did I have to be sitting thinking about taking mine, leaving my daughter all alone. It's not easy. As you know, Gloria, we have our good days and bad days, but we also have our memories within our hearts. Sometimes remembering the good times, happy memories can be the most painful thing there is, but it keeps them close to us.

Be brave, be strong, just like Caron.

I was utterly touched and humbled by that letter. Not only had this woman been through more than was imaginable, she was thanking me for giving her the strength to go on. Not me, actually, but Caron – she was thanking Caron. Caron had given her the strength to continue. All I had wanted to know was that Caron was missed, Caron was not forgotten, Caron had made a difference, and that one letter assured me of that. Of course, though, it wasn't the only one – my God, there were thousands of them. They came from all over the world, from men, women and children, and each one touched me deeply and somehow managed to comfort me.

In late October 2005 a letter came from Rebecca in Southampton. Her nineteen-month-old son, Joe, had died of a brain tumour just eight weeks after he was diagnosed. She read *Next to You* shortly before his death. 'Reading Caron's story at that time and seeing how she bravely enjoyed her precious time with her family inspired both myself and my husband, Steven, to cherish every day of Joe's last few weeks with us, despite his illness, and I must thank her for that.'

Yvonne's daughter was twenty-one when she died of colon cancer. Like me, she has two surviving sons. She wrote from South Africa, 'You have written this book as though it were me writing it, which I have so longed to do but do not know where to start. Thank you.'

Danielle kindly wrote the following letter to me:

My name is Danielle, and this May I will be running the Great Manchester Run in memory of my late cousin, Nik, who died sixteen months ago of a rare form of cancer. Recently I read Next to You *and, at the age of sixteen, was deeply touched by Caron's courage and could relate to so many things in it. I would like to raise money for the*

Caron Keating Foundation as well as Cancer Research UK. Nik was as brave and strong as Caron. I have run the race before. Nik was waiting for me at the end. This year she'll be running one side of me. Thank you for helping me through a difficult period in my life.

And still the letters continued to pour in. I have picked a few to include here; I could have picked a thousand. I think Caron would have been utterly overwhelmed by the response. I hope she is.

Dear Gloria,
    I just had to write and thank you for helping me through the last few weeks of my daughter's illness. My daughter, Hilary, known as Hil, was born with cystic fibrosis and was lucky enough to have a double lung transplant at the age of nineteen. This enabled her to live life to the full and attend a year at Canterbury University, which she loved. However, she suffered a lung rejection last May, and although we had the hope of another transplant, she died this January, surrounded by us, her brother, cousin and two of her closest friends. All over Christmas, while in Papworth Hospital with Hil, I read your book and it gave me so much comfort. You will never know how much it helped me to realise I was not the only one experiencing the sadness of my daughter's condition. Your book was the inspiration I needed to get through those difficult days.
    Ruth

Robin from London also wrote. Her sister, Pip, died of cancer and their father had died the previous year. Then she herself was diagnosed with pre-cancer in the breast and had a mastectomy and reconstruction. She had recently been given the all-clear.

Never felt upset for myself, just terribly sad that my sister had not been diagnosed early enough. It was touch and go whether Pip would be well enough to attend [our wedding], but she did come, which made our day. Her health deteriorated sharply afterwards and a lot of people felt she'd been so determined to be at the wedding that it was what had kept her going. [That was a fighting force I could recognise.]
   I drew a lot of strength from your book and from sharing in your feelings. It also helped me understand more about how it has been for my mother. I kept reading your book and thinking, What girls we have lost!
   Thank you for writing the book and for helping so many people in Caron's and your situation. We are not alone. And it's good to be reminded that ultimately it is love and families that matter.

Mrs Oldcraft from Lancashire wrote to me on 25 September 2006 to say:

I would like to thank you for the help you have given me through your book, as you were able to express feelings that I have, but am not able to put down on paper.
   Like you, I think of her every day and particularly on going to sleep and waking.

I was learning more and more about the human spirit, our endurance and capacity for love. I am almost ashamed to admit that in the beginning I had felt that my love for Caron was unique. No one shared the bond that we did. No one had felt loss like mine. As I've said, grief is selfish, it is all-consuming, and it is in many ways deranged. Having read so many testimonies to so many children lost, from stillborn to mid-fifties, I now knew that every one of these deaths caused the excruciating pain I had felt. In its own strange way, that too gave me strength. No two stories were the same – some were frighteningly similar; some were completely different – and yet a common bond united the letters and the people who wrote them to one another and me. Together we made a much stronger case for survival.

I just want to thank you for putting into words one of the most heartbreaking books – I just wish it were fiction. You made me laugh out loud and also made me sob so embarrassingly uncontrollably. Memories are wonderful things and remind us of the good times.
Michelle [whose dad died of liver cancer]

Another letter that came at that time read:

Dear Gloria,
I have just read your book and I must say it has helped me somewhat in coping.
My son was killed by his ex-girlfriend, who started a fire in his flat. She was given a seven-year sentence and served only three and a half years. He died leaving a boy and a girl, so much like their father in looks and ways it sometimes hurts.
Thanks for writing the book. You are such an inspiration to me. Different circumstances but the same end result unfortunately.
Eira

She is so right. I was only now beginning to fully understand that.

Liam got in touch with me by email. He lost his father to cancer when he was only twenty. This is what he wrote.

I put the book down and went outside to collect up all the autumn leaves, and I just totally broke down. Reading your feelings and thoughts was enough to reopen the past feelings that are still only hidden under the surface.

He was a strong man, Gloria, a police officer for almost twenty-five years, and I am sure that without his strength he would have lost the battle in six months. He never once moaned about what was happening to him and happily turned round and said he was a happy man and asked how many people could say that about their lives. His only sign of upset about the whole thing was how he couldn't be around to protect us from the pain we were going to suffer when he lost the fight. This was the only thing that brought him to tears. He said that he was going to end up causing us pain and there was nothing he could do about it. He was always there to protect us, but this was something he couldn't do. Many times he cried over this.

There must be no harder thing than to lose a child. How do you get over that? In short, you don't. Your life takes another road, a road that you didn't expect to take, and you learn to live with it.

I most certainly was on another road. Needless to say, I would rather have Caron here with me, her family together, the boys with their mother – I wish for that a million, billion times over, and nothing will ever come close to replacing what we have lost – but somehow the landscape of the path I was walking was changing. It's not that the pain eases, so much as alters. Where before I could see no reason to go on, now I did. Perhaps it is as simple as that. In sharing Caron's story, I had saved myself. Now it seemed not only was I not alone, I was actually one of the lucky ones.

I will never forget meeting a woman outside the Europa Hotel in Northern Ireland. She was bawling her eyes out. It was early on a Sunday morning and I was on my way to the airport. I went up to her and asked her if there was anything I could do. Through her tears she said, 'You will understand how I feel because you've lost a child, but at least you know what your child became. You know what your child sounded like, looked like. You were able to talk to your child. My baby died in my arms aged six weeks and I will never, ever know what my child would have looked like all grown-up, what she was like when she talked to me. I'll never hear her laugh.' That was a very defining moment for me. I had been so wrapped up grieving the loss of a daughter whom I'd been fortunate enough to have forty-one years with. Like the letters, it gave me a different perspective. That woman reminded me that I knew what it felt like to have Caron's arms round me, to hear her throaty laugh, to know the child she'd been and the woman she had become. I was lucky. I hadn't been feeling very lucky, but this woman gave me a real jolt. Suddenly letters from women whose children were stillborn had a much, much deeper resonance with me.

Katie from Devon wrote to tell me about her infant son, Lewis Neil:

My husband and I were devastated. Our world was crushed. We were told that we had created a pure spirit that would live eternally and, you know, that gave us a sort of comfort. We have had another little boy. He doesn't replace Lewis, but it brought us happiness beyond any words that describe fulfilment.

Their loss of Lewis was as significant to them as Caron's loss was to me, but at least I had memories. Liz from Milton Keynes wrote to me about her daughter, Violet. Her words summed it up: 'I wasn't lucky enough to have her as long as you had your Caron. Twenty-one IVF attempts, stillborn at eight months. I held her tiny hand for a short while, but I will hold her tiny heart for ever. I haven't slept since.'

My heart went out to them all. I now have a much deeper understanding of grief, and I realised more than ever that comparisons are futile. As that woman whose son was murdered by his ex-girlfriend said, 'Different circumstances but same end result unfortunately.' It has actually helped me to do my job as a presenter better, have more compassion as a person, to write this book, to sympathise more fully. In the beginning I got angry when people tried to compare the loss of their elderly mother to the loss of my daughter; now I know better.

I received a letter in October 2006 from a young woman whose father had died, aged sixty-eight, of bone cancer. Both she and her parents had read *Next to You*. I now treasure that letter, whereas earlier in my grief I may not have been able to understand it, may even have been slightly irritated by it. Now it gives me hope. Learning compassion is a lot of what 'grief-work' is all about.

I recall Dad saying how brave he thought your daughter was and how much he had always admired her and if he was in that position, he would handle it the same way –

*to let few people know. I remember distinctly thinking,
What an unusual thing to say, and immediately sensing a
feeling of great unease.*

*I know now that my father had already suspected he
had cancer. I spent quite a lot of time with him during the
last few weeks and he was able to discuss his dying with
me. For some reason, I feel that your daughter gave my
father the courage to accept his illness – I sense a powerful
connection. It made his last few weeks easier and he came
to accommodate his illness with great dignity and courage.
I just wanted to say thank you for that.*

*I have given many of my friends a copy of your book,
many of them mothers, and in every case it has awakened
something deep and profound within them. They were all
sincerely touched. I believe Caron's death was meant to
shock, and through her life and, more importantly,
through her death she has helped so many people awaken
to a deeper consciousness and to live life more fully and
with meaning.*

It makes me think of the exploratory journey Carol went
on in order to understand where Olivia had gone. Was
there a collective consciousness that could be awakened
by a single act? Could those no longer with us really
change the course of a future to which they did not
physically belong? I was beginning to think, see, hear and
read that perhaps they could. Among other great philo-
sophers, Carol studied Jung and I repeat just a snippet of
her huge and in-depth study because I think it goes some
way to calming the confusion of loss and in doing so help
the healing process.

The famous psychiatrist Carl Jung spent many years journeying through his own consciousness. From childhood, the Swiss scientist was aware of being two different personalities: one that lived in the outer world and went to school and was more or less the same as many other boys, and one that was more grown up, sceptical and withdrawn from the physical world. Somehow, he felt that his second personality, which he described as an inner personality, was more in touch with the beauty of nature and connected to the vast undiscovered universe and everything that lived within it.

Through many years of investigation Jung discovered that this inner 'subconscious' mind was connected to a 'higher' mind that he called 'the collective unconscious', which he described as a store of knowledge of all times and events past, present and future – like the hard drive. Jung felt that the collective unconscious was the reason people were able to become aware of similar information at the same time, even when far apart. Like the subconscious mind, it could communicate with the conscious mind through dreams and in other symbolic ways, including through meaningful synchronicities, coincidences. At death a person's spirit returns to its overall higher consciousness with memories of its recent life.

I have a friend whose ex-boyfriend suddenly repeatedly and vividly reappeared in dreams while she was on holiday with a new boyfriend, which, with reason, kind of freaked her out. On the way home from the airport, she thought she glimpsed him sitting on a bus. Then as she pushed the front door open after a week away, she saw on the mat a letter addressed to her in his hand. She opened the letter. Her ex-boyfriend's father, to whom she had always been close, had committed suicide. He was writing to tell her because he'd been trying unsuccessfully to track her down all week. She immediately walked back out of the house, boarded a train to Birmingham and made it to the funeral with an hour to spare.

Writing *Next to You* opened my eyes again to the world at large, the people in it, the suffering and the intense, acute love that we have the capacity to feel. It taught me to listen; it reminded me to read the signs. The letters that still come in continue to teach me something.

Sometimes when I see the news, or read the daily headlines, it is easy to be thrown right back into the confusion again and angrily ask yourself why any young person needs to die, ever. What lesson could possibly be worth learning that has cost someone else so unutterably dear? I only have to think of the recent story of Amanda Peak and her two little boys, Ben and Arron, and I find myself shaking my head at the pointlessness of it all. In June 2008 the two little boys were off on an adventure with their father to Silverstone when their car was hit by a drink-driver. The two boys were killed and their father seriously injured. In an instant one overindulged, arrogant man had ruined an entire family's life for ever. We all know drink-driving is evil. What do we learn from that? There seems to be so much suffering in the papers.

I remember going to the Courage of Britain Awards and seeing a table of seven children from one family all over-wrought with so much sadness I found it hard to watch. Their brother had saved one of his siblings from drowning, but had then himself drowned. We watched a reconstruction. It was awful. The children were distraught. He was so brave yet perished. Where is the sense in that? But the truth is, you can't let the anger take hold – it's like cancer and will consume you from the inside. As Caron did, you have to fight and keep fighting to prevent it from taking over, because otherwise the body count just keeps getting higher. None of the people we have lost would want that to happen. I would have liked to put many more letters in this chapter, so life-affirming was the response to *Next to You*, but that would be impossible. I have included just another three; they are simply meant to reflect the sort of letters I got and no way sum up anybody else's experience. They are in essence the same, but as you will read, so very, very different.

Sprotbrough, Doncaster

Dear Gloria,

I have just finished reading your inspirational book, a tribute to your wonderful daughter, and I feel compelled to write. My son, Christopher, died fourteen months ago, aged two years and four months, and since that day I have hardly had the will or the inclination to read a magazine or newspaper, let alone a book. Next to You caught my eye in the airport literally minutes before I boarded my plane. What made me purchase this one rather than replace it I could not say.

I was unable to put it down and I am sure I will open it again and again. At times I wept and cried constantly. Your daughter, Caron, was an amazing lady, courageous beyond measure, and the dignity and serenity she and all around her, not least yourself, portrayed was quite literally astounding.

My precious son died unexpectedly at a tender age, the cause of which remains a mystery. Just as your daughter did, he too touched the lives of all he met. His indomitable spirit was apparent from the day he was born (he was developmentally delayed) and amazed and mesmerised the health professionals he came into contact with. In his short life he introduced me to a love I had never experienced before.

I too have asked the question 'why?' Why us? Why Christopher? We will never know the reason, and I don't believe we are meant to, but I am beginning to realise the full extent of the phrases uttered a few times in those torturous weeks and months following my little boy's death: 'One day you will find a reason for the passing of Christopher' and 'Something good will come from all this sadness.' I see a strength in my daughter I never saw before.

Although I feel anguish, loss like I never imagined possible, I feel so privileged to have been given, in two years and four months, a lifetime of happy memories.

That is how your book read. It is inspirational, a celebration of Caron's life. Cancer sufferers everywhere will draw strength and tenacity to fight their battles in the knowledge that where there is life, there is hope. Mothers, myself included, who have endured such a monumental loss, who are still being flattened by that relentless steamroller, can and will empathise with your arduous, at times insurmountable grief. However hard the struggle out of bed in the morning is, though, with a purpose-driven life they will put on the mask and face the world. I thank you for your honesty, for sharing your private, innermost feelings and those of your family, and not least for the hope that through the mist of tears this book delivers.

Yours sincerely,
Rachel

Dear Gloria,

I write to you hoping that you have some ideas that may help me in setting up a fund in my daughter's name for counselling at Mind in Rushden.

My daughter, Anna, took her own life by hanging herself on 13 August 2006, aged thirty years, only yards from her home, here in Rushden. Anna had been bullied at school when she was fourteen and suffered from depression since that time. She first took an overdose at the age of sixteen. It was said then that she had extremely low self-esteem.

After leaving school at the age of sixteen, she had several jobs, including that of a nursery nurse both here and abroad. She then put herself through university as a mature student and obtained a degree in American studies. She was at that time living close to her university in Nottingham and, unknown to me, was still suffering from depression.

Anna returned home two years prior to her death and again found a job. She then made two suicide attempts in the form of overdoses within weeks of each other. After the second she spent two days in hospital. When she returned home, she was still visiting her GP and was given several different antidepressants. Anna was losing weight and feeling extremely agitated and unable to sleep. She was given sleeping tablets, but the situation remained unchanged. I remember her saying, 'What's wrong with me, Mum? Remember I used to be able to sleep for England?'

Despite her two suicide attempts, her own request on 4 August 2006 to be in hospital and a meeting with the consultant psychiatrist on 11 August, Anna was still considered 'low risk'. At the inquest the psychiatrist said, 'I was surprised she took her own life two days later. I thought Anna may take a further overdose, but not in the next few days.' Diagnosis on 11 August: 'depression and anxiety.'

Anna was a talented and beautiful girl. She had played the violin since the age of eight, had a good sense of humour, was artistic, loved animals and was a kind, caring human being.

Anna did not sit back and feel sorry for herself, but looked into every kind of therapy that might help her. She was my Peter Pan who never quite found her niche in life.

I could write for ever, but the only positive thing I can do is to try to raise funds for counselling at Mind Rushden. Anyone can have a mental illness in their lives and not everyone has the means or ability to travel to another town or even London to get help. Mind Rushden fills this gap. I understand that mental health is the lowest-funded area of the NHS, and the way things are going, I don't think this will change in the near future.

I am sorry about the bad handwriting and gabbling on like this, but I feel so strongly about this and no one seems to be doing anything.

Hoping that if you get to read this letter, you will be able to help me. There are so many other Annas out there.

Yours sincerely,
Patricia

She is so right: there are many Annas out there, male and female.

I got one letter from a woman whose physicist son had hanged himself in the family garage. Estranged from his father, confused about his girlfriend's religion and clearly depressed, he was found by his mother, who, when she first saw him, thought he was simply standing there before she realised his feet were off the ground. He had left all his things orderly for his mother, including a Bible open at Exodus: 'Do not bow down to their gods or worship them, and do not adopt their religious practices.' I wept for both of these good mothers, knowing that suicide brings an extra level of guilt and social stigma that cancer does not. I felt humbled. I know that most bereaved people see the time they received news of their loved one's passing repeat on a filmic loop over and over in their minds. My recurring nightmare is always of Caron's death and the lowering of the coffin lid. I can only begin to imagine what theirs is. I sincerely hope they have found support and guidance through their dark, dark days and endless nights.

Dear Gloria and family,

For an articulate person, I have no idea how to start this letter. I've been sitting staring at a blank page for some time, but I feel very strongly compelled to put words on paper and write to you.

On the morning of my twenty-first birthday I lost my mum to breast cancer after a nine-year battle. She was forty-five. That was ten years ago this July. I still cry, smile, talk to her on a daily basis and truly feel she is close to me.

Since your book was published, I've picked it up off a Tesco/WHSmith shelf many times, willing myself to be strong enough to read your words. But then I'd put it back down again, knowing that it would be a hard story to read.

This July my mother-in-law bought your book for me as a birthday present. I wasn't very happy when I received the wrapped present, as I don't do birthdays any more. Any cards I do receive go in the bin, and presents get left for another day when I can get my head around them. For some reason, I opened this gift on my actual birthday, the tenth anniversary of my mum's death. I didn't know whether to laugh or cry when I saw what it was – mixed feelings – but I couldn't read it straight away. I felt that I needed to leave it for a time I could completely concentrate on it and read it from cover to cover.

I finished your wonderful book late last night, in floods of tears for you and your family's loss and for my mum too. My husband normally complains that I'm being ignorant when my head is buried in a book, but he has not made one negative comment in the last few days. I got puzzled looks for laughing in parts and a hug for crying through others.

I just wanted to say thank you for publishing Caron's story for people to read. It is truly inspirational.

Thank you with warmest heartfelt wishes,
Michelle

> *Death is nothing at all.*
> *I have only slipped into the next room.*
> *I am I and you are you.*
> *Whatever we were to each other*
> *That we still are.*
> *Call me by my old familiar name.*
> *Speak to me in the easy way you always used.*
> *Put no difference in your tone.*
> *Wear no forced air of solemnity or sorrow.*
> *Laugh as we always laughed*

At the little jokes we enjoyed together.
Play, smile, think of me, pray for me.
Let my name be ever the household
Word that it ever was.
Why should I be out of mind
Because I am out of sight?
I am waiting for you for an interval
Somewhere very near
Just around the corner.
All is well.
Nothing is past; nothing is lost.

'All Is Well',
Canon Henry Scott-Holland

14

Time Does Not Heal

Say to yourself, 'This time will pass;
The sun will shine again.'
You've known the joy
That love can bring
And now you know the pain.
The loss of one so dear to you
Is very hard to bear,
So say to yourself each day you rise,
'The sun will shine again.'

'Time Does Not Heal',
sent by Libby Parr

London, May 2005

Dear Gloria,

I am not writing to you because you are a celebrity, but because you are a mother who has lost her only daughter. I'm not going to offer you platitudes, Gloria, because it's awful what you are going through. No one knows unless they have been there, and believe me, I have. Twenty years ago my beautiful only daughter, Jenny, of twenty-one years, went out with her friends at 7 p.m. and never came home again. She was killed by a drunken driver who left her dead on the street. I tried so hard to die

*simply from grief. Her loss was so terrible to bear I
couldn't cope with the pain in my heart.*

*Gloria, try to take each day as it comes. You will never
get over this terrible time, but you will, I promise, come to
terms with it. And you have your lovely grandchildren to
watch growing up. I have no grandchildren. Jenny wasn't
married. I visit Jenny in the cemetery each week and I tell
her all my thoughts and all the gossip; sometimes it helps.*

Mary

Time passed, as it does. The world went on turning. Days bled
into nights, weeks into months, and months into years. Years!
How is it possible that Caron has not been with us for years? It so
often feels as though it happened mere seconds ago. Every new
year posed a higher hurdle than the year before. Every birthday,
every celebration, every season to be happy was yet another
experience my daughter had missed. Charlie was a teenager
now. Where was she? Why wasn't she here to see him develop
into the wonderful young man he was becoming? It was a very
rude awakening for me to discover that, after all the soul-
searching and weeping and striving to rejoin the living, my sense
of loss was actually getting worse. As one letter expressed
strongly, 'People do try and tell you that time is a great healer,
but it's not. People do mean well, but truly don't understand.'

The woman who wrote that letter was right: time was not the
healer we are so glibly told it is. Not in this case. Every minute
since the time of death is another minute without her, another
minute missed, another minute robbed. In recent times I have
thought so much about what Caron is missing and all that she
is absent from. Pat in Essex wrote, 'I don't think you can ever
get over losing your child. All I keep asking is, "Why?" Every
day that goes by I miss her more and more.' Another lady,

Joyce, wrote after her daughter, aged thirty, died from breast cancer, 'No, time is *not* a healer. We just miss her more as time passes, but we can now discuss all the treasured memories we have of her.' That is all I want to do, but I can sometimes tell that there are those who feel that I'm 'going on about it'. If I don't, though, then she is absolutely committed to the past, and I can't let that happen. I understand that we all have different ways of mourning, but I hope this book goes some way to explaining why I will for ever need to talk about Caron, to place her in the now, with us, to let her accompany me on this journey, because without her I feel too bereft and start sliding backwards into the pit. If people don't realise that we need to talk about our deceased loved ones as much as we talk about those who are still living, then maybe they haven't taken the time to understand what it is that mourners go through on a daily basis to outlive their grief.

In her diary Carol Chase wrote:

Olivia wants you to think about her, but when you recall her earthly life and her time with you all, you feel a dagger through your heart, such sadness. She doesn't want this because she feels your sadness with you. Olivia wants you to think of her as she is now, with a smile on her face, still laughing at you – 'You're so dappy, Mother', 'Oh my God, what's Mum got on!' She has her arms round each of you; she is bound to each of you like a limpet to a rock, souls entwined; she shares each of your days. So when you think of her, think of her in this way, as she is now: such a beautiful soul who carries all of you with her as she continues to achieve.

Nobody would ever want to be thought of in the past, only in the 'now'. You will come through. You will see all

the pieces fall into their appointed places. Your
responsibility is to live for the now, the moment.

Brave words and a sentiment I agree with, but it is so hard.

As I touched on earlier in this book, my sorrow has in some
ways turned on its head. Early grief is about what *we* are
missing – we're sad for ourselves and what we have lost, and
that is where it is selfish, but we can't help it because we love
that person so much and we are missing them so much.
Sometimes you can rationalise elements of their death, take
comfort if the person you loved was in terrible pain or suffered
no pain at the end – we all clutch at straws – but mostly you are
just consumed with sadness. Now that I have made room for
the terrible gaping hole Caron left behind, now that I can put
the pain aside to enjoy a moment, a birthday, an outing, a
sunset, my sadness is no longer for myself but for Caron and
everything cancer robbed *her* of. This kind of sorrow leaves a
different taste in my mouth. Although I've always tried not to
go down the angry route, now I feel anger at all the things she's
missing out on. Of course I am still grieving for our pain and
loss, but on top of that there is the added weight of grieving for
what Caron has lost too. The permanent dull ache is something I am not always aware of any more, but when it hits, it
hits hard. Of course, mostly it is to do with the boys; not
mostly, everything; it is everything to do with the boys.

In her journal Caron wrote:

I find it really hard to listen to the stories of women who
have died from cancer and left children behind. My heart
breaks for those children – most of the time if I let it, it
breaks for my own. I don't want them to be motherless
boys – it's not the life I had planned for them. Who will

they run to with their hurts and worries? Who will tend to them, understand them, put treats in their lunchboxes, complete family dinner on a Sunday night, see their faces light up after school, hang the dream-catchers, share nightmares, tell them the chances of burglars coming are very remote?

Do we ever get the life we planned? I tell myself, There's a greater plan. There's a greater power and energy that I believe will look after all of us. I can't bear the thought of not being there with them and feel sadness for them. I look at Princes William and Harry and they seem to be coping, seem to be well-balanced young men.

I know lots of people who shine without their mother or acquire a kindly stepmother to love them dearly. It's just that it's not how I'd seen things working out. I intend to be there for their eighteenth and twenty-first birthdays, their first drinking sprees, first heartbreaks, their engagements. 'I just want to be with the boys,' I repeat to Russ for the umpteenth time. 'You are,' he replies. 'Get on with it.' And it breaks any emotional dramatic inner challenge and reminds me that for all of us, we only have this moment. At any time our families can be swept away. There is only now – ever; imagining the rest is ultimately a waste of time.

Not wanting the boys to grow up without their mum was one of the only references Caron ever made to death. Well, the harsh truth is that they are growing up without her. Even if she can see them, even if she is nearby, they can't see her and she isn't hands-on. She isn't in the audience watching Gabriel holding the stage as Elvis, his eyes flashing as hers used to do, filling the auditorium; she isn't here to hear Charlie's songs; they can't hear her clapping at their performances, laughing with that deep-throated laugh that I miss so very much. Even if she can see all of that, and I pray she can, they can't see her, and neither can I.

We are so proud of the boys, and she would have been too. They are settled now and developing into fascinating, funny, charismatic people, which is wonderful, but I really grieve for the fact that Caron isn't here to see it. When the boys and I were shopping at Spitalfields Market one weekend with Stephen and Michael, they were really taken by Banksy's cartoons and it made me think of my daughter. Nothing unusual about that, but Caron was so particularly visual, so creative herself, and it was a delight to see them take up that baton. Is it by osmosis? Or is it as that saying goes, 'Give me a child for seven years and I will give you back an adult'? Or does Caron still find a way to whisper direction into her sons' souls and lead them to this world of creativity and colour? The answers to those questions almost wholly depend on what sort of day I am having. On that lovely day in Spitalfields Market I could actually hear the conversations Caron and the boys would have been having if she'd been there. Charlie adored the second-hand shops and it was like watching history repeat itself. It wasn't that long ago that Caron was rummaging through the racks at Oxfam in Bristol in her constant pursuit of the weird, wacky and wonderful. I don't let it get me down when I am with them – I treasure our time too much for that – but later, when they have gone home, I find myself thinking about all the other conversations Caron cannot have with her sons. I don't know why I am becoming more conscious of that of late. Maybe with time you do defrost, and while that is an improvement, it is also a hazard, because once the blood begins to run though your veins again, you start to feel a whole lot more. Maybe not more, but differently.

When your parents die, devastating though it is, time does heal. It was a year and a half before I could talk about my mother without weeping, but time dealt with that. It was the right order of life, even though it was so deep at the time. So far, four years down the line, time has not healed the loss of Caron. The list of things she is missing gets longer: the pride of Charlie being a good sportsman, the pride of seeing Gabriel in his shows, acting, the pride of seeing Gabriel chosen to be form captain, the pride of seeing Charlie play his guitar and sing. And as for that hair gel! I can just see her fighting over the hair products with Charlie. Every event, every outing, everything; Caron is not there, so time can't heal that, because no one can turn back the hands of time.

Russ is absolutely brilliant with the boys, as he always has been, and he often says, 'Wouldn't Caron have adored seeing this? Wouldn't Caron have been proud?' I like it that we can still have those conversations. Russ has remained very close to Paul, and his family go to Cornwall at least three times a year, and he and Russ will often share memories of Caron at Polzeath on the beach, where they all used to picnic. I know not all widowers are so generous.

One young woman I know lost her mother in a terrible accident when she was Charlie's age. Shortly afterwards her father remarried and her mother's name was barely mentioned again. When she asked her father about this years later, he looked at her quizzically and said, 'I thought you'd put it behind you.' She told him she would much rather hear stories about her mother, even if it did make them sad for a while and even if her stepmother didn't like it. A day later they were sitting together in a beautiful spot and she tested the water by saying, 'Mummy would have loved this.' Her father looked straight ahead and after a while said, 'It was a long time ago for me now,' and said nothing more. Her grief has been stunted over the years. By being robbed of those conversations, she hasn't been able to weave her mother's death into her adult life. Fortunately this is not the case with the boys. Russ has been very careful to share the loss with both his sons and often refers to their mum. An enormous part of recovering from a massive bereavement is purely in accepting death. Looks easy on the page, though it is bloody hard in real life. I don't know if I will ever really be able to accept it; I continue to be hit by enormous surges of disbelief. Is it true? Has she really gone for ever? Sometimes it is disturbing to go to the graveside, each of us feels it, but it is a way of bringing up a subject that all too often people believe is better left alone. By going to the grave, the boys know that nobody is forgetting anybody, and if and when they are ready to talk about it or ask questions, they can.

What I wasn't prepared for was the loss of the 'unit'. Once, I had a daughter who was always on the phone, every day, sometimes twice. I never had to ask where she and her children were or what they were doing. They were there all the time and she would update me on the minutiae of their lives. Until Caron went to Australia, she; Russ, Charlie and Gabriel were constantly on my doorstep. Since going to Australia, I was on theirs. They were there – a unit, my family, an extension of myself. The truth of the matter is, I don't have access to that complete unit any more. I know I'm lucky, because Russ and his new wife Sally make sure I see lots of the boys, but no longer can I see Charlie and Gabriel with their mum and dad. Thankfully I see Charlie and Gabriel regularly – after school, weekends and school holidays. Those are the days I most look forward to, the days I most enjoy. All those years of having the entire family together, the fun of having several generations amassed round one table, all those performances in the conservatory, all the laughs that crossed the ages, even in Australia, are now more rare and someone is always missing.

From the moment Russ and Caron got together, I knew that he would always look after my girl. Over the years Russ and I have shared a great deal, never more so than when Caron was ill, and I am appreciative that we are still as close as we are. I am very aware that I'm not even his mother-in-law any more; I am his former mother-in-law. Most men can't cope with one and the poor man has two now that he has remarried. But I am his sons' grandmother and he has never forgotten that, as some do, and for that I am eternally grateful.

It is so hard to know what to do for children who have suffered the loss of a parent. I believe children have all the feelings of loss that we have but not the vocabulary to express themselves. This is hardly surprising. I am a consummate talker and I still can't find the words to convey what it is I feel inside. Gabriel was only seven when Caron died and I naturally want him to remember his mum. I notice these days he is talking about Caron more and more, not in a sad way, but in an inquisitive way, which soothes me a little because again it makes me feel that his mum is not being left behind. Over the last four years whenever we went to Hever he would always say, 'Oh, no, there Nana goes again, crying.' He'd either walk away or try and smooth it all over with a joke. Now he talks about her and of course I stop crying sooner.

On Mother's Day this year Russ sent me flowers; it was a lovely thought. He also sent flowers for Caron and handwritten cards from the boys for me to take to the grave. He always does something on those big days and always involves the boys. It would be all too easy to run from those difficult dates, but he never has. And I think it's also good for Charlie and Gabriel, as a foundation of understanding and respect in their future years. This year Paul and I went to the graveside to leave the cards and the flowers and pay our respects. I was doing pretty well until I saw the birthday cards from October that were still there, propped up against the stone, wrapped in cellophane. I have to be honest, it is seeing their little handwritten notes that breaks my heart all over again. 'Dear Mummy, I hope you have a really lovely birthday. I hope you have a nice time', 'Dear Mummy, I miss you so much. I wish you a very happy Mother's Day.' They always write to her in the present, as if she's alive but living in another space, which to them she is, and I suppose to me she is, but when I see it written down like that, the rational, spiritual place that I have crawled to caves and I go tumbling back to the bottom of the pit. They also tie balloons to the headstone, leave lovely pictures and bring cakes that they have made at school. It's just so extremely sad. My head keeps screaming, 'Caron should be here to enjoy birthdays and Mother's Day with her sons.'

It's interesting to see how we all live out our promises to Caron, spoken or otherwise. Paul in particular lives out his. Australia is a long way away, so when Charlie and Gabriel lived there, the cousins had few chances to be together, but now they are round the corner and Paul makes a point of calling in to see them all a lot. He does his utmost to make sure the boys see each other as much as possible – school allowing. Any time Charlie and Gabriel come to Sevenoaks they always ask whether Jake and Beau will be there and vice versa. Michael, on the other hand, lives further away, does not have children and therefore doesn't have the constant access he once did. Having said that, he always takes time out from work to join us when the boys come to stay in Sevenoaks or when we're off on another escapade, for instance recently in France, Michael relished taking them rollerblading along miles of espalanade or on an activity adventure in the mountains. Time plays both sides of the coin, because though it marches inexorably on without Caron, the boys grow up and one day soon they won't be boys any more. When that time comes, no doubt an uncle with a nice pad in central London will come in very useful! Michael visited Caron in Australia a lot. Though he looks very much like his father, he shares his sister's wicked sense of humour and ability to light up a room. That was why they were so particularly close and why he misses her so much. It is a personality trait he now shares with two others, as both Charlie and Gabriel have that spirit in abundance and I can imagine a fair few laughs in the years ahead. We took Gabriel to Paris and Disneyland for his eleventh birthday this year and he said to Michael, 'The best birthday present you could give me would be to come to Paris with us.' Michael did all the stomach-churning rides with the boys; Stephen and I stuck to the more sedate and safer 'It's a Small, Small World' and 'Peter Pan'. It was huge fun and a special time and you realise that even if you don't live in one another's pockets, there will for ever be a very strong, deep-seated connection that time has not eroded, as perhaps we feared, but made stronger.

Over and over I am made aware of what a double-edged sword bereavement is. She is gone, but she is not gone. In memory of who we have lost we must appreciate the life that we have, but life feels so empty without the person we have lost. You have to be brave and strong when you are weak and afraid. Joy and sorrow run concurrently. If daylight signals happiness and the night-time is despair, then life for a long-term mourner is for ever dusk. There are of course flashes of brilliant sunshine, like Disneyland Paris and Alldays Field, and the occasional heavy storm, like the anniversary of Caron's death. Indeed it is not unusual for one to follow rapidly on from the other. A kind and attentive friend will know that every celebration is bitter-sweet and will find a way to acknowledge that.

In the immediate aftermath of a death the world is a loud, fast, confusing place. In time, however, I believe you get used to it. For me, it is no longer an alien place, but I am still shocked when people shy away from mentioning the person who is so obviously missing. I know that people think by 'bringing it up' I might get upset. Well, the more time passes, the more upset I get when people fail to acknowledge Caron's passing. I really want to stress this for those who are in the very difficult place of dealing with people who have lost someone. I know how hard it can be, how hard *we* can be, but if you do not grant a bereaved person the chance to discuss the person they have lost, they will eventually withdraw the hand of friendship or, worse, you will incur their resentment. Time does not help in this matter. Time only makes us want to talk about them more, our memories and what they are missing. What time does do, is let us have the conversation without being so convulsed by tears that speaking is not possible. Time does give us that. We can talk about and listen to memories and they are music to our ears. Most people have only the best intentions, I know, and they truly think that not mentioning that person is saving someone from additional heartache, but our hearts are aching. Talking about the person after a while actually brings a little relief. Time does not heal, but it does let us appreciate the memories.

27 May 2006

Oh, painful, painful days. Does anyone who knows me truly know and understand the searing pain I feel inside at your loss, Olivia? A part of me is ripped away for ever. I struggle through these days trying to seem bright and normal, not wanting to drag anyone else down – just dying inside, aching for you. So long, two years since I've seen you. Daddy and I support each other. He's distraught too.

Whatever would we do without each other's support?
Daddy is the only person who talks to me in depth about
you and our loss of you. How I would hate to ever lose
that link. Who would talk to me then about you?

Clothes and personal belongings are so hard to cope with. I
was given the job of sorting Caron's belongings out at Menlo.
Russ was away on business for a week. Stephen and I looked
after the children and systematically went through all of
Caron's things. I spent hours and hours in the roof space. I
obviously took some precious things with me. Everything else
that was left was boxed up and taken to a barn belonging to
their friends Bill and Clare to store. Those huge clothes-
hanging boxes sat over there for many, many months, and
then one day I felt strong enough to go across to the barn. I
stayed there all day and distributing Caron's clothes sort of
dictated itself. There was Janet Ellis and her daughter, Martha,
Karen Fowler and her daughter, Francesca, Mallory Fletcher
and her daughter, Vita, and Clare herself. As the clothes came
out, it became pretty apparent what would go to whom. I
would hold up a garment and think, That would look terrific
on Karen, and I would put it in the corresponding pile. I have
subsequently seen Karen wearing one of Caron's suede coats
and I like it. It gives it dignity. It gives it life. Karen says it
makes her feel so close to my Caron. But my God, it is hard.
    As always, Carol Chase can empathise:

23 April 2005
Had a horrible week, sweetheart. I feel very jittery and
emotional. I plucked up the courage to sort through all
your things from school, all still in suitcases and bags from
when you died last year. All the lovely clothes you always

wore, pretty tops – I could see you in them, and when I
smelt them, *everything* smelt of you. So powerful, so
painful. I sobbed and sobbed. Oh, how I want you back.
How completely fractured my world feels.

None of the family ever went back to Taylors, Caron and Russ's
beautiful house in the rainforest near Byron Bay. Thankfully
our great friend Judith still lives in Australia. She was like an
angel who came and helped to look after Caron when she was
alive and subsequently after she died. She was a former girlfriend of Paul's and came up from Sydney and helped us all.
She's been doing it for three years. I admire and am utterly
grateful for her dedication. She is a wonderful woman. She
treasured the things that the family left behind and looked after
them. I would have really fretted if she hadn't been there to care
for Caron's things like that. Russ was eager to draw a line under
their time in Australia and at that stage didn't want much from
the house. Judith organised for the technology equipment like
computers to go to Russ's friend Mark, made sure all the
paintings were wrapped up and safely taken to their friend
Lindsay's house and ensured all the clothes were shared out
among Caron's lovely girlfriends there. Judith kindly sent me
back the Buddha that I bought Caron for her fortieth birthday,
the paintings that we had bought Caron and Russ over the years
and the musical instruments, which in time she thought the boys
would appreciate. She also posted all the love letters and cards
that Caron and Russ had written to one another over their years
together, which arrived with a red ribbon tied round them. I've
kept them with me and will put them in Charlie and Gabriel's
memory box. They are beautiful, wonderful proof of how much
their mother and father loved each other, through the tough
times too. Caron was always very flattering about Russ and how

brilliantly he'd coped and how thankful she was to him for that care. Her voice is very strong, even on the page, and I think the boys will one day treasure them hugely. Last Christmas in the local church hall they had a sale of all the rest of the smaller things, the toys and books, but the furniture stayed with the house for the next chapter.

I look back over the time we've had without Caron in our lives and I can see with hard-earned hindsight and perspective resulting from a treacherous climb that the first year is the hardest. Your loss remains as deep as ever, but the time you spend at the bottom of the pit lessens. It is very, very hard, but if you can get the key to celebrating the life your loved one had and the memories they left behind, rather than dwelling on what might have been, you have a better chance of survival. It is really the only constructive thing that time gives you. Time is not an elixir; the healing is entirely down to you. And it takes time and energy. To be honest, it is virtually impossible to find the positive in the first year – every single significant day was in essence crucifying – but since then we have found a system that enables us to manage those dates better. On the third anniversary, 13 April 2007, Michael, the boys, Stephen and I went to France. We took them to La Colonne d'Or, Caron's favourite restaurant in the village of St Paul de Vence, high up in the mountains above Nice. The house we bought there as a family is now full of Caron's favourite pieces of furniture and paintings. I feel very close to her there. Hanging on the wall in the sitting room is a stunning portrait of Caron and sometimes it feels like she's the custodian of the house and welcomes us all home whenever we go there. I can see her sitting in the village square, La Place, watching the old Frenchmen rolling boules.

I've had many letters from people who have built a refuge in a new place, but this one, from Pat in Merseyside, stood out.

Her family bought a house in Spain after her twenty-three-year-old son, Karl, died from an incurable illness.

This house here is my refuge. Its beauty, its peacefulness and its smells remind me that the world is still a lovely place even though for me the most beautiful thing in it has been taken from it. I truly know your pain, and from one mother to another who has lost a child I send you a hug.

Before dinner on that third anniversary we went up and sat on the steps of the medieval church, lit candles and said a prayer. The church was closed, but in a way the less formal setting made it easier on the boys. The restaurant doesn't normally have candles, but we asked if we could light our remembrance candles at the table, which they let us do, and it was dignified rather than morose. I never want to labour the point when commemorating Caron's death with the boys, but it's nice just to say, 'This is Mummy's anniversary and we're going to light some gorgeous candles for her,' and leave it at that. It is not a closed subject, but they aren't obligated to talk about it either. I suspect that though the boys are doing really well now, missing a mother may become more apparent as they grow up. No matter how many years pass, that single, enormous fact is never going to go away.

On 26 July 2007 I received a letter from a young woman in Sussex called Louise. Her father had sadly died, leaving her heartbroken, partly because she'd also lost her mother, years before.

My mother died when I was twenty-seven and never got to see her beautiful, wonderful grandchildren. The pain my mother went through will never leave me – I just choose to put it away in that safety box in my head that I keep closed, not permanently closed, but I avoid letting it open in the early hours of the morning. I feel envious when I see mothers with their daughters out shopping. There is no one to tell when my children do something amazing, achieve something we are proud of . . . I have many friends, but they have their own lives and children.

I don't think the boys will remember much of Caron's illness because she was so positive, but there were things she couldn't do. She would tell them, 'I may not be able to ride bikes or rollerskate, but I can read to you and paint with you and talk to you. There are other things I can do.' Sadly, though, that wasn't always enough and the boys would ask, 'When your back is better, can you come on the trampoline?' Michael remembers Russ tweaking his back one day on the beach. Charlie went white as a sheet: a bad back has terrible connotations for the boys. They are far removed from that place of fear, but I doubt it ever completely goes away. Losing your mother at whatever age has a very profound effect on us all. The lucky ones have their mothers around to a ripe old age, but even then losing them is so hard. Having your mother taken away prematurely is something I, with everything I have been through, still cannot comprehend and I thank all the people who've written to me explaining the multitude of ways they take their mothers' spirits with them as they move on in life.

We make birthdays much more celebratory now, for all our sakes. I think we've got them more under control and ensure we always do something fun. It's not easy, but it is important. I want to celebrate Caron's life in order to carry her memory forward – not a memory of death and illness, but the memory of the girl she was and the woman she became.

Linda from Cheshire wrote to tell me about her sister, who

died of cancer, and about how she'd then 'lost' her brother-in-law when he had emigrated to Australia with their two children because he couldn't see the point in staying in the UK. She suffered a triple loss.

The road ahead is long and painful and sometimes seems impossible to travel, but we owe it to those wonderful mothers to keep their light shining and their memory strong in their children's hearts and minds. I will think of Gloria each day over the coming months and years, and hope my Kate will walk beside us as Caron walks with her.

The hardest year was of course 2004. I was not in the place I am now and could not feel anything but the loss of my girl. It was, however, a major achievement launching the foundation in her name. Raising £90,000 on that first night was exceptional and really gave me something to hang on to. In 2005 it was the publication of *Next to You* that was an amazing way of celebrating Caron's life. More than anything I was so proud of *her*. I treasure every letter that comes in starting with the words 'I've just finished reading *Next to You* and felt compelled to write . . .' Each person has taken something from Caron and been altered in some way for the better. No grieving mother could ask for more.

In 2006 we went to France and sat outside, under the stars, and raised a glass to her, and in 2007 we did the Strictly Tea Dancing event, which was fantastic because the boys were a real part of that and were the living embodiment of Caron, which as my friend Jenny Parnell says, now brings 'much more solace than pain'. Time does not heal, and that is empowering in some respects. Time will not make this go away. Time will not bring them back. All time can offer is memories. The future is up to you.

15

Hope, Faith and Quantum Physics

When you get to the end of all the light you know and it's time to step into the darkness of the unknown, faith is knowing that one of two things shall happen: either you will be given something solid to stand on or you will be taught how to fly.

Edward Teller

Perhaps if we could see
The splendour of the land
To which our loved are
Called from you and me,
We'd understand.

Perhaps if we could hear
The welcome they receive
From old familiar voices –
All so dear –
We would not grieve.

Perhaps if we could know
The reason why they went,
We'd smile and wipe away
The tears that flow.
We'd wait content.

extract from 'Miss Me But Let Me Go', Anon,
sent by Dr Mike Cornelius
from the children's charity Variety Club

Letters of hope started arriving shortly after Caron died. I read them, acknowledged them, but couldn't really take them on board. They provided a spark of hope, but it was extinguished almost as quickly. This is very much a solitary journey and one you take at your own pace. Julie Nicholson, the vicar whose beautiful daughter was killed in the 7 July London bombings, was told many times, 'At least you have your faith.' It puzzled her. What did faith have to do with it when she was so full of sorrow there was no room for anything else? It was reported that she gave up the Church because she couldn't preach forgiveness, but actually she stopped being a parish priest because she didn't have the resources within herself to do the job. She never gave up the Church or stopped believing in 'this mystery we call God'. Faith, hope and light are all lost to you in this vast universe of sadness, but that doesn't mean they aren't there. For a while you can't reach them because you don't know where to look. If you are lucky, you may accidentally stumble across something that lights the way, a chance encounter with a medium, a beautiful piece of writing; for me, it was the poem 'Sometimes' by Frank Brown, which I included in the Prologue, but more often than not the positive thing you need in order to counterbalance the negative that has befallen you has to be actively sought out by you.

One thing that has given me great comfort is that just six months after my son Laurence (Loz) died, for some unknown reason I went to a hotel where there was a clairvoyant day. This was something that I had had no interest in before and I have no idea to this day why I should suddenly decide to do such a thing. However, I did decide to do a reading. I sat down and said nothing but my name. This lady was very accurate in everything she said to me about myself, even going back as far as my birth. Still I said nothing. She then went on to say she would see if there was anybody in the spirit world. She held my hand and said that she had a young man. 'All the weight has gone from him,' she said. 'He is talking about his ankle.' I fell off the chair. His melanoma had started in a birthmark on his ankle! 'And Dolly,' she said. 'He is talking about his Dolly.' Loz had a Dolomite Sprint car that he and his dad had spent a year restoring. He always referred to it as 'his Dolly'. I was then told I was not to worry about him – he was only ever a step away. Also, he was happy as he had gone home. Those words sent a shiver down my spine, as the night he died he had hugged me and said, 'I am so happy I am going home.'

I am now a firm believer that mums like you and I are very privileged to have had such special children and that they were only lent to us to love and cherish until they were needed for a much better place.

Keep your chin up, and please rest assured there are those who understand your pain.

Pam

Do I believe in life after death? The spirit world? Yes, I do. I don't know what it is exactly, where it is, how it looks, but I have a fundamental faith, for which I am intensely grateful. I have had it all my life. I prayed every day when Caron was ill, prayed all the time. You could say my prayers weren't answered in the ways I was looking for because of course I wanted her to live. Instead of rejecting my faith, getting angry with God for not choosing to listen to my desperate pleas, I have chosen to hold on to it. Sometimes this is very hard, other times it is less so, but I have to believe I will see Caron again. I have two sons, a husband and grandchildren who need me to function much better than I was able to after Caron died. That is why I need to believe. That's why I need spirituality in my life. Trusting that I will see Caron again is the only way I can muster the enormous amount of energy I require to enjoy life.

I, like every bereaved parent I know, asked the question 'Why?' I will never forget my friend of many years from Belfast, Jimmy Galway, the flute player, taking my hand and saying, 'Maybe you just don't know the reason yet.' Let me be clear, I still do not see a 'reason' for Caron dying, but it was a concept I could take on board. It was something concrete to work with, an anchor round which my tormented thoughts could swirl. He enabled me to turn the question on its head. Instead of dragging myself down with asking, 'Why did this happen to us?' I could focus my thoughts on 'This has happened to us. Now what am I going to do about it?' Turning that question round has had a huge impact on how I cope with Caron's death. It led me to the foundation, it led me to writing *Next to You*, and the book led me back to Caron. Working on the book, I got to rediscover my daughter and she has been my greatest teacher. Time and time again it is her voice, her words that get me through the difficult days. What gives me faith and hope? Caron.

I believe many of us are led by those who have passed away. Olivia had already bought a card for her father's birthday. He found it all ready but unsigned in her bedside-table drawer after she died. Usually she gave him humorous cards, but this one was different. On the front was a picture of a man and a little girl walking away. It read, 'Parents hold their children's hands for a while but their hearts for ever.' It must have been an extraordinary gift to find a card like that after Olivia had been so suddenly taken from them. As her father says, a strange but wonderful choice of card. It provides just enough light to help find a way out of the dark and allows him to hold on to his belief that she is not completely gone.

Illness is traumatic enough, but I acknowledge that if my daughter had been blown up, or run over, or stabbed, maybe I wouldn't be able to turn that question round. We all have our own journey. Maybe I would have been totally consumed with anger, but personally I didn't have anyone to blame for Caron's cancer. Of course we all desperately wish that hideous disease didn't exist, but there is little to be gained from being angry at cancer and I couldn't be angry at the patient. It's not as if Caron neglected herself and left herself wide open for something. It's not like she was taking heavy drugs or abusing her body. I'm angry she's not with me, yes. All I can think is that the cancer was ignited by a clash of hormones, a weakened immune system and an anguished mental state following the death of her beloved father. Of course that's only my theory about what led to her breast cancer; I certainly have no proof. No one seems to know yet what causes cancer. What I do know is that because of her illness, Caron went on an exhaustive spiritual quest to answer her own questions. It was a journey of discovery, self-discovery and an exploration of faith and fear. Caron arrived at the simplest conclusion – what mattered most was *love*. She knew she had been truly loved and had known what it was to love. Cancer or not, she was one of the fortunate ones who'd had a wonderful life. It was not a life she ever wanted to leave, but she was at least at peace with herself towards the end. She was able to accept what would be. As Russ said, 'She had stared death in the face.'

Caron gleaned so much from the hundreds of books she read, from what the Buddhist monks had shared with her and what all the other counsellors, therapists and practitioners had given her, and she was generous enough to share much of the journey in her journals.

> I don't know what the future brings or means – I will 'expect' good. Try not to judge what is happening to me – remember it is always passing and live the best I can for me and others around me. Surrender to divine will – whatever it is – with as much generosity, humility, egoless attitude as I possibly can.

Spiritually Caron had clawed her way out of a dark and fearful place, and had been rewarded with ongoing hope and faith that in the end all would be as was intended. She had found inner peace. Whatever this was going to bring, she was going to deal with it as positively and as well as she could. And my God, she did. I have no doubt she wavered during those frequent sleepless nights. I know only too well how a long, dark night can play havoc with the mind, but overall the churning had lessened and she was ready to let it be. There was a calmness about her. It has been a privilege to watch someone go through that and come out the other side as an enlightened person, and as a result it is the one aspect of her passing that offered me great comfort. This has given me the ability to hold on to my faith. If she could believe in angels and a higher place right up to the end, so can I.

Faith presents us with the notion of a soul, a spirit, and in times of loss that is about all we have to comfort us even if we doubt it. I have explored the notion of the soul, and when I think about Caron's, it does not require such a great leap of faith as I would have imagined. Caron's spirit has always been there in abundance. Every letter written from a person who knew her testified to that fact. As far back as the Brownies, my little girl had been spirited, inquisitive and buoyant. As Stephen always says, 'Do you brighten a room when you walk into it, or does it brighten when you leave?' Well, Caron always brightened the room when she walked in and it dulled a little when she walked out. That brightness is hard to replicate or reproduce, as Michael says. Despite the ravages of cancer, that was never more the case than towards the end of Caron's life. Russ said at the funeral that Caron was never more beautiful than at the end. Though her physical form had changed, he was right. It radiated from within. Her spirit did not diminish, not one iota. If anything, it grew exponentially as her body started to give way to the disease.

Caron never gave up. She would never have done that. Unfortunately for her and us, her body was surrounded, overwhelmed; all her defences were breached. I believe the fact she held on as long as she did is down to pure human spirit. Again and again I think about that last doctor in Switzerland, who looked at her X-rays and was staggered she was alive, let alone still walking. I think of those young men in the armed forces who time and time again save their fellow soldiers despite suffering horrendous injuries. If anyone needs proof that a person's spirit can exist outside the boundaries of the physical form, read the stories coming out of Afghanistan. Caron's body may have lost the battle, but my God, her spirit was still so strong. That helps me in my dark hours because it leads me to the same conclusion over and over again. Proof of eternal life had been staring me in the face for forty-one years. Spirits don't get sick; people do. Spirits don't suffer, they don't tire, and they don't age. Is it such a leap of faith to believe that they don't die either? I have felt Caron's presence sometimes when I am asleep. I can't feel her or touch her in my dreams, but I have a strong sense of her being with me. Do I take it as a sign? Wouldn't you?

I witnessed such phenomenal bravery, tenacity and positive strength in my child. You wouldn't ever wish to go through it in a million years, but paradoxically it was a privilege to witness and be part of. I feel fortunate that I had that time to share with Caron and didn't have her life suddenly taken away in a terrible accident or crime. Though I didn't want to accept the possibility of Caron losing her battle, and in fact still can't accept it, in those seven years I was given some marvellous times that we would not have had, were we not being held under the sway of cancer – times to say and do things together, time to pack in a lifetime. Our relationship was always good but, like Russ and Caron's, it went to a new level. Unbeknown to me at the time, we were all making our peace, using that time to come to terms with what was to follow. Some directly; others, like me, unwittingly. She fought as hard as anyone could and in doing so she taught us to fight. She also succeeded in living beyond the lifespan she was predicted by her doctors. That not only gives me comfort, it gives me the impetus I need to fight on and not let the b*****d grief pull me down.

In another entry in her journal she wrote:

What an extraordinary time. I'm having conversations with God on an almost daily basis. Am I imagining it or going mad? No, it's happening. I've had fear coming up about Monday's check-up. Although I know in my heart that all is well, it's as if I've been clinging on to the fear – afraid to let myself believe I am completely healed. What this brings up in me is a sense of powerlessness, which is what

happened every time I was told there was something
wrong – all my power left me. Right now I feel strong. I
feel like I'm finally saying goodbye to the cancer, stuff is
leaving me, this is letting go of five years of being
consumed by fear and uncertainty, and this is a dawning
of a whole new era.

It's not that I could ever forget her courage, but when I reread
her writing, it reminds me to be strong. Once again the person I
seek refuge in, gather strength from and seek the guidance to
carry on from is Caron. Doesn't that mean she is not gone?
Doesn't that mean that although she is not here in her physical
form, she still influences my life? I still have a relationship with
my daughter, and I realise now, in hindsight, that in the madness
of the first year, when I rushed back to work, created the
foundation and started writing the book, what I was really
doing was searching around madly for Caron. After an exhausting but ultimately beneficial process, I found her. It turned
out she'd never actually left me – her strength was inside me all
along; I'd been looking in the wrong places. It takes courage to
step into the darkness of the unknown. I was lucky because all I
had to do was follow in someone else's footsteps.

Caron bravely searched her soul to find the faith required to
believe that all would be well and was then told that, despite
everything she'd done, she was not clear and in fact the cancer
was worse than ever. She did not give up. Instead she managed
to find the resources deep within herself to remain positive and
find light and joy in a life that could easily have been eaten up
by darkness. I cannot read her journals and notes without
being touched by her strength. I owe it to her to keep my faith,
search out hope and continue to love.

Paul, Michael and I, have been forced by events to have

conversations we wouldn't ordinarily have had, to share thoughts that we wouldn't ordinarily have had. I never thought I would have to talk about tragedy and death with my children; my job was to protect, nurture, love and keep them from pain, not bring it in. I never expected to talk to the boys about the things we have had to talk about. I never wanted them to see me so broken. We have all gone to such depths of despair that we find ourselves saying things that are probably not usually discussed round kitchen tables, but those conversations have helped immeasurably and forged a stronger bond than ever before. Feelings erupt from deep within. They are brought up from a place inside yourself you never knew existed. They allow you to make some sense of the darkness and guide you towards the light. Some people may believe those feelings come from a higher place. I think they come from a deeper place. To be honest, their source matters less than where they are taking you, as long as that place is one of greater understanding and compassion.

Greater understanding and compassion are a common bond between many people who've lost loved ones. We have learnt, the painful way, to appreciate life. Perhaps we are stronger for it. As a Tibetan monk said, 'The lotus flower grows in mud. The human spirit, like this beautiful flower, will only grow in grim conditions. In order to gain wisdom you must have the obstacles of life, its suffering.' Death sometimes alters those who have been left behind, sometimes exaggerates their qualities, but there is rarely no change at all. It is a common misunderstanding that the death of a child is often the cause of divorce. Though of course this does happen, I haven't found it to be the case. If there were problems before, a cataclysmic event will no doubt bring them to the fore, but my experience has been that the strong relationships in my life have become stronger and the weak ones have faded away. However, this forging of bonds takes time and energy too. You have to walk each other's path to get there. For instance, I could be upstairs in a great frame of mind and then all of a sudden I can look at a photograph and find myself in tears. Stephen will say, 'What's happened?' but of course nothing has *happened* – I just got hit by one of those unforeseen waves. He is extremely patient. I have often said, 'Poor Stephen, he doesn't know what woman he is waking up to,' but when we were talking about this book, he told me that actually that has never been the case. He has always known exactly who he is waking up to. As I said in an earlier chapter, he simply alters his mood in response to mine. I suppose I am being micro-managed. He just does it so well I don't realise it is happening.

I can see why grief can drive a couple apart in the beginning. Men and women look at things differently; they do things differently; they react differently. The book *Men Are From Mars, Women Are From Venus* fits well into the pattern of bereavement, as it does almost everything else. Men and women grieve differently; ergo, mothers and fathers grieve differently. Don died before Caron became ill, so personally I will never know what it would feel like to see her other parent 'get on with life', as so many men try to do. I don't think that a father feels the loss of a child any less than a mother, though for a mother maybe it is more basic, more primeval. You just watch a mother with her newborn baby. She is in tune with the baby's needs without the use of words, expression or touch. While a newborn's physiology is incredibly advanced, they are a long way from being developed. These tiny creatures that cannot hold up their own head can somehow communicate their needs to their mother and have those needs met. You don't have to have given birth to experience that depth of feeling for a child – mothers of adopted children feel the loss just as acutely if their child dies – which leads me to believe that understanding the difference between mothers and fathers lies more in the difference between the sexes than anything else.

It's not just parents; it's brothers and sisters, husbands and wives. Learning to walk one another's path is as much a part of the grieving process as navigating your own. It's not just Paul and Michael's path; it's Russ's, Stephen's, the boys' and my own. That is not an easy thing to do when you're still so consumed by sadness that you can barely get dressed.

Carol Chase's quest to understand what happened to Olivia and why has taken her on an extraordinary journey. She says she is a completely different person to the one she was before Olivia died, and therefore her husband isn't married to the same woman. Nor is she married to the same man, though; their respective journeys, though very different, have ultimately brought them to the same place and they are closer than ever before. Olivia died at six o'clock on a summer's evening. Now, every day at 6 p.m. Carol and Clive sit down in a quiet room, open a bottle of wine and talk about their respective days, their family, the difficult bits and the good moments. Of course they do it to remember their daughter, but what they are also doing is remembering one another. And that is very important.

Not long before the first anniversary of Olivia's death Carol Chase wrote in her diary:

16 March 2005
How I would like to build a cocoon of concrete around myself. So much pain to bear, terrific trapped-nerve pain in my shoulder, and the pain of no more Olivia in my life

just gets greater every day – feeling totally overwhelmed, want to shut out the world because I can't cope with anything other than this pain and I can't cope with that. So hard to try to be normal for the family. Will I ever know what it is to feel normal again?

The important thing is to be brave, not put your life on hold. Push your life forward. One of life's major lessons is learning to be alone and to enjoy your own company. It's at these times that we develop our spirituality.

When I was looking through my diaries for this book, I was absolutely staggered that I had gone back to work so soon. I don't know how I did that. Not that I knew it at the time, but Caron must have led me much further down the path of adjusting to her loss than I realised. I was using all the tools, tricks and templates for grief I had already picked up thanks to my daughter: live in the now; do not give yourself over to fear; love; find the positive; appreciate what you have; be brave.

Carol, on the other hand, like many others, had to go and discover her own tools, on her own. Completely contrary to my whirlwind life of doing, Carol's life came to a grinding halt. She just stopped and allowed it to be. That was her way of accepting Olivia's passing. She too realised that in order to survive you have to accept what has happened. This is almost the hardest part of grief. Her GP offered her antidepressants, but they made her feel horrendous, and three members of the Church could not shed any light. No one and nothing can make this better. Like us all, she had to find her own way, and that was why she went on a quest to find hope. Part of her journey, like my own, was fully appreciating the person she'd been lucky enough to have in her life. Carol got a letter from a boy who had known Olivia and who had pronounced scoliosis of the spine. He recalled sitting in a corner at a disco, alone, because none of the girls wanted to dance with him. Olivia was at the disco and, noticing his sadness, came over and sat with him for an hour. He said he would always remember what she said to him that night: 'You're a lovely person. You've got to remember that it is the beauty inside that is important.' Another girl wrote to tell Carol what Olivia had written on her school shirt when they were leaving junior school, aged twelve: 'A true friend is someone who you can sit next to for an hour in silence but get up feeling you've had the best conversation in your life.' Olivia was a kind soul in life.

I have been fortunate enough to read much of Carol's diary and almost the strongest voice I 'hear' is Olivia's. It comes across as powerful, kind and much older than her fifteen years. Isn't that what Olivia and Carol are doing, sitting next to one another in silence but still having those wonderful conversations they'd always had? Believing that, researching where Olivia has 'gone' and hearing all those lovely insights from Olivia's friends, Carol tries not to look at Olivia's life as one cut tragically short but as a rich life or, as another friend wrote, 'a life of goodness spent'.

I will never forget going to a charity event and bringing along one of the paintings Caron had completed during her art class in Bryon Bay and which we had made into a limited print. A young man bid £4,500 for it. I went over to thank him afterwards for the wonderful amount of money he'd given to the charity. He said he'd been at university with Caron at Bristol, and although he hadn't known her very well, he'd never forgotten her. He had been in hospital and Caron had visited him, then phoned his mother to tell her how he was. He said he'd always remembered that understated act of kindness.

Buying the painting was his way of saying thank you and remembering.

I sympathise with the suffering of all the people who write to me of their loss, but I am even more touched by their descriptions of the people who've passed on. So often they are described in exceptional terms: memorable, influential, kind, generous, loving. There are so many examples of humility, courage and humour. In almost every letter the sender writes, 'I could go on writing for ever.' In the beginning it felt as if we were losing a lot of utterly wonderful people. Now I try to look at it another way. Instead of focusing on the life they didn't have, I focus on the life that they did have. How very life-affirming it is, how awe-inspiring, to read about these big-hearted, generous people and know that we have been touched by some beautiful souls. What we, left behind, have to do is find it within ourselves not to be overwhelmed by the loss, but to strive to focus on what we have gained. Carol, myself and most of the mothers who write to me would say that as excruciatingly painful as it is to have lost a child, we were blessed to be their mother. Aren't we lucky to have had a child like that and to believe, in our hearts, that death isn't the end?

Mr Pritchard from Beaconsfield wrote to me about his son, Matthew, who died aged twenty-three from a brain tumour. His humour, bravery and positivity made the ordeal easier on his family. When told the tumour could be malignant or benign, Matthew bravely joked, 'I'll go for the benign type, please.' Matthew's loving mother wrote a piece about her son for the *Daily Mail* to raise awareness and money for the Iain Rennie Hospice at Home (IRHH), a pioneering organisation that provides at-home care of the same level that patients would receive in a hospice. Like Caron, Matthew was surrounded by his family when he passed away on a beautiful sunny day. He woke and, in a moment of lucidity, asked whether 'today' would be the day he would die. When his mother asked how he felt, he replied, 'Today would be good – I'm so weary.' She has written that since his death she has felt a deep sense of peace and calmness, as if an invisible force has given her the strength and spirituality to cope. She likes to think it's Matthew.

Her husband, by her own words, is a 'fixer' and English in his outlook and, by his own admission, has no strong religious beliefs. However, it was he who wrote to me, included the beautiful article about his son and shared with me an experience he'd had six months after Matthew had died. He began his letter, 'I guess you will receive tons of mail, and naturally, many readers will want to compare their experiences with your own. Comparing is futile, because everyone is different.' He went on to say that several months after Matthew died, his twin sisters took their A levels and later that summer they all anxiously awaited the results. They deserved to do well since they had worked hard despite Matthew's illness and Matthew had really wanted to see them go to university. He continued:

In the early hours of the morning I was in a light, semiconscious sleep when Matthew appeared in the doorway of our bedroom. His facial features were totally clear; I had forgotten some of the detail. He was about seven foot tall and dressed in a shiny emerald-green robe. To his right was an elderly Indian gent dressed in a black shiny robe. He was only about five foot tall and had to look up to Matthew.

Matthew was in a state of excitement similar to that which we had seen when he was a little boy and opened his presents on Christmas morning to find that he had got exactly what he wanted. His words to me were, 'In Eng. and hist. the notes are down.' I said, 'What?' He repeated exactly the same statement with an element of frustration, as though I was stupid, but still smiling and full of excitement. I turned to Nicky and repeated what Matthew had said. When I turned back, both figures had disappeared.

He told his daughters and they were instantly relieved because to them it meant they would get As in English and history, or 'Eng.' and 'hist.', as it was abbreviated in our day. And they did.

Five years later Matthew's father was clearing out his mother-in-law's old house and checking nothing had been left behind when he found some paperbacks left in a cupboard in the spare room. One was called *Life After Death* and had sold for two shillings and sixpence. Skimming through it, he read, 'Very often the deceased appear as being very tall and dressed in a brightly coloured cloak.' That was good enough for him.

I am now convinced that the spirit of our loved ones does live on, and there is one sound, logical reason why mankind should not discover details of the afterlife. The reason is that if it were proven that the afterlife is 'better', then would not everyone take an overdose and get on with it?

People will say, 'Are you nearly back to normal?' or 'Have you moved on?' They can't possibly understand that the only way to be back to normal is for a miracle to bring back your loved one. But your strength and personality will help you adjust to life without your daughter, enabling you to channel your strength and support into your family and friends.

I have read many experiences like the one above and it gives comfort. I choose to believe. If all this is sounding too far-fetched, too much like wishful thinking, there is always a little bit of science to fall back on: quantum physics. It was first proved experimentally in France in 1982 that two previously connected quantum particles separated by vast distances remain somehow connected. If one particle is changed, the other is also instantaneously changed; at the quantum level all energy is connected. Not only is it connected, it can't be created or destroyed. All it ever does is change state. Caron's spirit was once encased in her physical form. It isn't any longer. If there is even the tiniest chance that she 'lives on' elsewhere and that we are still connected on a molecular level, then as her mother I owe it to her to continue the path she was on: I must take the very best out of this life, enjoy and be thankful for all that I have right now and let tomorrow take care of itself.

It is fairly well documented that Caron believed in angels, and when she saw an isolated white feather, she believed it to be an angel's calling card. As I mentioned earlier in this book, I see white feathers at times when I most need help to keep going along this positive path I am trying to carve out for myself and my family. Choosing a book title is never easy. For my last book, while considering titles with my editor, I repeated to myself, *Next to You, Next to You*, over and over, trying to get a feel for whether it was the right one. Just then I saw a long, white feather in a bush right beside me, as if to say, 'Yes, Mum, that's it – I'm next to you.'

Edinburgh, October 2005

Dear Miss Hunniford,

   I am seventy-four years old and my beloved grandson of twenty-three took his own life last month. As you know,

*everything is very raw at the moment and he is in our
thoughts every day – sometimes sorrow, sometimes anger.
Anyway, I watched you on* Parkinson *last Saturday when
you talked of angels and white feathers. Well, today I
went into the garage, which was Mark's domain and I
have not had the courage to go before. I could not believe
my eyes, as right in the corner were two white feathers. I
suddenly felt so much better and believe it was a message
to let me know he was being looked after by his guardian
angel and is OK. Thank you for sharing your grief and
for giving me a bit of peace of mind.*
    Yours sincerely,
    May

It isn't always feathers: Alice from County Down wrote, 'I
believe Michelle is looking after me and is beside me all the
time. I have even smelt her perfume when times were tough.' I
was told of another experience that I would like to share, this
time from a father. I suspect fathers often get overlooked;
mothers are probably cared for more tenderly, for longer and
more intensely by their girlfriends and family than fathers are.
I suspect some feel left out, playing second fiddle to grief and
second griever to the lead. The story I'd like to tell you once
again concerns Olivia Chase, who had told her family that she
would like to be married in a poppy field. Poppies were her
thing. One day a few weeks after Olivia died her father, Clive,
wrung out bereft and racked with grief, had to pull the car
over, unable to drive on. Out loud he asked Olivia to show him
a sign that she was Ok. Moments later as he was about to
continue driving, through the open sunroof floated a poppy
flower, dried and a little battered, but nevertheless . . . a
poppy flower. Staggered, he searched the source of the

coincidence, but as he was parked just off a busy junction in the middle of town, there was nothing but asphalt and concrete as far as the eye could see. He looked upwards, now calmed, and thanked his daughter.

On the first anniversary of Olivia's death, Carol Chase wrote in her diary:

On 24 May I went to the cemetery and just surrounded you with the most beautiful flowers and plants – orchids, sweet peas, a huge basket of lilies, flowers either side of your bench. It was like a flower garden. You were surrounded by love and it made me happy to be able to do something for you again. Hope you like it, sweetheart.

I picked two poppies from the churchyard, one in flower and one in bud. They wilted on the way home, just like me. I put them in a little vase next to me and within twenty-four hours the poppy bud, encased in its living shell, had shed its shell and the shell was lying lifeless on the windowsill. Yesterday it had been green, lush and living, today pale yellow and dead, but out of its encasement had blossomed the most beautiful scarlet poppy, with gentle, delicate petals, like you. I likened the shell to your body in the cemetery: lifeless, served its purpose, and from it had emerged this glorious, vibrant, delicate flower – your spirit, which I can't see (yet), but something quite magnificent. So many lessons in nature if only we open our eyes to see and understand. You will know how much we have been thinking of you, loving you and missing you. We have a lifetime of this ahead, Olivia – it seems like such a long road, darling.

Love you more than ever,

Mummy x

Teresa from County Tyrone sent me a CD with a song called 'Postcards From Heaven'. She had lost her son, Connor, in the terrible tsunami that hit South-East Asia on Boxing Day 2004. His body was not found immediately and only with the help of the Irish government did the family finally locate him, on 10 January, in a temple that had been converted into a temporary morgue on the island of Krabi.

Connor sent four postcards from Thailand. One arrived a few days after Connor was buried, and shortly after that one arrived to our home, but Michelle, my daughter, hadn't received hers, so she went to the grave and said 'Connor, where is my postcard?' Later, when she went home, the postman arrived with her postcard in his hand.

Hence the title of the beautiful song on the CD, 'Postcards From Heaven'.

It isn't just the mystical stories that ease my aching heart and help me to stay focused on the positive. I got a very generous letter from a woman who'd married a widower.

My own husband's wife died of cancer four years ago, after a five-year battle. She fought bravely, with always the thought she wanted her youngest child to have a mother for as long as possible. My husband was truly devastated when she finally let go of life, and spent a long and lonely first year hardly able to live, except with the knowledge that his child needed him to carry on. She was the one who finally said to him one evening, 'Daddy, I need you to feel better.' He realised he needed to change. Six months later, when I met him, he still could not talk about his loss and said he realised there were still so many memories that were too

*painful and tearful. Perhaps because I am a coach/
psychologist, I did get him to talk and to cry and really to
look even deeper at what his first wife gave him – and he
realised it was the gift of love. The wonderful memories of
their happy marriage, and of her selflessness, also enable
him to be able to love deeply again. We have now been
married for over a year, and it is a truly spiritual and
rewarding union. I frequently want to thank his first wife
and her own spiritual nature, which has enabled and
empowered my husband to be so happy again.*
   Abigail

Four years down the line Russ is happily remarried to Sally
and they have a new beautiful little girl, Tilly Jennifer, whom the
boys call TJ. Charlie and Gabriel are thrilled with their baby
sister and seem to have taken very willingly to helping to look
after her. It's cool to hold a bottle to feed her, but they 'don't do
nappies'. Sally and Russ have provided a very stable and loving
home life. As Russ says, there's a lot of laughter around the
house. The boys are happy at their school in Esher and love
pursuing their passions – for Charlie, football and music, and
for Gabriel, who just can't wait to go to Stagecoach every
Saturday afternoon, the theatre and gymnastics.

The press made much of the fact that I had 'refused' to go
to their wedding; the real truth is that it was never in the
framework that our side of the family would go. Russ and I
discussed the wedding well in advance and decided it would
be more comfortable all round if we weren't there on the day.
Better also not to have the press report on how *we* were
coping. We had our own family wedding celebration dinner
with Sally, Russ and the boys a couple of weeks ahead of the
actual day, all the family were there and it was much more

personal and private for us. It does, though, bring into focus that the grieving process is different for each individual and that people 'move on' at different paces. As a grieving mother, I need to continue my relationship with Caron, and understandably Russ had a need for the sake of the boys to start a new life. On a general level how many times have you heard grown-ups saying, 'I can't believe my mum, in her seventies, has married again so soon after Dad's death'? There is that old saying, 'If you've been happily married once, you want to be married again.' When you're consumed with grief, nothing is simple, nothing is obvious, and it's a case of each to one's own. No one deserves happiness more than Russ and I am truly delighted for him and the boys that Sally has brought that into their lives.

Charlie and Gabriel are happy, energetic, gorgeous, not-so-little boys. They are my future in terms of carrying Caron's spirit forward. They are so loved and appear to be in a great place. They are certainly exuberant, high-energy and very cheeky in their sense of humour. More than anything they are tremendous fun to be with. I know Caron would be so pleased that they are being well looked after. As an entire and now extended family unit, we are united in caring for the boys. In fact Russ said in his eulogy that Caron only let go because she knew in her heart the boys would be well cared for. And they are.

Now there is new life in the family: gorgeous TJ. I understand what a gift a daughter is. New beginnings. New life. Any new light brings with it renewed faith, hope and maybe just a touch of quantum physics.

Back to the Beginning

Love knows not its own depth until the hour of separation.

Kahlil Gibran

What have I learnt? I have learnt so much, but I still understand so little. I have learnt that the human spirit is miraculous and yet we do terrible things. I have learnt that there is infinite goodness in this world, but this is not enough to guarantee safe passage. I have learnt that I am not alone, yet I know the true meaning of loneliness. I know that sometimes I can feel things I cannot see and see things I cannot feel. People have shared their grief with me and in doing so have helped me deal with my own; I in turn have tried to pass on what I have learnt. Haven't I seen those words before?

Sometimes I really believe I have a handle on this thing called grief and feel a great sense of accomplishment for all that we as a family and foundation have achieved. I feel connected to Caron; I still feel her love and love her in return. I can see her in her sons; I laugh with her when I laugh with her sons; I hear her when I hear her sons and know that wherever she is, she is OK. During those times I know that death is never the end, just as Ann, the lady who wrote to me back in August 2004, said. I have moments of pure joy – for instance, hearing Charlie and Gabriel laughing in the background, watching the four cousins together, seeing Gabriel as Elvis on stage, gathering friends round the table for my birthday, having a sing-song – but then suddenly a wave hits and that joy is savagely interrupted by a searing, shocking stab through my heart. It all becomes too much and I realise I have learnt nothing at all. My heart is broken. My soul is shattered. I ache, hurt, keel over with pain. I am bereft, cut loose, adrift, lost. I am no longer myself. I am empty, closed down. I am scared and angry. I feel out of control. I weep, sob, shout. I rage against an unjust world. I realise I was mistaken: she isn't here at all. She died. I watched her take her last breath. I cannot see her or hear her, and I miss her laugh more than ever. Ninety per cent of the time I can put on my mask and keep the lid on this volcano, but sometimes when I am alone, I just have to let the emotions come to the surface and weep them out. I let the grief take over and cry.

Sometimes I feel that time splintered the moment Caron died. Part of me stayed with her, locked for ever at 6.15 p.m. on 13 April 2004, and wherever she is, I am too. The rest of me moved through the wilderness of time, trying to figure out how it was that the earth continued to revolve. For all the progress I have made, I am constantly being thrown right back to the beginning.

I still wake up every morning with the same feeling of disbelief. I have given this subject as much thought as a human being could. I have tried hard to understand, but my limbic brain, my instinctive brain, is still struggling to catch up. The truth is, I am not able to make sense of something that makes no sense at all. I go to functions and I hear myself talk about Caron and I still feel as if I'm watching a film, seeing myself being played by a woman who looks oddly like me. I shuttle between two times. Either it is now, this very moment, or it is then, 6.15 p.m. on 13 April 2004. So far I haven't found that the time in between makes any difference to my grief. Time hasn't filled in the pit; time can't. It breaks my heart all over again when I see the boys experiencing new things that Caron would have loved. I pray I get to see them at university, getting married, having children of their own, but I know it will hurt like hell.

It's method, rather than time, that heals. Now at least I can cling on to things that are helpful. I look forward to seeing the boys for the weekend and holidays and having them to stay. This last half-term was really glorious for me and I consciously decided to follow in their footsteps and think like a child. As Paul says, children are in the present and it's a shame we lose that gift as we grow up. I told myself, I will enjoy every second of this. I won't spend it watching them and mourning the fact that Caron isn't here too. And I succeeded. Maybe I'm wrong. Maybe time gives you the method to cope with time. Either way it was a genuinely fantastic half-term. Now at least I am able to make the most of what I am doing right now. That is a long way from the person who thought she would never laugh or smile again. I nod my head to those people who have to find something from nothing. I have the boys. Some people don't.

When I am feeling low, I imagine Caron to be alive and back at Taylors, her and Russ's house in Australia, floating around the exotic garden amongst the palm trees, although of course in my heart of hearts I know she's not but I don't want to go back and see for certain. That would be another dose of realism I couldn't bear. It would take away the last grain of escapism that I allow myself. Imagining her there, alive and well, is respite from this interminable loss. Caron always used to say it was paradise, and I wonder if maybe, just maybe, she was right. Maybe she is there. In the letter I got from Matthew's father, telling me about his son visiting him in the early dawn draped in an emerald gown, there was a PS:

PS You mention that you feel your daughter is still in Australia. Perhaps she is. I say this because two of Matthew's favourite places were the islands of St Lucia and St Vincent. We often sail those waters, and my wife in particular has a powerful feeling of his presence when we sail past St Vincent.

Once again in my darkest hour someone lights the way. That someone is Caron.

I said earlier that I've always believed something, someone, 'this mystery we call God' occasionally moves the big pieces around, which either makes you take up a new challenge or move on to a new life. When Caron was too ill to go and see the Tibetan healing monks when they visited Bryon Bay, they came to her. Though deeply spiritual, the focus of these particular monks is medical and they perform healing chants, making an amazing guttural sound that resonates deep within. They care for people's spirits. No spirit more than Caron's. They did her so much good and brought her such peace. Although she never became a Buddhist, they turned her round so many times and gave her the inner strength she needed to let go of the past, no longer fear the future and realise the power of now.

Thursday, February 2004
I am innocent and forgive myself for whatever I think I did.
Just meditated – light and space in amongst the junk.
Give it over – minute by minute.
Peace – allow the body to be in that space.

This is where Caron's story takes an incredible twist. The monks who came to Taylors so many times and chanted for four days to help Caron's soul pass from this world to the next, who were so pivotal in her quest for peace, have set up a healing centre at Taylors for people who are ill, to go to for respite. Maureen, the Northern Irish woman who brought the monks to Caron in the first place, is now living with them and helping to run the centre. A benefactor bought the property for them. I can see the monks in their bright-orange robes moving steadily and quietly against the waxy deep-green leaves of the tropical garden, in amongst the trees, going from the house to the summer house, performing their healing chants, providing a retreat for troubled souls. This they do in the very same summer house where they chanted for Caron's health for four days continuously, where Caron herself meditated daily and wrote her journals about what she wanted to pass on, based on what she'd learned over the course of her seven-year journey fighting cancer. It seems astonishing to me to think all of that is going on in the house, which Caron put so much energy into and loved so much, the place of so much pain, so much laughter and so much peace. She always said the house was so special that she knew it was only on loan to them for a period of time, and she was right. I think that's an amazing move of the big pieces. You simply couldn't make up an ending like that.

Caron's spiritual well-being was a long, arduous search. The monks and her tenacity helped get her there. Again, she wrote much about it:

Often I felt in the past like there was nothing but fear and I would be completely consumed by it. Then I was able to quiet my mind and get a sense of what story this fear and anxiety were appearing in. I realised that I am the presence that does care and doesn't leave. These emotions are not who I am. I am not even this body or mind, but rather a great ocean of love and everything else that goes with it. The silent witness that watches the dream of my life unfold. I have this real sense that if we could see for a few minutes the reality of our lives, we would laugh and laugh. We are so invaded by what we 'think' is happening and yet it's all an illusion.

Thinking about the monks and all they did for my daughter gives me comfort. It reassures me, or I allow it to. It also reminds me to think about the beautiful garden, the palm trees, how much happiness that house brought us all. I look at photos and see we were always laughing, having dinners, making music, holding parties, jamming with Cliff. There was so much joy in Caron's life that the boys will scarcely remember her being ill there. It was a wonderful way to live. I know now how much pain she was in and it is incredible how little the boys or I saw. Australia is the gift that goes on giving. I hated it at first. The distance was immeasurable. I have come to realise, though, that is one of the things that has given me a degree of sanity because not only did it teach me to be without her on a daily basis, but I can imagine her there for the rest of my life.

And so this journey continues, on a daily, sometimes hourly basis. I keep myself busy, too busy maybe, I focus on the love of my family, and I try to avoid the big waves. Some, of course, are unavoidable, and when they hit me and the darkness descends, it is 6.15 p.m. on 13 April 2004 all over again. Even there, though, I find refuge. Even there I find something to hold on to that stops me falling to the bottom of the pit. Even there I find hope. When Caron died, she smiled. When I close my eyes, I can see it. A soft, beautiful smile. A cynic might think that her smile was simply the body relaxing; a realist might think of it as a release from the anguish she'd carried with her for seven years. I think differently. Caron never, ever wanted to die. She never wanted her sons to grow up without a mother, so while there was without doubt a release from pain, she was not happy to die. She wasn't smiling because she was leaving; she was smiling because she was being welcomed somewhere else. A higher consciousness? Paradise? Taylors maybe? I like to think it was Don, her silver-haired dad, a glass of wine and some peanuts in his hand, welcoming his child back as one day she will welcome me. I hope, I pray, I wish, I need to believe that, because if I thought I would never see my precious child again, I wouldn't manage to operate as I do, to cope with the enormous hole that Caron's departure has left at the very core of me. I raise a glass to my girl and all that she gave us – her laugh, her eyes, her inner beauty, her spirit, her children and her love.

To climb out of that pit, I have had to learn to let her go. The future is no concern of mine. I try to do as my daughter taught me and live in the now. And right now I miss Caron.

Where did that smile go?
The one you saved just for me,
A smile between mother and daughter
There for all the world to see.
Created in an instant
At the moment of your birth,
A smile that warmed your soul
And gave me heaven on earth.

Where did that smile go?
The one that was mine alone.
I cannot seem to find it;

Always With You

It isn't in our home.
I've looked everywhere in your room.
I've hunted high and low.
I'm feeling lost without it.
I really miss it so.

Where did that smile go?
The one that could melt my heart.
I would have hidden you away
If I'd known we'd have to part.
It's lonely here without you;
It's a shadow life I lead,
And tucked in every moment
Is a sad and painful need.

Where did that smile go?
The one where love shone through,
Where each day was very special
If I shared that day with you.
That smile is now my comfort;
It's in my very soul.
That smile is breathing life
To fill an empty hole.

It isn't in your bedroom,
A silly place to start.
That smile has never left me;
It's living in my heart.

'Our Smile', Sue White

ACKNOWLEDGEMENTS

As with any book there are so many people I would really like to acknowledge and give my appreciation to.

Gay Longworth, who has interviewed and researched so many members of our family and friends. She probably knows more about us all than any other person! Huge thanks Gay for your extremely valuable contribution and for helping me to search through thousands of letters in such a sensitive way. The book may not have happened without you.

To the thousands of people who wrote such personal and detailed letters, which in turn have provided much insight for this book.

Friends of Caron who continue to be great friends of our family. In particular, Johnny and Cathy Comerford, who raise thousands of pounds for Caron's Foundation every year. Yaz and Fiona, who carry on those fun dinners that Caron adored. Karen and Simon Fowler, and Mallory and Mike Fletcher who never fail to turn up at family and Foundation events.

My manager **Laurie Mansfield** who is still the wise Buddha, and worked closely with Eugenie Furniss and Rowan Lawton, my literary agents.

To **Rowena Webb**, Publishing Director at Hodder, for her faith in this book and the belief and hope that it will help many people through the loss of their loved ones. Also for her guidance and endless patience.

Juliet Brightmore, my picture editor, who spent hours and hours sifting and sorting through hundreds of photos.

Fenella Bates for her long-sufferance in taking in my copious notes and changes to the manuscript but never losing her patience.

And to **everyone at Hodder**, including Sarah Christie who worked so tirelessly designing the cover; Emma Knight who dealt with my publicity; Laura Collins the copyeditor and the gallant girls of Hodder who walked/ran a marathon in the Pink Power Walk to raise money for the Caron Keating Foundation.

To the many, many people all over the country who endlessly support the Foundation all year round.

And finally to **the Chase family** who opened their hearts and shared the pain of losing Olivia in this book.

'Sometimes' by Frank Brown

'A Child of Mine' by Edward Guest, taken from *The Collected Works of Edward Guest*

'We Give our loved ones back to God' by Helen Steiner Rice. Taken from *The Poems and Prayers of Helen Steiner Rice*, published by Baker Publishing

'Footprints in the Sand' by Anonymous

'Do not Stand at my Grave and Weep' by W.H. Auden. From *Collected Poems*, published by Faber & Faber

'She is Gone' by David Harkin from *The Life of Rhyme*

'Always a Face Before Me' by Anonymous

'When I Must Leave You' by Helen Steiner Rice, taken from *The Poems and Prayers of Helen Steiner Rice*, published by Baker Publishing

'Masques' by Karen Nelson

'This is my Oath as I am Born' by W.G. Royce, used with permission

'Brave Heart In Memory of Caron' by W.G. Royce, used with Permission

'Let There Be Purpose in this Suffering' by Sharon Stanton Keep

'I'm Looking back on Childhood Years' by Anonymous

'There's Always Another Tomorrow' by Anonymous

'May You Always have an Angel by your Side' by Douglas Pagels from the book of the same name

'Look To This Day' ancient Sanskrit poem

'What God Hath Promised' by Annie Johnson Flint from *Annie Johnson Flint's Best Loved Poems*, published by Evangelical Press

'Miss Me, But Let Me Go' by Anonymous

'The Deeper Sorrow' by Kahlil Gibran. From the book, *The Vision . . . Reflections on the Way of the Soul*, published by Penguin Books

'All is Well' by Cannon Henry Scott-Holland, taken from *Sermons of Cannon Henry Scott-Holland*

'Time Does Not Heal' by Libby Parr, used with permission

Extract from *Memoirs* by Edward Teller, reprinted by permission of Basic Books, a member of Perseus Books Group

'Love Knows Not its Own Depth' by Kahlil Gibran. *The Vision . . . Reflections on the Way of the Soul*, published by Penguin Books

'Our Smile' by Sue White

The Caron Keating Foundation is a fundraising partnership set up by Gloria Hunniford, Paul and Michael Keating. The foundation offers financial support to professional carers, complementary healing practitioners and support groups dealing with cancer patients, as well as individuals and families who are affected by the disease. It also financially assists a number of cancer charities with their ongoing quest for prevention, early detection and hopefully ultimate care.

For more information about The Caron Keating Foundation, please visit www.caronkeating.org, or write to PO Box 122, Sevenoaks, Kent, TN13 1UB